IN THE
SHINING
MOUNTAINS

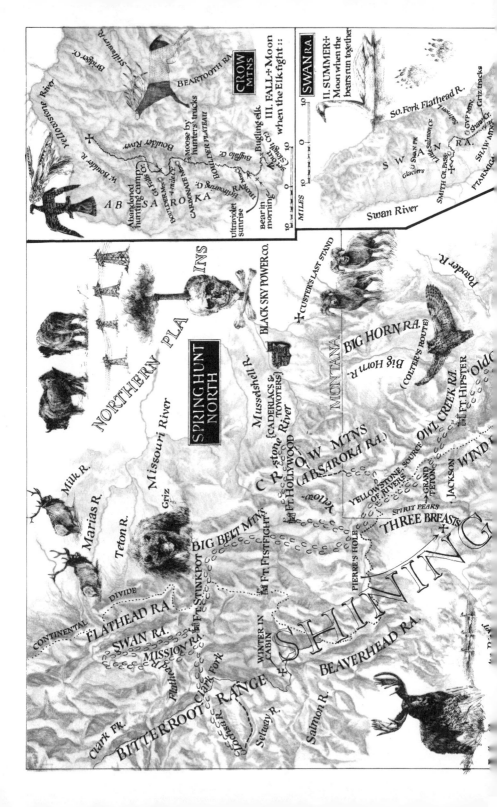

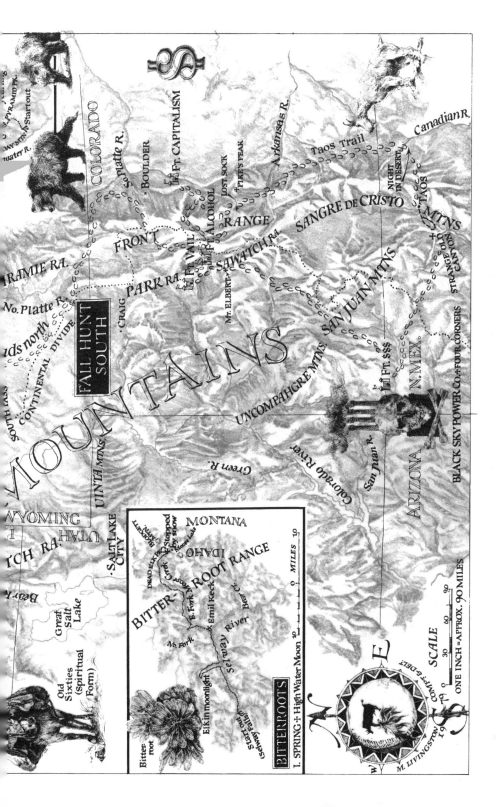

IN THE
SHINING
MOUNTAINS

A WOULD-BE MOUNTAIN MAN IN
SEARCH OF THE WILDERNESS

DÁVID THOMSON

ALFRED A. KNOPF
NEW YORK 1979

THIS IS A BORZOI BOOK
PUBLISHED BY ALFRED A. KNOPF, INC.

Copyright © 1979 by David Thomson
All rights reserved under International
and Pan-American Copyright Conventions.
Published in the United States
by Alfred A. Knopf, Inc., New York,
and simultaneously in Canada
by Random House of Canada Limited, Toronto.
Distributed by Random House, Inc., New York.

Library of Congress Cataloging in Publication Data
Thomson, David, [date]
In the shining mountains.
1. Rocky Mountains—Description and travel.
2. Thomson, David, [date] I. Title.
F721.T46 1979   917.8'04'30924   79–2126
ISBN 0–394–42755–6

Manufactured in the United States of America
First Edition

In Memory of

MICHAEL TERRY THOMSON

He asked not of anyone,

he gave freely of himself to all.

CONTENTS

THE SHINING MOUNTAINS
I

THE BITTERROOT MOUNTAINS
6*1*

Fort Hollywood
*II*9

THE SWAN RANGE
*I*27

Fort Hollywood
*I*79

THE CROW MOUNTAINS
*I*87

Goodbye, Fort Hollywood
244

THE
SHINING
MOUNTAINS

GO WEST, YOUNG FOOLS

I ALWAYS WANTED to be a mountain man, so one day a few years ago I packed up my outfit and headed out west. Wide-open spaces and freedom, I thought, the ledges and crags of the wilderness, that was my calling. I'd build a cabin back on some little creek, put a pack on my back, and make it on my own in the mountains. Be a free man.

I wound up working as a night clerk in a motel in Denver.

Denver is like a miniature Los Angeles with rabies. At night the streets snarl and flash, and it has a vast collection of the weirdest signs you ever saw. Down West Colfax they rise ever higher against the skyline in a chaotic assortment of gaudy colors and gawking shapes, each one crowding over the next in what seems to be an attempt to make you hit a telephone pole near enough to their front door to do some business. Madness trying to outdo madness, I thought as I drove down that long strip. In the background, through the buildings sometimes, the mountains appeared shimmering in the early-summer heat, and I compared that skyline to the skyline of the signs. They can't be serious, I thought. But they were.

Denver sits on the Front Range of the Rockies; it is the place where the rising plains first meet the mountains. For hundreds of miles a gently rolling flatland collides with a wave of mountains along that front; foothills begin to rise with a new and exciting abruptness. The city itself is growing in a sprawl to the north and south, as if great bushel baskets of cars, warehouses, high-rise apartments, and corporate office buildings were being dumped further and further along the base of the mountains, leaving slums festering back near the middle. It was a familiar pattern to me. It wasn't exactly the clean-aired gateway to the Rockies that I had imagined.

Back at the motel desk I answered the phone and received

guests. My face burned. It was no place for a mountain man to be, but I was broke. I saved my money, holding on to the imaginary map of the Rockies I had in my mind: it was a huge region, plenty of unpopulated spaces, and there were still some wild places left in it. The last frontier in the 1970's; an old American dream was waking and turning to the West. The idea of being a mountain man sent fire into my spirit. Building a cabin, wandering through the mountains, living by my hands and my wits. You didn't have to have a college degree to be a mountain man; nature judged you for what you were and what you could do. There'd be some freedom left out here for me, I thought. The wilderness had always called to me. I'd make it on what was in my heart, even if I was poor.

I just had to get out of Denver.

I dreamed those dreams while I worked at the motel. The boss kept calling me to check whether I was answering the phone correctly when the desk was busy. Most of the time I wasn't. An Aspen businessman would come walking up and ask for his key, another suit and tie with a coat over his arm would come up to register, and a cloud of perfume with frosted hair would come up to find out which room Mr. Out-of-Town was in. In the midst of all that the phone would ring. I'd pick it up and say, "Yeah, whadda you want?" And it would be him, the sneaky bastard, anger in his voice like a switchblade as he reminded me how I was supposed to answer the phone. He was a short, pudgy man who wore an expensive suit, and soon he had my number. He stayed on my back, and I started to get mad. Finally, about the fifth time, he came down a little in his tone and told me gently that he thought I had a problem with my attitude and wondered what it was. I told him that his motel made me feel like puking. He told me I was fired.

I was happy. That was the way any good mountain man would have handled it.

I was beginning to realize that the Rocky Mountains had come a long way since the days of the free trappers. Traditionally Denver was the jumping-off place for prospectors and fortune seekers in the latter part of the 1800's, a place where they bought their grubstake and then took off into the mountains from. They called it Cherry Creek. Now Cherry Creek was a wealthy residential suburb, and Denver was the jumping-off place for the jet-set skiers. It didn't shine no more.

I got another night job, working in a hospital for the state. It was dreary. Bright fluorescent lights at three in the morning. In the late hours I doodled pictures of unmapped mountain ranges. I had to get enough money together to get out of Denver. It was damned expensive to be a mountain man in the 1970's, and it was going up all the time. During the day I worked on an article, and at night I worked in the hospital, filling out insurance forms. My spirit ached. I almost forgot what the mountains looked like.

Finally I sent in the article. I went out into the city to wait. I climbed a twenty-five-story building and went out through the fire door and onto the roof. Lots of tar, small rocks, aerials, pigeons flapping about. A little bit of breeze, but the air mostly still and yellowish. It was a day of inversion, when the atmosphere forced the smog back down on the city, and I couldn't believe how potent it was up there. The air was yellow, as if hazed with smoke from a poisonous fire, and I could see little brown particles drifting along like an ethereal sewer running through the atmosphere. It stung the eyes, so I had to rub them, and it caught in the throat. New York, Los Angeles, *Denver*. Off in the distance, obscured by the sick yellow haze, stood the snowcapped mountains. My destiny, I thought. I had to get to them.

I went back down and checked the mail, but there was nothing. I read at night to pass the time. I lived on a major ambulance route, and I would read until one came by, then stop; the sound would fill the room, as if the vehicle were entering through the window, the red lights flashing around the walls, then it would speed past, and its penetrating scream would recede into the neon squalor of the inner-city night. The ambulances were busy in that part of the city. The Chamber of Commerce had moved out into the suburbs.

Captain Clark, my imaginary leader, had let it be known that back in the States he was preparing a map of the western territory at the wishes of President Jefferson, particularly the country of the upper Platte River, so I sketched in the details of this huge outpost, and dubbed it Fort Capitalism, for its manic preoccupation with money and expansion. There appeared to be no wild game left in the region.

The day after I finished my map sketch a big check came in the mail. I picked up the broomstick and danced around the kitchen. It was enough money to get out of Denver. I bought some wine and had a party with the other inmates of the building that night. I told them I was heading for the mountains to be a mountain man. They wanted to know if I was going to trap beaver. I told them I hadn't really thought about it. They wished me luck.

HIGHTAILING IT OUT
OF CHERRY CREEK

I CLOSED out my business in Cherry Creek, bought some flour, packed up my mule, and headed west on the trail that led out of the encampment and up into the mountains. Run into a prospector headin' for the high country, scattered trappers on horseback trailin' toward some summer doin's, bands of 'Rapaho movin' up as they follered the elk. The sun was shinin' and the mountains looked clear and cool as I climbed higher over them foothills, and I was happy seein' country I'd never seen before.

Actually it wasn't a trail, it was a four-lane freeway called I-70, which cut a big swath through the foothills as it climbed up off the plain where the city lay. And I didn't see any prospectors or trappers; instead I saw Porsches and Mercedes-Benzes whiz past me, a part of Denver's elite heading for their condominiums in the mountains. No Indians, and no elk. But every so often I imagined it the way I wanted it, that I was on a trail, heading into country that was open and free. The mule's name was Spirit of the Sixties, and that mule had an eye for the horizon. The dialect of the mountain men was creeping into my thinking.

I traveled up into those hills and went southward till I hit a creek that wound back and forth past several small forts and settlements nestled beneath the hills. Actually they weren't forts, but I pretended they were. Finally I came upon a run-down fort at a bend in the creek where the valley opened up some; a gas station, a post office, a sewing store, and several bars. There an old German carpenter rented me a lodge, and I stowed in my outfit and took a breather.

I walked around those hills looking at pine trees and small rock cliffs and clear streams flowing over the rocks. The air was fresh; the smog hadn't reached up that far yet. The snow was just going out of the highest parts of those hills and the flowers were coming up through the pine needles. I saw a lone doe with a tiny fawn; it was the Moon When the Deer Were Born. I explored around till I found a branch of the creek that ascended into a region that seemed wild, with small side valleys and hills and lots of cool pines. I found a trail going up into a little valley with a grassy opening that was perfect for a cabin site. I camped there for two days, exulting in the sunshine and the wandering sense of freedom I felt at getting out of Denver. It was the wildest place I could find around there. It also turned out to be a State Park. On the second day I ran into a Forest Ranger, who smiled when he told me that if I built a cabin there I'd get put in jail.

I went back to the lodge and hung up my ax. I spent the summer working for the old man and making excursions into the surrounding countryside, looking for sign. I found lots, but it was mostly on posts. *No Trespassing.* There were houses going up all through that country, and the old winding dirt roads were dusty with new traffic. I explored back and forth, working north, and early one Friday evening I happened to come out on a small rock promontory overlooking the freeway. It was full of vehicles. A long line of campers, vans, boats, Winnebagos, sports cars, hang-glider enthusiasts, and Cadillacs were traveling in an endless procession of winking red lights westward up into the mountains. It seemed as if half the city of Denver was on its way into the Rockies. It was a stunning realization. On my map for Captain Clark, I duly noted the major recreational artery I was witnessing, sketching in some details of the surrounding countryside, and I christened the promontory I was standing on Sad News Butte. Captain Clark would have shit his britches if he could have seen this. Saddened, having had enough, I trailed back toward my lodge.

As the summer wore on I found in subsequent explorations

that the game was all shot out of those hills, that there were scarcely any deer or elk left. The streams and lakes further and further west were fished out too, most of the native trout populations extinct. People streamed up that highway from Denver, and they pulled fish out of the creeks and rivers as fast as the Department of Fish and Game could plant them back in. Increasing crowds were inundating the mountains there, every day there was more and more sign of it. The developers were having a field day.

It was no place for a mountain man to be. I began to cast about for a different direction, uncertain at that point which way to go. Fall and spring were the two seasons when the mountain men made their living; those were the times when the beaver's fur was glossy and thick, at its commercial prime. Summer fur wouldn't sell, and during the winter the beaver were frozen in, nearly impossible to catch. So the early journals of the mountain men spoke of the spring hunt on the upper reaches of the Seedskedee River or the fall hunt in the Snake River country. They boiled their traps, sometimes in concoctions of bark, to remove the human scent before they started trapping. So, since I didn't have any traps, and since I figured the beaver would freeze their genitals off if I harvested their fur right before winter, I boiled my socks instead, hoping to remove both the powerful human scent which they had developed and a particularly vicious Asian fungus which was feasting on my toes at the time. A symbolic tribute to the mountain men. I figured it was an authentic enough preparation for the fall hunt, which I did want to make, and which I was looking forward to more and more now.

THE TAOS TRAIL

IN THE BACK of my mind I was beginning to lean toward the southern stretches of the Rockies, down toward Taos and Santa Fe. I figured that the rush of development which was spreading out from Denver would slacken off the further south I traveled, and that down there land might still be cheap enough to be able to build a cabin somewhere. So I started laying plans for a southward loop, following the major rivers as the mountain men used to do, which would swing down along the Sangre de Cristo range, hit the Taos country, then meander back up through southern and western Colorado. It would be a good hunt. A hunt for a place, somewhere that wasn't being overrun. A place that was still wild.

Back at my lodge in Fort Alcohol, I made some jerky and laid in quantities of beans, salt pork, and flour for the journey. My supplies didn't come up the Platte River by keelboat or packtrain as they did for Jim Bridger; I bought them in the Safeway at Fort Image, a few miles up the creek. Alas. But my socks were boiled, I had a good skinning knife, and I had a long eye for the horizon.

I took off early one morning about the time the first frosts were beginning to color the high mountain slopes, in the Moon When the Berries Ripen. I ascended Bear Creek past Fort Image to its rocky headwaters and on up over into the higher country beyond. It was rolling, timbered, with occasional rock bluffs protruding from the dark green of the pine forests. Once in a while I could see a good-sized valley off between two mountains, but the signs of the realtors were stuck prominently at the approaches to them.

The sun came up and I went down a long, long hill, which I sketched in on the map for Captain Clark as Crow Hill, for the preponderance of those black and rascally birds which circled the rocks near the top. Then I went on, southward, crossing two different mountain passes which were difficult to climb but still suitable for wagon travel, and finally came to what I believed to be the South Platte River.

If it was indeed that same water, I was standing on the furthest point that a white man had yet set foot up the course of that drainage. I made some calculations and drew it in on the map; then proceeded to ford it on horseback. Even though it being the time of lowest water, my horse stumbled on a boulder in the strongest part of the current and was rolled once completely over before it regained its footing and struggled ashore, dragging me incidentally along with it. I lost two traps in the mishap.

Actually I knew it was the Platte River by the sign on the

bridge. I didn't lose two traps, I lost one sock, which floated away while I was swimming. Still I was close enough to the head of that long western river to feel some of its history. The South Platte ran up to the Continental Divide thirty miles west of where I swam, and headwatered; from there it wound down out of the mountains, back through Denver, on northwest out of Colorado and all the way back across Nebraska, where it finally emptied into the Missouri at the Iowa border. The first wave of mountain men went up the Missouri River and into Montana, on the heels of Lewis and Clark. The second wave went up the Platte in the early 1820's, following the North Platte into Wyoming toward Yellowstone. That route was later to become the Oregon Trail, the first wagon road over the mountains.

At first they came up in keelboats, pulling them with ropes or poling them against the current for upward of 2,000 miles. Those boats carried twenty-five tons of supplies, drawing two and a half feet of water: muskets, pistols, flints, fire steels, gunlocks, powder, lead, bullet molds, hunting and skinning knives, saddles, rope, picket pins, awls, chisels, files, cups, kettles, wool blankets, coffee, sugar, salt, tobacco, alcohol, rum, and various Indian trading goods. Green River knives and Hawken rifles, tools of the trade. The journey up the Platte or the Missouri took three or four months. After a few of the keelboats snagged their masts on overhanging trees and sank, they switched to packtrains, which trailed up the Platte with horses and mules.

As I looked at the river I began to realize that the journeys the mountain men made were extraordinary in their distances and their hardships; that there was nothing in my experience with which I could even begin to compare them. After that long drive across the plains of Nebraska, when I first caught sight of those snowy mountains rising on the far horizon, I felt a sudden thrill and a great sense of relief, and I could only guess at what fraction that feeling was compared to someone who had pulled a keelboat across, starting out in the spring against high water. More than anything else that began to interest me about the mountain men: the distances that they traveled across the wilderness and survived, sometimes alone and on foot.

I got back in my mule and crossed the Platte, angling south toward the Continental Divide. When I struck the Arkansas

River, I followed it down as it swung southeast around the beginning of the Sangre de Cristo range, seeing that mighty chain of mountains for the first time. Some of the peaks were 14,000 feet high. The passes were over 10,000. Snow-covered eruptions of rock swung into view as I rode southward, the sun burning out of the southwest with a heightening force, floods of color and light, the deep blue of the autumn sky. High massive meadows and sprawling forests. I drove my mule up to the ends of roads and wandered around murmuring and tripping over things, eyeing those heights. It was a mountain man's range. I'd probably still be there today, except that I ran into a Forest Ranger, who told me it was a National Forest and I'd get put in jail if I built a cabin there too.

But there were too many people anyway. I ran into them on the roads, on the trails, everywhere. The Forest Ranger told me that most of the trails leading up into the Sangres got between twenty-five and fifty people a day, all summer. They came down from Fort Capitalism in droves on the weekends, and from all over the country the rest of the time. The trails were like mountain sidewalks. There warn't any griz left in them mountains, they was all killed off. There warn't any wolves or wolverines left either. It was no place for a mountain man to be.

I kept on a-goin', following the Arkansas eastward, back out toward the plains. When I broke out of the mountains I veered south, following the Sangres down toward the New Mexico territory, picking up the Taos Trail. Mountain men trapping in Wyoming in the early 1830's made trips on horseback down to Taos along this route, sometimes on a trading excursion, sometimes for a winter sojourn. Out of the Yellowstone country they rode down the Wind River, picked up the Sweetwater River and wandered down that toward Colorado, along the North Platte, across the grassy hills where Fort Capitalism now stands, and on south along the eastern front of the Sangre de Cristos.

What a ride. The mountain men rode down the Taos Trail for an adventure, for a drunk, for dark-eyed women. Jim Bridger made that journey in the winter of 1833–34. One way it was a distance of five hundred air miles from Jackson Hole, Wyoming; probably close to eight hundred the way he rode. They followed the big rivers. There were trees and cover along those rivers for deer; there were elk and buffalo, roots and berries, fish, and they usually did not want for food. If the country was open they made twenty or twenty-five miles a day, camping under the stars and the canopy of the cottonwoods along the river. Now that journey can be made in one full day; then it took thirty-five days. One month of riding down the big western rivers into the Southwest, through a land of mountains, plains, and deserts that had no human scars, that was all wild. Over and over I wondered what a trip like that would feel like; the size of the emotions they must have felt seemed beyond the grasp of the times. I wanted those feelings, the long and wild journeys. Where and how?

I kept on a-goin'. As the miles slipped past, the country began to change. I saw fewer and fewer people, and there was more and more distance between the forts. I began to feel more at ease, more alone in a good sort of way. The country became drier and spread out more, with solitary plateaus rising in the distance. Mile after mile it rolled past, flattened and somnolent, red sand washes, the Southwest beginning to spin its old, amazing spell.

Finally I crossed over into New Mexico and rode out onto a desert, with low and jumbled mountains to the northwest. *I was on a horse, with a pack mule, and I had ridden all the way down from Wyoming!* The spears of the yucca plants rose scattered across the flatness; an old riverbed cut a deep and winding channel through the sand with some green plants at the very bottom. The sun turned huge and bloody and began to set in the west; the silence was overwhelming, buzzing in the ears. Flinty stones, red gravel, and sand underfoot, I wandered out toward the river. The spell in those vast stretches was something that made my heart sing. I rolled in the sand, I gave praise to the earth. It wasn't crawling with people, and I began to have hope. I found an old railroad bed with the tracks torn out, and a square pit with old rotting timbers which held the desert back. It didn't look as if it had been touched in years. Finally when darkness came down I rolled my sleeping robe out in the sand and lay there until the stars began to blaze, feeling the touch of millions of lights spread out over the vastness of the dry desert landscape. I felt freedom that night, and as I stared at a nearby yucca plant I wondered if it was whispering. But all the space around me, the dark flashing sky and the mountains and plains, were one vast message: a whisper of mystery and freedom. *Stop them from desecrating me, and I will enrich your spirit and your children's spirits, for as long as the sun shines. Stop them; let me shine as I have always shone!*

Voice of the earth. If only that reverence were a truth.

ON INTO THE TÁOS COUNTRY

THE NEXT DAY I traveled south with a growing sense of hope and optimism, the seed germinating in me that I might have discovered country in which I could build my cabin and begin to be a mountain man. The trail began to swing west again, back toward the mountains, and I continued to faithfully make annotations on my map for Captain Clark. I noted that the dangerous yellow gas which seemed to emit from the vicinity of Fort Capitalism was conspicuously absent in this region, as were the blaring hordes of traffic and the throngs of Hollywood stars who were penetrating into the mountains west of the fort. Indeed, I noted that the inhabitants here seemed to be fairly normal.

Late in the day I reached the mouth of a large canyon, which I suspected to be the Taos River canyon, ascending into the mountains to the west. I made several identifying sketches of surrounding landmarks where the river flowed out, and then began a three-day ride up that wild and rugged canyon. Deer were not absent from those reaches and I did not want for fresh meat.

Actually I stopped about halfway up the canyon and cooked some sausage on a fire grate along the river. It *was* a wild and rugged canyon, though, with sheer rock walls laced with cracks, of a dark red color, which rose up to the sky. I was getting up into the mountains again, more water, a strong growth of big pines which lent the canyon a cool, dark air. Yet it was a dry-land growth, without heavy tangles of brush on the forest floor. I was beginning to like this country more and more.

I came down into Taos in the evening and strolled around the town. It was an art colony with scores of galleries, adobe hotels, adobe bars. It had an easygoing, half-paced atmosphere that I liked. I stayed in town that night, listening to a pretty black-haired woman play a fine Spanish guitar. Dreaming out old dreams. The next morning I got in my mule and rode out into the country west of the settlement, scouting around. I loved the countryside. Adobe ovens out in the yards, chickens scratching around, a poor countryside with hardly any billboards, plateaus rising up in the distance of the plain, small rivers cutting deep, looping canyons out across the flatness. The Sangres steep and green by contrast, rising to the north, country that was high and difficult, but beautiful. It began to interest me and I wondered what lay beyond those mountains to the north. I wandered up that way.

Finally I found a place that had horses and gave five plews rental for a strong-chested mare, and I rode it up as far as I could, crossing and recrossing a little creek, out across a clearing and up into a stand of aspen on a mild hillside where I could see. I let the horse feed and sat there gazing about for a long time. There was too much downed timber to get further on a horse, so I started to think about making a trip from there on foot, taking a pack and a rifle and just starting north with a compass and seeing where I came out. From what I remembered of the highway map I could go all the way up into Colorado before I hit a highway. The idea began to take over my mind; I imagined myself walking through wild valleys, up long sparsely timbered ridges, hunting for my food, pushing north through a wild and uninhabited region of mountains. Like the trips the mountain men made; the real thing. I was fired on it, but I couldn't figure out how I could keep my mule and the rest of my outfit from getting stolen. I decided to talk to the rancher that I rented the horse from when I got back down.

Twilight came on, and I sat against a tree thinking about the trip, eating some cheese and sausage I brought along. Finally I slept there in half an old log, covered with the horse blankets, the animal haltered to a tree. The stars were fierce in the sky. I froze. Always the horse stood there peacefully, her head hung a little, dozing. A little thing like cold didn't bother the mountain men, I thought.

I woke up at first light, the birds singing, and saddled up the horse. I started out walking, leading her, to get warm. When the sun rose I climbed on and rode. The creek shone with the morning. The aspen were just starting to turn yellow; the Moon When the Berries Ripen was dying, slipping into darkness toward the birth of the next moon, the Moon When the Elk Fight. Autumn was coming on. The air along the creek was sweet and crisp as it circulated into my head. I liked this country and I wanted to find a place to build a cabin. I figured I must be getting close.

When I got back down to the ranch I talked to the foreman as he took in my horse. I asked him what would happen if a guy just took off to the north from there with a pack and kept going —what would he run into?

He shot me a once-over glance. "You'd run into the biggest goddamn logging operation you ever seen," he said. "They're logging the shit out of that country up there." And he walked away, carrying the saddle into the barn.

A MYSTERIOUS INCIDENT

I RODE DOWN out of the mountains and onto the plain west of the settlement, wandering around for part of the day, vague and displaced thoughts of land and a cabin circling around in my head. I got on a bumpy dirt road and headed toward the river I had seen out on the plain, figuring to see if there were any beaver on it. The road wound over mudholes and around sharp corners, past small, poor adobe homesteads that appeared beautiful to me, rickety fences, garden patches, beans and pea vines, goats and chickens foraging about, fire ovens, naked brown-skinned kids swimming in a muddy pond. Old wrecks of cars picked over for parts. The road wound past there, went a long way over sagebrush and nothingness, then dropped sharply downhill toward the river.

When I got down to the bottom there was a suspension bridge. I crossed it and turned off the road down some tire tracks that followed the river next to the canyon wall. Nightfall was coming; the canyon rose up fifty feet on either side, leaving a winding trail of shadowy sky overhead, a few stars beginning to wink. Desolate and age-ridden it seemed, so old my bones felt green. It went back to a time before the missionaries came, before Bridger rode down to see this country, before any white man had seen it. Back to a time when this land belonged to the Indians.

I stopped and got out of the mule. That canyon felt old in the open air, closed to my comprehension. The darkened river flowed slowly past like the blood of the Southwest. It traveled back beyond the worm-eaten bones of the missionaries, back to the spirits of a pueblo way of life, a collective way of life. There was pain in that river, dark pain.

I walked up a ways and found where an old campfire had been. It was almost dark now and the atmosphere of the canyon seemed lonely and beyond my grasp. Unconsciously I knelt down and put my hand on the ashes, looking around. Suddenly a burning sensation hit my palm and I shook my hand vigorously in the air. There were hot coals under those ashes.

The hair began to rise on my neck. Whose fire was that? Where were they? Why hadn't I seen them coming down the road? I was out in the middle of nowhere; *I should have seen them.*

I went back to the mule. I had the feeling I was being watched, by someone native. I was in their country, I had driven through it; maybe that's why I felt it. But I felt that I was being watched by an Indian.

I scrounged some dead sage, got some meat out of the mule and cooked it. I looked up and down the canyon, listened, but didn't hear a thing. I had the feeling that I was an intruder. But the only thing moving was the blackened river, drifting past as slowly as the passage of the stars. It was an eerie feeling. Finally I pulled the meat off and folded it in a piece of bread.

I was just about to take a bite when a great clattering of steel filled the canyon just up around the bend, as if someone had thrown a heavy pan down onto the rocks. My heart jumped and

I stood up, listening. The sounds died away into silence. The river moved past. Nothing stirred anywhere.

I threw my things into the mule and backed it up all the way to the bridge. I drove up out of the canyon and when I got to the top I didn't look back. I just kept going. Maybe someone didn't want me there, and had thrown the pan over to scare me off. I thought of the eeriness, the fear; I thought of some mountain man a hundred fifty years ago making a camp down here somewhere, the vast emptiness, no safety for a thousand miles, the darkness full of that fear I had felt. And the other side: a pair of native eyes, full of rain and sun, plains and far rivers, looking down from a place of concealment at the very first camp of the white intruders. Upon their land. I drove on through it, the darkness erasing the years. They would come back at dawn.

THE SPECTER OF
50,000 MOUSE TURDS

THE NEXT MORNING I drove up a dirt road about six or seven miles, back toward the mountains to the north. I figured to talk to a rancher about land. I passed several unlikely-looking places, then curved into some big timber and pulled up in front of a large log house, a real log house, not a prefab. The logs were old and dark, but they had been varnished. There were other log outbuildings scattered around, a big fuel tank, a small bulldozer. I went inside the entryway and saw rattlesnake skins mounted on boards. I knocked.

The man who answered was balding, of middle height, but had a sloping, powerful build, like a bear. He pierced me with a distrustful stare, then softened a little and invited me in. We drank coffee and I told him what had happened the night before. He told me that was a dangerous place to go, that I could have got my throat cut. By who? I asked. Mexicans, Indians, he said. I was tempted to say that if he were walking in their shoes he might feel like cutting a few throats too, but I held off.

I turned the conversation toward land.

"What land?" he said.

"I was looking to buy some."

"You and about ten thousand other people."

At those words my heart sank. Not here. "Is it hard to get?"

"There's none left. You can get desert for six hundred bucks an acre, but you'll dig to China to hit water. Who the hell wants to live on the desert with no water?"

My throat began to feel dry. "What about up here along the mountains?"

He grunted sarcastically. "Can you raise fifty thousand bucks?"

I couldn't raise fifty thousand mouse turds.

"Forget it, then."

"Is that true?"

"It sure is. Two thousand, four thousand, six thousand bucks an acre for the good land with water. It's gone crazy."

I swallowed and looked out the window. Goddamnit, I thought.

"You know what done it?" he said, in a more calculated tone. "Those goddamn hippies."

I couldn't believe how old that sounded. "What do you mean?"

"They started comin' here about ten years ago. Some of 'em had money and they bought land. *That's* when it started. Land's gone up four times since then."

He sat back tapping his finger on the table and looking at me. I knew what he was saying was true; that was indeed the historical turning point. The hippies were only one of its symbols. It was the same pattern, after all, as Colorado. For some reason a picture of a bear running flashed into my mind.

"Are there any grizzlies left around here?" I asked.

"Nope. Ain't been a griz here for years."

I began to feel the formation of an arrowhead in my guts. I stood up and headed for the door.

"Where you going?"

"I'm going to build a cabin."

Goddamn Easterners, he might have thought.

A MOUNTAIN MAN'S
SENSE OF DANGER

I RODE HARD back toward where I had rented the horse. I rode through a thunderstorm. I rode through hail and lightning. I rode across raging rivers. When I got to the place where the road ended I grabbed my ax and followed up the creek until I hit a side creek, and then I followed up that. After about a half mile of timber I came out into a grassy clearing on the south side of the creek. Rich pricks, I thought. There were enough straight pines around for what I needed. I walked over to one, sized it, and raised up my ax.

At that moment something stopped me. It was nothing I heard or saw; it was a sense, something in the air. That sixth sense that the mountain men developed, when they could feel in the air that something was impending, that some danger was near. There was no material explanation for it; just a wild sense that they developed after years in the mountains, living amid the dangers of grizzlies and Indian attacks. By God, I had it, and it was singing strong.

I held perfectly still, the ax poised, and slowly looked around me. Whatever it was, it was very close, and it felt as if it was about to strike. I could see nothing or hear nothing, nothing moved, but I felt that strange wild tingling in my nerves.

Then I looked above me. There, in the seventh branch of the tree I was about to hit, sat a young man in a green uniform with yellow patches on his shoulders. His hair was blond and well groomed; my mountain man's sense told me that he was from southern California and had just graduated from college. He was a Forest Ranger. He had a brown paper bag next to him, and he was eating a peanut-butter-and-banana sandwich, watching me with scarcely any expression on his face, except that of observation. Finally I spoke.

"What would happen if I built a cabin here?"

He picked a banana slice out of the peanut butter and flipped it into the air, like a coin. It landed neatly on his tongue. Chewing it up, he said, "You'd get put in jail."

That's what I thought.

"Don't work too hard," I said, and I walked away.

IT WAS pushing further into autumn, and there warn't nothing there for me any more. The fall hunt was getting late; it was time for me to start heading back toward Fort Alcohol. I packed up my outfit and headed over the divide west toward the San Juan River, figuring to swing up along the Green River into Utah. The harsh land floated past, low mountain ranges in the distance of the plains, a solitary mesa off in the desert that made me think of an ancient sea, vast stretches of sagebrush where scorpions tickled the sand and rattlesnakes lay like the embodiment of a century, dozing in the sun. The enormity of it, the vistas stretching far and empty with such relentless beauty, the harsh bright colors shimmering through the dry air—it was like a peyote dream. It uplifted me, disembodied me, made me wander in spirit along those far horizons, made me wonder at the sheer size of the land and the sky. I felt an ache at leaving this country, a sad ache that wouldn't let go for miles, images of the land and the people and the way of life that floated hauntingly in my memory. If only the prices hadn't gone crazy.

A CLOUD ON
THE SOUTHWESTERN HORIZON

I RODE ON. Early in the afternoon I looked ahead and saw a long and unnatural-looking smudge trailing along the horizon. It looked like a cloud, but the color was ugly and lifeless. Something big was burning there, but in all that parched nothingness I couldn't imagine what it was. It looked like it was fifty miles away, maybe more. I drove on toward it for over an hour, watching it gain magnitude as I approached, seem to rise higher and more grotesque into the sky. It was inky, something foreign in the landscape, with a hint of yellow bile scattered into its depths. I began to be suspicious.

It was a power plant, the Four Corners power plant. I got out of my mule and stood there staring at it. There were four different smokestacks scattered along a robot-like consortium of buildings, all of them pouring a silent burden of smoke steadily into the sky. The four smokes joined as they drifted up and away, becoming one massive inky blotch which covered the whole lower end of the sky. It was both awesome and satanic. After the clear and natural landscape I had come through, it was like a nightmare of financial power, born somehow into the bright heart of the desert. The wild and lonely spell of the countryside stamped with smoke. I sat there for a while, a breeze coming up over the dry wisps of grass and arid soil. Off in the distance rose a big, prow-shaped mountain that I knew to be Shiprock, the unmistakable landmark the early mountain men used, from a hundred miles off.

I copied extensive notes onto the map I was preparing for Captain Clark. The river is warm here, I wrote, unsuitable for drinking, and there are dead fish along the shoreline. There are no bear, few fowl, and the deer which remain in the area seem to be losing their fur. The source of this destruction is a mysterious combustion of smoke and fire, very foul-smelling, the origin of which I could not determine. Plant life downwind from it seems to be withering, and the soil contains a high degree of acidity. The rain that falls here burns the eyes. All in all it seems to be a dying region, and I recommend a wide detour through the canyons to the east. The smoke is visible for nearly a hundred miles across the plains.

GOODBYE, BIG SKY

THE ORIGIN of the smoke and fire was not mysterious in the present-day Rockies; it was a plant which burned coal for electricity, and they were springing up all over the West in the seventies. The West had been declared an energy Sacrifice Area by the federal government. I rode on into nearby Fort $$$ and found some magazine articles about the Four Corners plant in the local tobacco shop. One of them said, "Hello, Energy—Goodbye, Big Sky." The Four Corners plant when it first fired up put out over 300 tons of pollution a day, more than New York and Los Angeles combined. It burned 22,000 tons of coal every day. It was owned by Western Energy Supply Transmission Associates, a conglomeration of private power companies who dreamed up that acronym so they could be known to the world as WEST, the largest utility conglomerate yet known to man. There were over twenty of the companies scattered from California across the Southwest, and they got together and drew up massive plans for the Four Corners plant and five others in the region. The smoke would stay in the southwestern skies; the electricity would go out to big cities like Los Angeles, Phoenix, and Tucson. Plants were under construction along the Green River, along the Colorado River, and west of there toward the Taos country. The Peabody Coal Co. was in on the deal. When all the plants were running by the end of the seventies they would connect the pollution of the industrial East with the pollution of the West Coast. A high trailway of soot and sulphur poisons drifting across the southern end of the Rockies. The mountains down there wouldn't shine any more.

I put the location of every one of those companies on my map for Captain Clark, naming them all the Black Sky Power Co. I put a skull and crossbones where each one of their plants stood. I noted that the Indians in the vicinity of Fort $$$, whose long-sacred lands were being torn up for the coal, considered Black Sky Power Co. to be a conglomeration of rich liars who bought their way into the tribal councils with promises of color television sets and new pickup trucks, claiming that it was fair to trade those things for a black sky over their land. The Indians said that the power company's tongue was like a snake, that the only reason they were pushing so hard to burn coal for electricity was because they could make an enormous fortune doing it, and that it was never right to make the sky black for any reason. The Indians said that down in the Southwest the sun had great power, and all the power the people really needed could come from the sun and the wind.

I also noted that the Indians were very angry, and that they spoke with deep feeling and wisdom on this subject. On the basis of my own observations I made some other private recommendations to Captain Clark, and then dispatched that missive with a small band of trappers who were returning to St. Louis. Word had come up the Platte River that Captain Clark had recently been named Superintendent of Indian Affairs, and I deemed that it might be timely and important for him to receive the letter.

STÁRVIN' TIMES
IN THE VÁIL COUNTRY

D ARK THOUGHTS tumbled around in my head as I headed north over the San Juan Mountains, trailing back toward Fort Alcohol. Someday the Black Sky Power Co. would get theirs. In the meantime I held on to my evolving map of the Rocky Mountains, making mental notes about the way the sunburst ranges of central Colorado slipped gradually into the long dry stretches of the Southwest. I recalled that the long-timers among the mountain men learned the Rockies from end to end by riding along the big rivers and the major ranges, and their maps were locked in their memories. Jim Bridger stayed in the mountains for seventeen years without going back to St. Louis, and he knew them well. In *A History of the Mormons* by John W. Gunnison we are told that Bridger traversed the Rockies from near the Canadian border in Montana to the Gulf of California, and was the first white American to see the Great Salt Lake in Utah. "His graphic sketches are delightful romances," Gunnison wrote. "With a buffalo skin and a piece of charcoal he will map out any portion of this immense region, and delineate mountains, streams and the circular valleys called 'holes' with wonderful accuracy."

The thought of it fired me up again. He knew the Rockies by memory, by what he had seen on those horseback journeys; he could ride down the Green River into Utah, watching every day the way the river turned in relation to where the sun rose in the east, to where it set in the west, the mountains that served as major landmarks, and the time that it took him to travel those turns in hours and days of riding, and then years later sit down with someone and trace out that changing course in a scale of miles accurate in its length and its relationship to the surrounding chains of mountains. One of his chief claims to fame as a mountain man was his remarkable geographic memory; he had only to see a region once, and then it was locked in his memory from any direction, scaled and fitted in with the other pieces of ranges and river valleys that he had traveled, part of an enormous tangle of mountains that were then unmapped and unknown, but that spanned the continent.

That same quality was true of the other early and best-known mountain men, men like John Colter and Jedediah Smith. They were at heart explorers, although they seldom got paid for that. They bought their supplies with beaver skins—plews, they called them—and it was their business to be looking for new beaver streams. But some of them seemed possessed of an incorrigible inner urge simply to take off and explore, to use whatever excuse was necessary to travel into country where no one else had been, to see where the rivers went, to find a pass through a mountain range that no one else had crossed. For some of them that was their real love in the mountains.

That aspect of their lives I began to lean toward more strongly than anything else about them: those long journeys they sometimes made, roaming into some unknown region with only a rifle and a knife, a few rudimentary supplies, living from wild food as they went, and coming back out weeks or months later, walking back in among the other trappers as matter-of-factly as if they had just gone out to check on the horses. The country they covered, the wildness and ruggedness of it, continually haunted my imagination.

I thought of going up into British Columbia, but I knew my heart was down here and I couldn't leave it. I wanted to be a mountain man in America, not Canada. I knew from two years of living outside the country that I was an American, that I loved the country and cared what happened to it, that I was glued to the political process by which it would work out its destiny. I didn't want to escape from it. I just wanted to be a free mountain man.

Different schemes sailed through my thoughts as I rode north, rising into spectacular country; I started thinking more and more about long trips into the mountains. I dreamed of doing it myself for real—a light pack with a few essentials, a small-caliber rifle, a compass; traveling into the wildest country I could find. That was the closest I figured I could come to what they experienced—the feeling of being alone in all that wild country, the challenge of its size and sweep against a lone human, that strange thrill of exploring country I had never seen before. The test of being able to survive it and come back out. That was what I wanted; at the point that I arrived there I figured I would stop playing mountain man and start being one, as near as I could be in the seventies. But where to do it I didn't yet know.

I rode north to the east of the Sawatch Range, passing through Fort Leadville in a strange feathery snowstorm. The weather had turned, the autumn was growing late, and the remainders of the elk herds were starting to move down. I camped in a high and lonely stand of pines with a creek flowing through, and listened to the wind moaning through the tops of the trees. *You're too late*, it seemed to whisper.

I kept on a-goin', boys, up over the top of them mountains in snow that woulda bogged down one of Hannibal's elerphants, snow as tall as the tallest trees, a curious mountain lion on my trail, me just a-pushin' on through them drifts till I come over off the north side and started down into the big valley of the Vail country. About the time I come down out of the snow I hit on starvin' times. I run out of jerky and I didn't have no more flour, and that old hunger was eatin' at my legs by the time I got to the creek. They was hungry mountains all around there, boys, and I set out to raise me some meat.

I didn't have much luck. Fort Vail was crawling with people; the ski hills above the town looked like white anthills. Expensive cars were pouring into the valley in a steady stream, bumper to bumper. Everywhere you looked they were building new lodges. The deer and elk had to cross the freeway in a big steel culvert —there was no other way for them to get over.

I was hungry. I didn't have no more sausage and I barely had enough plews to feed my mule. I set out hunting, but I couldn't get away from them lodges. They was everywhere. They were shaped like a big "A," and they had lots of glass in the ends and balconies for people to be seen from. They stood up there with drinks in their hands, dressed in fine sweaters and tight red or blue leggings, and glanced down their noses at me with looks that would injure a cactus. I went on down the valley and it was the same everywhere. It was all glass, envy, and lipstick. They all had big champion dogs that cost a fortune and chased deer. When they came back from killing one of the few deer that were left the people put them on leashes, put on their jazzy outfits, and strolled through town, pretending what a hard time they were having with such a big, handsome, and extraordinarily stupid pedigree dog. I almost shot one of them to eat but its owners came out of the store. They walked on down the street, smiling at the people who obviously had money. At night they murdered each other in their dreams.

I was down and out. I kept on hunting. Game was fearsome scarce. I looked in the aspen groves, up the draws, and over the ridges of low hills. All I found were the A-shaped lodges, and huge gleaming gas hogs driving up and down over the hills. One man came out on his balcony in a silk robe and yelled at me to get off his property. He took off a pair of twenty-two-dollar fireplace slippers and threw them at me one after the other, yelling that he was going to call the police. I told him to shut up; I retrieved the slippers, went into town, and sold them to an aspiring young hotel clerk for four dollars. I continued hunting. Finally I caught sign of some Big Macs. I trailed them across a broad expanse of Formica counter, and kilt two of them near a painting of a river bordered all around by plastic elderberry bushes. I hated myself when I kilt Big Macs. I was convinced they were laced with heroin.

I had enough. It was no place for a mountain man to be. In that town you had to have a Master Charge card to take a deep breath. That night I found a Cadillac parked behind a building and siphoned enough gas to drive to St. Louis and back. I took off in a snowstorm. The fall hunt was over.

I went north on the Blue River, then east up the Colorado River and across the slopes of Shadow Mountain, where the aspen trees stood bare against the sky. It was growing in me to quit the Colorado territory and strike out for the Northwest. Vail was like a suburban nightmare, a twisted mockery of all the mountains could mean for human beings. Colorado, for all its height and color and beauty, was full of millionaires, politicians, and glamour junkies. It was like a full-color advertisement beaming down into the middle of the Rockies. There were no griz left; the last one disappeared ten or fifteen years ago, replaced by a ski resort.

I commenced to climb the Continental Divide up a series of steep and narrow switchbacks, laboring with my mule until I reached the summit. There at the heights I found a large fake Indian trading post, run by white men, which did a considerable business in plastic eagle feathers, vinyl moccasins, fiberglass wildflowers, and a limited supply of what they claimed were buttons from William F. Cody's underwear. Not being in a mind to trade, nor having the plews to do so, I continued down the eastern side of the Divide, seeing a band of wild goats at a salt lick, and descended a river whose name I do not remember, but which I faithfully transcribed onto my map for Captain Clark. After a mild storm and many days' journey down the canyons of that wild region, I finally ascended the middle fork of Bear Creek, and on the twenty-ninth day of October in that year I once again passed through the historic gates of the fort.

THE FLÁVOR OF FORT ÁLCOHOL

FORT ALCOHOL was where I wintered that year, working up a grubstake and replenishing my outfit. It was called Fort Alcohol because most of the people there drank whiskey for breakfast. Small businesses came and went broke, but the bars never closed. The people were broke, broken; they drank and managed to keep alive. There was a little money in gas and tires, in a pile of lumber, a junk car, a poached deer when someone could find one. It was the flip side of Colorado, the poor side. The glamorous dreams the people there bought were always getting repossessed, and they couldn't understand why. They couldn't believe they were getting taken; they still thought that someday a piece of Hollywood or Vail or Aspen would fall in their laps. It never did. Instead there were explosive fights with broken bottles and chairs, stolen pickups, a shooting, and borrowed money that was never paid back. There weren't any mountain men left in that town that I could find. A few honest fishermen was all, and they were giving up on it. The fish weren't native any more.

By the time the first heavy snows were burying the grizzly in its high and inaccessible den far to the north of Fort Alcohol, I was already dreaming about the spring hunt. I made up my mind that I was going to take off for that country to the northwest where there were still some grizzlies left. I would build up a grubstake over the winter and take my mule toward the Yellowstone country and on into the Montana territory. There warn't no wolves left in Colorado, and there warn't no wolverines. I wanted to get into country that was wilder, country where there were a few grizzlies left, where there were more wild animals to follow. I wanted to learn how to track. I wanted to find a place that was wild enough to build a cabin.

I got a job building concrete bridges for the new middle-class settlers who were pouring into the surrounding canyons, who wanted them so they could get to Fort Capitalism faster. I got my outfit together. I sharpened my ax. I bought a chain saw. I got a good Green River knife and a Hawken rifle, and at night sitting by the old man's big stone fireplace I dreamed about a place somewhere up there to the northwest where it was still wild, where there weren't any subdivisions or throngs of people moving in, where there were deer and elk in the woods, bears, where the price of land hadn't gone crazy, and I could make the trips that I dreamed about making. Take a rifle and a pack and head into some of those ranges up there, travel wild, live off the land like the mountain men. I would pick several ranges and see if it could still be done.

Actually my rifle wasn't a Hawken, it was a Remington 66 that weighed four pounds. The Hawken was the favorite of the mountain men, but it weighed ten pounds and shot a .50-caliber ball, for buffler and griz. And there warn't scarcely any buffler or griz left. So I pretended mine was a Hawken. American history was eating a thousand new holes in the old distances, the old wildness.

As the winter wore on I could barely wait for the snows to begin melting away from the high mountain passes. I held the fervent hope that the country to the north wasn't all sliced up yet. I began to plan the spring hunt up the South Platte and into Wyoming, west over the Snowy Range, north through Muddy Gap till I hit the Sweetwater River, and up the Sweetwater till I hit the tar springs at Lander and the beginning of the Wind River Mountains. That was the way some of the first mountain men moved into Wyoming in the 1820's, once the central Platte route opened up to regular travel.

As the deeper snows came I began to think more and more about long trips into the mountains, about finding some wild country that I could do it in and what I would carry. A kettle and a spoon, a flint for emergencies, compass, flour and jerky, fishline and hooks, ammunition, knife, signal mirror. Travel as light as I could. Every time I thought about actually doing it I felt a magnetic pull so strong it sometimes made me stand up and pace. If I could find someplace to do it, the mythology I was pursuing would become real to me; I would be living out my own myth, for myself. I dreamed of what it would feel like to be back in the mountains and totally dependent on my own resources for my survival; I dreamed of following moose and bear, living in the wild with them, learning their ways. The idea of long trips off on my own stuck with me and grew stronger. I would do it when I got up into Montana and Idaho.

To kill time I went to the library at Fort Image up the creek to read about the mountain men and some of their adventures and journeys in the wilderness of the Rockies. I read about Jedediah Smith and the extraordinarily hazardous trips he made across the deserts from the Rockies to California and back; I read about the scattering of Colonel Andrew Henry's trappers from the Three Forks region of the upper Missouri by Blackfeet in the summer of 1811, the lost wanderings of those men over great areas of the northern Rockies. I read with amazement about Hugh Glass and John Colter. I read about the travels of Ashley's trappers over the Wind River Mountains and beyond in the 1820's, into the Yellowstone country, down into the Green River country in Utah. I read about Hugh Glass's famous 250-mile crawl, and James Clyman's 600-mile survival walk down the Sweetwater and the Platte when he missed a meeting with some other trappers. I began to realize that some of the journeys the early mountain men made, by accident or design, were extraordinary. They involved great distances, sometimes over unexplored territory, often under extreme conditions. Not just the physical hardships they faced, but the mental and emotional strain they took on in facing a tract of wilderness the size of Montana, alone or lost or in trouble, and still made it through. Those epic journeys seemed to illuminate the qualities that I admired most in the mountain men: gut-level endurance, a refusal to give up, something in the human spirit that hangs on in the face of adversity against odds that seem impossible. There was something inside some of those men that was awesome; by choice they put themselves 2,000 miles deep in a mountain wilderness, taking on the enormous odds of weather, freezing, grizzlies, lone injuries and winter starvation, the bewildering vastness of the mountains themselves, and somehow their spirits rose up to it, they learned to exult in it. Instead of shrinking in the face of those odds something in them climbed up to meet them, swelled in spirit to the size of the mountains themselves, and sometimes soared beyond them in a personal victory. The mountain men were in a contest with the mountains, they felt that contest, had superstitions about it, lived its fine lines every day they were in the mountains. They wanted to live in the mountains and they wanted the mountains to stay wild. Although they didn't formulate it as such, their challenge was a contest of the spirit, a confronting of fate—their life against the reach of the mountains. The final result of the game was simple: either they made it through alive, or they went under. The challenge of staying alive, of playing their fate against the wild and cold of the Shining Mountains was what gave them their stature, made their spirits big and exultant, made them seem mythical to us today. That the ones who survived loved the region was indicated by the name they gave the mountains, for that is what some of the early ones called the Rockies: the Shining Mountains.

THE WRITER'S SECRET HERO: THE FIRST MOUNTAIN MAN

As THE WINTER began to lose its grip I dreamed of those journeys I was reading about, the test of the high mountains, the challenge of the spirit they held, and of making trips like them on my own. I dreamed of heading up into the northern Rockies, into the wildest mountains that were left, and making my own trips.

I found one more story of a lone trip by an early mountain man that dumbfounded me: the winter journey John Colter made when he discovered Yellowstone in 1808. A painfully brief account of it was published by H. M. Brackenridge in 1811, to wit: "This man, with a pack of thirty pounds weight, his gun and some ammunition, went upwards of five hundred miles to the Crow nation; gave them information, and proceeded from them to several other tribes."

Aside from being one of the greatest single feats of exploration made in the Rockies by any mountain man, that trip was also a feat of endurance that is difficult to fathom. He started out in the late fall, alone, and returned in the spring, long after the other trappers had given him up for dead. He traversed the high mountains in the middle of winter, crossing the Continental Divide twice. The country he covered was all unexplored. He was the first white American to set foot in Wyoming, the first to see Wind River, the first to set foot in Yellowstone. He was the first to cross the Tetons. The mountains he found his way through in that area were high and rugged; it seemed impossible that he could have picked his way through them in the winter.

But it was true. After six years in the Rockies, Colter went back to St. Louis and told William Clark about his lone journey.

It was published on Clark's map of 1814 as a meandering dotted line through the mountains, and called "Colter's Route." Clark called his map *A Map of Lewis and Clark's Track Across the Western Portion of North America from the Mississippi to the Pacific Ocean*. That dotted line was the only official recognition Colter ever got while he lived. Now western historians generally recognize him as the First Mountain Man, and open the era with the day that he left the returning Lewis and Clark expedition in North Dakota and turned back toward the Rockies with two other trappers in 1806.

Back at my lodge I got out my map and titled it *Bicentennial Explorations of the Shining Mountains Region, Including Its Major Valleys, Rivers & Peaks, Concentrations of Wild Game, and Some of Its More Sublime as well as Depressing Aspects, Including Its Ravagement by the Rich and Super-Rich*. It was a long title, but that's the way they done it in them days. I drew in Colter's Route as best I could. I had to find out more about him.

Finally as the winter started to break and hints of green grass showed up on the south hillsides I began to feel something inside me that wanted to explode, that wanted to break out of Fort Alcohol and Colorado like a stack of dynamite, sending things flying, riding high through the springtime and north into wilder country. See them mountains that Colter first went into. I couldn't take the glamour junkies and I couldn't take the *Playboy* mentality, and I couldn't take the sadness of seeing the beauty of that part of the Rockies developed to death. *Don't Californicate Colorado*, the bumper stickers said, but it was already done. At night I ground my teeth; in the evenings I oiled my Hawken, sharpened my skinning knife, and began packing my gear in ammunition crates I got from the back room of Fort Safeway. I boiled my socks in preparation for the spring hunt, and I sat watching the sun come up before I went to the concrete pits. I listened to the water dripping off the eaves in the wet evenings, the new birdcalls, and dreamed of the unknown trails.

One bright spring morning at the pits, I looked around and noticed that the snow was almost all melted, the birds were singing in full, and the sun was shining down out of a big blue sky full of warmth and freedom. I put my hammer down, walked up to the boss's younger brother, and told him I thought he was full of shit. I had been carrying that for five months. He didn't say anything, he just stared. The birds were singing away. I picked up my tools and walked off the job.

I was done with it. I sailed back over the asphalt trails to my lodge, feeling dizzy with freedom. The creek was full of the power of melting snow, shining in a steady roar. I hurried old Sixties around from the corral and packed it up tight with everything I owned. I whistled to the pines. I ran around in a daze saying some goodbyes, and finally I burned a little juniper in front of the bars. Then I lit out north along the Platte River.

OLD GABE

I *pushed that old mule as hard as she'd go, boys, hair flyin' and the dust a-rollin' behind me, away north from the Platte and on up into the Wyoming territory. I rode through spring thunderstorms and over swollen rivers, I rode on day and night without stoppin'.* In my mind a character appeared: an old mountain man with long grizzled white hair and beard, buckskins, feathers and beads, riding alone with a Hawken rifle and a rolled buffalo robe, someone free to roam from one end of the Shining Mountains to the other, seeing and feeling the heights, living off the earth, before the expanding American economy began to take over the Rockies. He was shrewd, joyous, devilish; he was free and he loved it. I invented him to help maintain my sanity, a panacea for temporary helplessness. Every time I saw a new second-home subdivision springing up in the foothills I imagined him in its place, riding over the location scornful and free, chewing and spitting tobacco. He was a free trapper and he didn't take any shit; hunger was his only boss. He had friends among the Indians. The other trappers called him old Gabe.

Actually old Gabe was Jim Bridger's nickname among the other mountain men, and I liked it so much I couldn't think of a better one. But he wasn't only Jim Bridger, although there was a lot of Bridger in him. There was some of Colter's daring in him, and some of Jed Smith's visionary urge to explore, and some of old Bill Williams' mania for solitude. He was a mixture of a lot of them.

I went over the Snowy Range and it was still early up there, huge snowdrifts and a wind that was freezing cold, yellow flowers just starting to come up through the snow. They were the first big range after the plains, moving up the Rockies from Colorado, and they were high and running with snow water, lots of quartz outcroppings, small pits where they had been prospecting for gold. Some of the peaks pushed past 11,000 feet; it was a high and beautiful range surrounded by plains, and there was more remoteness in it than I had felt anywhere in Colorado. I was getting into wilder country.

THE OREGON TRÁIL

T HIT THE PLAINS again and pushed northwest toward the Sweetwater and the tar springs at Lander. The plains were empty except for fences, scattered cattle, and oil rigs; a vast ancient seabed that stretched far toward the horizon, overwhelming the spirit with its barren, windswept distances. There were mesas where the ancient waterlines showed to mark off centuries; there were low and barren mountain ranges off in the sunlit haze where dinosaur bones lay buried, spearheads frozen in the rock. I took off my shirt and shoes, rolled down all the windows in the mule and *rode for days on end without seeing another human, once in a while some Indian smoke way off in the distance where they was doin' up buffler meat, nothin' else but all that space and sky that made me feel like I was floatin' in another world. And then one of them spring thunderstorms would come across the openness, and soon enough there'd be thunder a-boomin' so big it like to rattle my insides, and I'd get down in one of them washes and wait, soon drippin' and soaked, spears of lightnin' hittin' so close the hair on my neck would raise up. By thunder, I jes' kept on a-goin' toward them Wind River Mountains, for it was the sweet time of year and the storms and the lightnin' made my soul sing with joy. Old Gabe was friends with the sky, and he was always hopin', poor child as he was, that the sky was friends with him.*

I was on what was to become the Oregon Trail, the first road over the Rocky Mountains.

WIND RIVER LAW

I RODE into Lander in the evening and made my camp in a park by the river. About three in the morning a police car pulled up and told me if I wasn't out of there in a half hour I'd get put in jail. I told him I was a free mountain man and I warn't hurting nothing. He told me if I wasn't out of there in a half hour I'd be a free jail man. I stuck some porcupine quills in his tire as he left, then I packed up my outfit and pulled out in the predawn darkness, brushing away my tracks as I went.

The next day I rode up into the long high foothills south of the tar springs to get a look at the country. I was again on the front range of the Rockies, the end of the plains stretching back to the east. The Wind River Mountains ran for about a hundred miles, angling northwest toward the Yellowstone-Teton country, the heartland of the mountain men. I had read about these mountains when I was about twelve, and the name always stuck in my memory. Now I found myself next to them and I began to think about making a trip into them.

I couldn't see them, they were hidden by massive foothills. Those hills angled up toward the west in long smooth runs, treeless, the wind coming over them with great power from far away. Late in the day I watched a lone eagle soaring on the wind, high over the immense hills. It appeared as if it needed nothing in life but food and wind. The sun dropped into a red pile of clouds and the wind turned cold. I was left hanging with that eagle, wondering about both its freedom and its lack of emotion.

The next day back in town I ran into a wilderness ranger who made long patrols into the Wind River Range on horseback. After some talk, and some double-talk, he agreed to let me ride in with him. It wasn't exactly the kind of trip I had in mind, but it would do for starters. I wanted to see how wild those mountains were. I gave fifty plews rental for a speckled gelding and we rode in for ten days. Trailing one of the pack horses behind me, I dreamed of getting into parts of that range that were wild, where there were no people.

We ran into four hundred people in ten days. People were swarming over the Wind River Mountains like ants. Church groups, Boy Scout groups, National Outdoor Leadership School survival groups, a family of nine from Iowa, a high school biology class, a scourge of backpackers, and a high executive from the Colonel Sanders chicken corporation. Every day it was like that. The ranger told me that he had been patrolling the Winds for five years; on his very first trip he saw three people in ten days. Now he saw three hundred and fifty, and he hardly saw any wild game any more. It was all going downhill fast, he said, more and more scars.

I went back to Fort Hipster and got my outfit together. The ranger told me it was the same story in the Big Horn Mountains, which lay a hundred miles to the northeast. I had to get further northwest. Warn't no griz left in the Winds.

I said goodbye to the ranger and started up Wind River toward the Yellowstone country, on a long heavily timbered pass that kept climbing and climbing. I worked on my map of the Shining Mountains, sketching in the Winds and making notes. They were more pyramidal, they stretched more than the ranges in Colorado. The whole range had a grandeur of design, spaced with sharp peaks which sloped down gracefully to merge with the valleys, as if they had been shaped by an awesome wind. More room, a bigger sky between the peaks. Which was, I realized, true of Wyoming in general. Big open plains and badlands separated most of the mountain ranges; after the tightly scattered and sun-shot eruptions of the central Rockies, the mountains were separating into big solitary ranges whose outlying spurs sank finally into long stretches of ancient and dry country. The Big Horns, the Laramie Mountains, the Snowy Range, the Wind River Mountains. Big, solitary ranges.

On up the canyon I went, leaving the dryness behind. I saw some big mountains rising to the north, bare volcanic-looking humps, high and massive, fissures and holes in them filled with snow, mist hanging around their tops. They had an air of darkness to them; it felt as if the country beyond them would be wild and without human habitation. Looking at them I felt a twinge of fear and wonder; at first sight they struck a nerve in me. They looked old and dark, wild. I stopped at a gas station and asked the man there what mountains they were. Them are the Crow Mountains, he said. Are there any grizzlies in there? I asked. There sure enough are, he said.

I made up my mind that one of my survival trips would be into those mountains.

I kept going on up Togwatee Pass. This was the route it was generally agreed that John Colter used when he discovered the Tetons and Jackson Hole. I got the feeling that the land of the entire region was rising, in a long and gradual way; the forests were deep green and the country far into the distance looked high, like the thickly timbered hills of a huge plateau, teeming with glimpses of water, covered with wild and dense-looking forests. It would be a long, long way to come up this pass on snowshoes, but what a journey. Twenty years after Colter trailed it other mountain men were using this pass to get up over into Jackson Hole and the Yellowstone country north of it, although their supplies came over South Pass, near where I had seen the eagle. By the mid-1820's the Yellowstone-Teton country had become the heartland of the fur trade. The summer trading rendezvous was usually held in Jackson Hole, and from there they fanned out in four directions for the spring and fall hunts: north through Yellowstone Park and into Montana, west into Idaho, east into lower Wyoming, and south along the Green River toward the Great Salt Lake in Utah. It was some country they covered on those long journeys, and they always seemed to wind up back in the vicinity of Yellowstone and Jackson Hole. That region itself was rich in furs, and it was a natural crossroads in terms of routes through the mountains. It was the closest place to home that most of them had.

THE THREE BREASTS

I CAME up over the top of the pass and there, rising out of a large flat plain, were the most awesome mountains I had ever seen. I stopped and got out of the mule. They towered up like giant pyramids above the surrounding plain, white and shining, so big that even in the far distance they made me murmur under my breath. At their base they formed a massive wall; at the tops their sheer white peaks cut into the sky, higher than the passing clouds. Trois Teton, a French trapper named them—the Three Breasts. The Three Paps, the more businesslike British of the Hudson's Bay Company called them. Pilot Knob, some of the American mountain men called Grand Teton, the biggest of the three, for once seen it remained forever a landmark in the memory.

Standing there with the wind streaming past, cars passing and tourists stopping, I wondered again and again at the experience of John Colter entering into this region on snowshoes when it was still wild and far, after the long and arduous trip from the bottom of the pass and beyond, looking over the top to the plain and those ethereal mountains rising up, the spread of the dense wilderness all around; it would be as if he were entering someplace unearthly, mythical. They were so high, the region looked so pristine and wild, that he would have had to remind himself that he was flesh and blood and this was the earth, still the same large region of mountains that he had previously been traveling in. It was that different, that amazing. I was nearing the heart of the Shining Mountains.

I drove down across the plain and into the town of Jackson Hole. It was full of millionaires and glamour freaks. Everyone had posters of Robert Redford and other movie stars pinned to their walls and land was a million dollars an acre. It used to be the home of the mountain men.

I continued north along the Lewis River and into Yellowstone

Park. Somewhere up the Lewis I stopped at a place where they had float trips; there were cars, buses, and hundreds of tourists milling everywhere. I got out of the mule and went down by the river, taking my maps, driven by some inner sense of being close to a discovery. The surrounding forests were dense and wild-looking, the river pristine and clear; there was something in the air that was rare and high and mysterious, wilder than any place I had been in the Rockies, despite the throngs of people. I squatted there by the river, sensing it for a while, feeling the power it had to obliterate the noise and clamor, but unable to put my finger on what it was. Then I began to study the maps.

It dawned on me. The rivers. This was the height of the Rockies, the headland of the big western rivers. It was the altitude I was feeling; I was on a massive wilderness plateau. The rivers in all directions flowed down off it. It made rivers flow to the north: the Yellowstone River, the Gallatin River, and the Madison River all fanned out of the park and flowed north into Montana for fifty miles or more. The Snake flowed south into Idaho, the Shoshone flowed east into Wyoming, the Wind River flowed southeast into Wyoming. It was the very beginning of the Missouri River. Water that began on the Yellowstone Plateau flowed 2,000 miles down the Missouri to the Mississippi and the Gulf of Mexico on one side, 2,000 miles down the Snake to the Pacific Ocean on the other side. The Continental Divide ran through the park, and there was a creek called Two Ocean Creek which split on the Divide so that half its waters flowed into the Gulf, half into the Pacific. Two Ocean Plateau. The region was the violent and volcanic headland of the waters of the Rockies. The Green River started up just south of here and flowed all the way down into the Southwest. It was the symbolic as well as the actual birthplace of the Shining Mountains. I had made it back to the beginning, the home of the mountain men.

Finally I wandered on through the park, taking it all in, trying to fathom how John Colter found his way through this high and jumbled region of mountains and timber in the dead of winter, when the nights were 20 and 30 below and the snow twelve feet deep. I wondered over the wild and lonely feeling of the Rocky Mountain Fur Company trappers who followed his footsteps twenty years later, roaming and exploring and hunting wild meat, when they began to find out that the things he said about boiling mud springs and exploding geysers were indeed true, when they saw and felt for the first time the wonder of the Tetons and this high wilderness plateau that was 2,000 miles west of American civilization, at the mythical height of the Shining Mountains. And they looked around, feeling the wildness and beauty, and they said: By thunder, I'm going to stay here, *I ain't going back*. That was what made a mountain man—when he decided to spend the winters in the mountains instead of going back to St. Louis. Then he could call himself a true *hivernan*, a winterer. At that point something was born in them, and America had one of its deepest and most fetching myths. It became a lifestyle, an identity in itself. And this region of the Teton peaks and the hot baths of the Yellowstone Plateau was the region they called home, felt was their home.

THE NEED FOR Á HOME

I RODE on out of the park, thinking about my own need for a home base. I had been on the road for too many years, and the American status system was wearing on me. The law of the land was that if you didn't have a dollar you weren't worth a nickel, everywhere you went, and I was tired of it. I was tired of getting kicked out of parks at three in the morning. I was tired of the Fort Images and the glamour freaks; I was tired of middle-class hipsters, ski groupies, Jesus freaks, and fashionable ecologists; I was tired of mountain rock stars and racist businessmen. I was tired of John Denver's smiling teeth. The Rockies were being overrun by status, and I didn't have any. I needed a place to hang my hat. The rich now owned the home of the mountain men; it had turned into a little Hollywood. It seemed as if the country I was now riding into was my last chance—I had to find it here. I was almost to the end of the American Rockies. Once again my grubstake was running low. I was running out of country and I was running out of gas. As I rode on up the Madison

River valley and into Montana, watching a low-spreading range of mountains rise up on the left, I held on to the hope that there was a place left for me up here somewhere. That if I got back into country that was off the beaten track enough I could find some cheap land that hadn't been hacked up into a subdivision. Then I could build a small place, hang my hat, and lay in some firewood, and I could write and survive even if I was poor. I would be free; I would be a mountain man. My American dream.

And then I could make the survival trips I dreamed about. Get a good rucksack, some cheese and jerky, my Hawken, and head into the wild. Deep into the Crow Mountains. Maybe try the Swan Range up near the Canadian border. Set out into the Idaho wilderness in the springtime when there weren't any people, work my way across, see how wild it was, see if I could get into some truly wild country. Explore the wilderness in the seventies, and be a real mountain man. I wondered if I could do it.

I rode on with a certain grimness of intent, pressing old Sixties harder with the knowledge that I was running out of time. That poor mule was starting to take a beating as the seasons of the seventies came on. Somebody kicked it in the shoulder in a Safeway parking lot, out of spite, and a gravel truck spit out a rock and cracked its windshield. A city councilman in Casper, Wyoming—an energy boom town—said one night in a bar that old Sixties wasn't worth a shit. I said that by comparison he was worth a lot of shit. He agreed. I polished up the headlights and put in new sparkplugs. By God, I'd keep ridin' it, for there was good things about it and it had a place in my heart.

The surrounding countryside as it spread out caused a low moon of hope to rise somewhere in my emotions. I followed up the Madison and turned on the main Bozeman Trail, heading west out across the Montana territory. Off to the south distant ranges rose up one after another, still white with snow, looking remote and untouched. I rode over rolling hill country and across wide plains; the sky was blue and immense, peopled with white clouds, and weeds were blooming away from the rivers. Wherever there were horses the mares had thin new colts close at their sides. The air was fresh and windy. The land was so good and big that it made me ache. I kept on a-goin', boys, for I was bound to find it.

FORT STINKPOT

I CROSSED the Continental Divide over a region of round-rocked mountains, riding hard, and finally followed down a steep canyon of the Clarks Fork and into Fort Stinkpot. Fort Stinkpot was the major fort in western Montana, located in a big valley rimmed around by high mountains. Known in earlier times as Mis-Sou-La, it is now called Fort Stinkpot because a huge corporate mill there puts out a form of pollution which on certain days makes the whole valley smell like a stale dog fart. Especially in the winter, when atmospheric inversions hold it down over the settlement for days at a time. The people who own the mill live up above the odor in the mountains. "Farts are a natural part of everyday life," they say in the newspapers anyway, defending the smell they have created. Fort Stinkpot was also a big branch office for the Montana Black Sky Power Co., and I found out they were busy with plans to swallow one of Montana's rivers whole and turn the skies dark in eastern Montana, where there was a great deal of coal under Indian lands. The same pattern I had seen in the Southwest was just beginning up here. I marked the locations down on my map for Captain Clark.

I was running out of plews; the spring hunt was almost over. I hit north, up the Flathead River, along the Mission Mountains and almost up to the Canadian border, but I didn't have any luck. The valley was beautiful, there were grizzlies and wolverines in the Missions, but the real estate business was booming, the price of land had quadrupled, and people were pouring in. There was a new colony of glamour freaks up at Fort Whitefish. I passed it by and crossed the mountains in the region of Glacier Park on the Going to the Sun Trail, seeing mountains so big and spectacularly beautiful that they fractured my consciousness. I'd probably still be there today, except that it was a National Park. If they caught you building a cabin up there they'd put you away for 99 or life.

THE SWAN RANGE

I WENT BACK SOUTH, my mule starting to go lame, my moccasins worn out, till I hit the Swan River on the eastern side of the Missions. It formed a dense, relatively narrow valley which drained back to the south. As I rode down that valley I was struck with its depth and beauty; in the evening the sun streamed over the Missions in bright gold shafts which shone across all the dark timber at the upper end of the valley. On the left side was a strange, wild-looking range of mountains—the Swan Range—the upper end of them high and moon-blasted, the southern end softer, a mixture of mysterious greens and browns blending into each other. I found out that on the other side of the Swans lay a million acres of classified wilderness. There were griz in there, lots of them; it was one of the wildest stretch of mountains left. I would make one of my trips up there. I'd start in about the time the snow was gone from the high country, the Moon When the Bears Run Together, climb to the top, spit on my palm and see which way it flew. All that wilderness to explore. Travel light and see if I could survive, see which way the calling led me. Feel that freedom on the wild side of the mountains.

But first I had to find a place to hang my hat. I pushed south, past Fort Stinkpot, and by the time I trailed down into the Bitterroot Valley the spring hunt was over. I was done in from traveling, fur was sparse, my socks were stinking again, and my mule could scarcely walk; rear wheel bearing was thumping. I rested, camping out in the foothills of those mountains, and fixed my mule. A full moon rose up. High water was passing in the Bitterroot River. I knew I was at the end of the line. One more hunt. I was in the wildest country left in the Shining Mountains.

I got a job driving a fifteen-yard dump truck and started caching plews. The Bitterroot Mountains haunted me through the day and the night. They were a deeply powerful range, broad with scattered peaks, and on the other side of them lay a million and more acres of Idaho wilderness: the Selway River country, the Salmon River country. The Bitterroots started out way above Fort Stinkpot and ran for over two hundred and fifty miles, forming nearly all of the western border of Montana. Below Fort Stinkpot they formed the western heights of the Bitterroot Valley for about seventy-five miles. It was a huge sunny valley of a beauty which sent my spirit reeling. Through large hazy gaps in the mountains it seemed as if I could look all the way across into the mysteries of the Idaho wilderness.

But the Bitterroot Valley itself was already heavily subdivided when I got there; land was two to three thousand dollars an acre. Rich people liked to retire there. Fake log cabins were going up everywhere.

I planned the fall hunt up the West Fork of the Bitterroot River, which wound some thirty miles back in toward the Idaho border. There was a little private land up there, and some mining claims. The rest was National Forest. That was it for me. Somewhere up there . . .

The summer floated past and I got my outfit ready, a lone spark of hope burning in my soul. I counted my imaginary plews and put them in imaginary packs; I drove the big fifteen-yarder up and down the mountain, hauling riprap, blasted rocks to fill in the logging road where a river coming down from the Idaho peaks was eating it away. All day the logging trucks came down out of Idaho, hauling big cedar logs, and I wondered what that stand would look like when they were finished. I wondered if there were still places left where you could see big virgin stands of cedar and ponderosa, see what a four-hundred-year-old forest looks like. Maybe in the Selway wilderness. I planned to make one of my trips in there as I bounced down through the heat and dust, early in the spring when there were no people, traveling light and wild across a hundred miles of wilderness, seeing what wild places I could get into. I dreamed of it through the heat and dust. The High-Water Moon.

Finally, about the time the big rocks started to show up out in

44

the river, I sharpened my ax, packed up everything I owned, spit over my shoulder at the racist owners of the dump trucks I drove, and took off south, along the Bitterroot.

I was riding a thin line, traveling on hope. I went up the West Fork and followed it mile after mile as it wound into the mountains, shining water, yellow sunlight through the trees at the bends. Past houses and ranches, more and more into stretches of forest. I asked around here and there. Finally I met a man who knew about some land way up near the Idaho border, on Hughes Creek, and he said he'd show it to me. We drove on up till the road turned to dirt, climbed a mountain, rode past a reservoir, and kept going for seven or eight more miles into the mountains. Then we turned up a smaller dirt road and followed that for eight miles, up a narrow mountain valley with a lot of willows along the bottom, steep forested hillsides rising up on either side. It was forty miles down the mountain to the nearest fort. It looked pretty wild.

Finally we came to a cluster of weathered log buildings overlooking the creek. It was an old gold camp that the man owned; there was a tool shed, a cookhouse, a wash shack, and several cabins. He was a good man, straight with me. He knew I didn't have much money and so he told me offhand that I could stay up there for nothing and watch the place if I wanted. It was what I needed, and I told him I'd do it. After he left I picked out the oldest cabin overlooking the creek, and I unpacked my outfit. I hung my ax on the porch. I hung my lantern from a rafter. I hung my hat from a peg on the wall.

In the next few days I laid in some firewood and cleaned out the cabin, getting things in order. I trapped a wood rat and stopped up the cracks between the logs with old newspapers, pounded down some boards where there were holes in the floor. Mornings I went scouting up and down the creek; there were a few moose in the willow bottoms, some deer roaming through the lodgepoles. It warn't long afore I decided to spend the winter up there. By thunder! Be a true hivernan. I'd bring in some flour and sugar, a bunch of potatoes, hang up a deer, get some snowshoes, live wild up there and look for my cabin site.

I had to lay in a small mountain of firewood to make it through the winter, so I started working on that every day, hauling in six-foot lengths. I figured I'd cut them up later. Afternoons I went down the creek looking over various sites on the higher ground. Most of the good sites were on the road side of the creek; yet it didn't look like it got much traffic. There were plenty of cabin-sized lodgepoles. I couldn't believe it—was this it?

I was due for another disappointment. I ran into an old miner who had some claims on the lower end of the creek, and he told me all the private land on the creek was subdivided. He said that ten years ago all the available land in the valley was one long mining claim, and it sold then for less than two hundred dollars an acre. Now it was divided into ten-acre chunks, and the good ones were selling for two thousand dollars an acre. Well-to-do people from the East were buying them. The wave of subdivisions that came in the last ten years had hit everywhere. All up and down the Rockies.

Something broke in my spirit. I didn't admit it to myself but something broke. I went back to the cabin and worked on the woodpile the rest of the day. The country didn't seem wild any more, and it didn't seem free. It was as if the suburbs I had fled from in Minneapolis had already staked their claims in the Rockies. The property lines had been drawn all up and down the Shining Mountains; it was just a matter of time until they were filled with envious neighbors. There was no place left to be a mountain man, unless you were rich.

The woods turned gold and red beneath deep blue skies, and the creek fell lower, shining at the bottom with the amber colors of the autumn. I worked steady hauling in sawlogs, and when I figured I had enough to get me through till spring I went into Fort Fistfight, the nearest town, and brought up a load of supplies—rice, macaroni, potatoes, beans, flour, canned goods, coffee. The nights were freezing by then, heavy frosts coming down, and there was a small tight shed where I figured meat would stay cold during the day. Time to lay in some meat. Early one morning as I was packing my rucksack to go out hunting I heard shots down the valley. I waited for a time, and soon a shiny blue-and-white Blazer came bouncing up the road. They told me that hunting season had just opened. It was the first hunting season I had ever been close to in the Rockies. I was in for a shock.

They came up the road in new four-wheel-drive vehicles day after day, week after week, in numbers that were difficult to believe. The remote valley I had been living in became like a sporting-goods convention, with people driving past the cabin from dawn to dusk in sleek, flashy vehicles. Every so often one of them would go back down the creek with the head and rack of a big six-point bull elk hanging out the back. Or a deer, or a young moose. Big volleys of shots rang out just after first light, and again late in the evening. The logging roads above the valley hummed and droned with trucks, horse trailers, and jeeps. It was an invasion, one which seemed without sense, without feeling or thought for the land or the wild animals that were left. Just a manic onslaught, a kind of wilderness infantry charge against the deer and elk. Something else broke away inside me. I hung up my Hawken; I wouldn't hunt. Hunting had gone insane. The deer and elk were getting blasted out of the mountains. I would buy beef for the winter.

Finally the first snows came, and stayed. Ice began forming in the creek, and the grouse flew up to higher country. I bought fifty pounds of beef, some chickens, and ten pounds of ham, and hung it all in the shed. The hunters dwindled off, the season closed and with it the valley. It turned wild. Lynx tracks began to show up below the cabin.

One day an old trapper came in and set a trailer up near Mine Creek. I spent time with him, following him up the trail and watching him make his sets. He caught several beaver and a few marten. The mountain men waded into that icy water in leather moccasins; he used rubber waders. He told me that he had trapped for fifteen years in the Idaho wilderness, packing in alone in the fall, on foot, and coming out in the spring. He didn't see another human all winter. He said he didn't carry a sleeping bag; I couldn't believe that and I asked him how he managed to survive. He told me that mostly he slept under the spruce trees in the bottoms; after December, he said, the snow built up around them four and five feet deep, making a round cavern under the branches. He crawled in and built two fires against the snow wall, one at his knees and one at his chest, so the heat reflected back on him. Then he cut some pine boughs to lie on, and he said he slept warm, down out of the wind, keeping the fires going all night. He kept a deer or an elk hung up along his trapline, and cut frozen chunks off with his ax as he needed them. He said he ate a lot of beans those winters.

Finally the beaver ponds began to freeze solid and he pulled out of the valley. Heavy snows fell toward the end of December, and I was left alone with the snow and the atmosphere. I snowshoed up the creek three or four miles and tried out sleeping under a spruce tree with two fires, lying on top of my sleeping bag on some pine boughs. It worked just as he said. The heat radiated off the snow and I fell asleep. I knew he had done it. You could survive nights that were 20 below that way if you had to. That was the way the mountain men had made their camps when they were in the high mountains.

The moon rose and fell, deep snow buried the creek, and the last of the elk came down off the mountaintops and left the valley, heading for lower country. Only a few big moose stayed up there, and I marveled at their strength and hardiness, following their tracks through snow that was four feet deep as they made their long feed loops. They were phenomenal survivors. The weasel and marten hunted pine squirrel; the lynx hunted the snowshoe rabbit. I never saw a lion track all winter; they were shot out of that valley. Blizzards came up the valley and howled past the cabin with blinding force, pushing snow dust through cracks in the west wall and forcing the smoke back down the stovepipe and into the cabin. I felt how slowly the seasons turned into one another; I began to fill in gaps in my knowledge as to how the animals traveled through the seasons, how they survived the drastic changes. I felt something of what the mountain men felt when they holed up against the mountain winter with a few large chunks of frozen meat and five moons ahead of them, how hard it was. If they were near friendly Indians it was easier; they wintered in tepees with plenty of warm buffalo robes and usually enough meat, seedcakes, and dried berries. But if they were alone they wintered in crude shelters with no windows and no stovepipe, smoky and dim, and they ate the same meats day after day, week after week. As the winter wore on I wondered how they could stand it, the same stinking suit of buckskins, the maddening taste of the same meat week after week.

Most of all that winter I wondered about John Colter and that epic winter journey he made, a pair of snowshoes, a flintlock, and a thirty-pound pack, traveling 550 miles into the dead of winter and the heart of the Shining Mountains, going alone from fall until spring through the high mountains. Spending the winter up there made it even harder to believe that he did what he did. The most I stayed out on any trip that winter was three nights, and I was so glad to get back to the cabin by then that I couldn't conceive of someone staying out and traveling all winter. But Colter did it. He was a quiet man who seldom boasted and never lied.

All my experience in the Rockies, all my longings and imaginings, were pointing toward the experience of long journeys like that. The changing moons, the wild animals, the wilderness itself: traveling into it on my own, the calling, the unknown it seemed to hold—that was what I wanted. To learn how the animals survived, what they ate and how they moved under the moons; to learn how to survive through it myself. That was my dream. Somewhere in the Shining Mountains a place where I could do that, make those trips for myself.

But it had been broken in me. Everywhere in the Rockies tens of thousands of middle-class people had swarmed into the mountains in the seventies, all with the same idea. The Great Escape. They had money behind them to pay for suburban homes. Land everywhere was being chopped up and subdivided, suburban homes were springing up all over the mountains from New Mexico to Montana, motorcycles and pickups were tearing up into the foothills. The wildness was being bulldozed and shot out so fast that you barely had time to say it was going before it was gone. It was sad, sad beyond the words you could find to describe it. I couldn't stand it any more. I couldn't stand seeing it and feeling it all up and down the mountains and not being able to fight it in any way. It wasn't just "progress"; it was a high-powered onslaught of exploitation against every natural resource in sight, an insane race to convert the mountains into social status and private profit. And it had already reached up onto Hughes Creek in Montana. I knew from what I had seen of the hunting season that Montana was only ten or fifteen years behind Colorado. Give it that amount of time and the streams would be just as fished out and the deer and elk just as shot up as they were west of Fort Capitalism in Colorado. The dream I had of a cabin off in the wilds somewhere was just about gone from the mountains.

As the spring came on, word came up the creek that there was 1.237 acres for sale on the West Fork for $2,000. I went down and looked at it; it was part of a subdivision, all that was left. I could have bought it, but finally I thought fuck it, I didn't want to be part of a subdivision. Someone else told me about a lawyer in Salmon, Idaho, who specialized in remote mining claims in the Idaho wilderness. I called him up and it turned out he had some to sell all right, but they were running from $60,000 to $150,000 apiece.

"Who's buying them at that price?" I asked.

"Rich people back east mostly," he said.

"What the hell are they going to do with them?"

"Well, they figure that if things go all to hell and the ship starts to sink, they'll have a place to go and hide out."

Anger flashed through my gut. I told him that, just between him and me, since they were the ones who were steering it maybe they ought to stay at their posts, and if it did go down it would be a good place for them.

He hung up on me.

THAT WAS the end. I went back up the creek. The new High-Water Moon was in the sky, and the creek was surging up its banks. I packed some things in my rucksack and started up Burrell Creek toward the Divide to say goodbye. It tasted sad, sad in the throat. I had learned a lot about the mountains up there, felt a lot. I had lived alone under nine full moons; I had learned why the moon was such a strong part of the consciousness of the Indians and the mountain men, both as a measure of time and as a mysterious subconscious lodestar amid all the loneliness of the wilderness. I had seen the first autumn moon, the Moon When the Elk Fight, heard their whistles and grunts and seen their tracks where they fought. That moon was the turning point of the season. I had lived under the winter moons, the Moon When the Trees Pop, the Moon of the Deep Snows. I had ached through the spring moons, the Moon When the Geese Come Back and the High-Water Moon. I had lived under all those moons, and they had put haunting rings in the pith of my memory. I had followed the best climbers in the mountains, the elk, and marveled and cursed at their strength and cunning. I had seen where a bear came out in the spring, and I had followed the moose through the deep snow of the upper valley. I had seen how completely the lynx ate rabbits, leaving only a scrap of fur and one or two of its feet, and how the winter haunted the coyotes, how they hunted field mice in the snowbound meadows, listening and then pouncing, crunching bones and gristle to ward off the cold. I had felt some of the wildness, and learned how hard it was for animals who lived wild to survive. I had gotten some of the romance rubbed off the mountain man myth, learning how cold and dirty and rough their way of life was, the hard price they paid for their freedom. Still I wanted that freedom more than ever, but the price for it now wasn't cold or loneliness or hardships. It was hard cash. All the available land was being subdivided; the rich were moving in on the mountains.

A SAD FAREWELL

I WENT on up to the end of Montana, the Idaho Divide, and stayed up there for three nights without a sleeping bag, sleeping on pine boughs by an open fire, learning the way the deer slept, dreaming old dreams, saying goodbye. I could see seventy-five miles across the Idaho wilderness from up there—the Salmon River country off to the south and the Selway wilderness spreading to the west. I thought of the trip I had dreamed of; I longed to take off into that country with a pack and a gun, felt the call of it so strong that it raced around in my blood like a fish caught frantic in shallow water. The freedom of it, my freedom, my identity. A mountain man? It was no good any more, I thought. They were cutting the mountains up with a big shiny butcher knife. The rich were the only ones who could afford it; a person couldn't make it any more with just a pair of hands and a strong heart. And even if you had the cash you were doomed to watch the Shining Mountains, the last wild region left in America, lose their shine, lose their wildness, year after year. I couldn't see any way to fight back; if you were poor all your energies went into just making a living. Let the rich have the mountains, I thought, let them pull their political strings to tear into the Rockies to make their mountains of money. Let them sell the last of America's freedom, let them trade the big sky and the rivers of wind for smoke and suburbs, until the region was ruined and the wildness was gone. I wouldn't be a part of it.

GOODBYE FOREVER

I WENT back down the mountain, packed up my outfit, and headed east for the first time in four years. I rode hard, grinding my teeth through the night until my fillings began to drop out. The last range of mountains was the Crow Mountains, their very beginning in southern Montana fifty miles above the Yellowstone country. Again I felt that twinge of fear when I laid eyes on them, their size, their ruggedness, the darkness which seemed to lie behind the peaks. I realized that the Crow Mountains were nearly a hundred miles long, curving down past Yellowstone Park to the east over the heart of 'the Rockies, looking down on the birthplace of western rivers. The range John Colter first explored, on that long winter journey.

But I didn't even mark it down; my map of the Shining Mountains was down at the bottom of my trunk. I was leaving old Gabe behind; my dream of a trip into those mountains was finished. I was quitting the mountains. Even if I had the money I didn't want to stay and see them ruined. I vowed that in my heart I was leaving the Shining Mountains forever.

I TRAILED on back across the badlands to Minnesota and got a job building swimming pools for rich people in the suburbs. My heart was full of thorns. Every time I thought of the mountains I pushed them out of my mind. At first it was easy; I pulled a big curtain of darkness shut between me and the shine that lay far to the west, as if it didn't exist. But as the spring gave way to the heat and humidity of summer it got harder and harder. Little glints and visions peeked through the curtain, and I had to keep pushing them back into the darkness.

I figured I would be a swamp man. Sigh. Up in northern Minnesota there were large wet tracts of forest and swamp, and land up there was a few hundred dollars an acre. It was quite a comedown from being a mountain man, but it was the only cheap land left that I knew of in the whole country. Weekends I went up and looked at some of it. It was tangled, wet, and there were millions of mosquitoes. It was as flat as a continental breadboard; warn't no landmarks to travel by. I could write about birds, lizards, snakes, and mosquitoes up there, I thought. My heart sank a little more.

Back on the job it got harder and harder to keep the shines out of my mind. Every time I faced west I found myself gazing at the horizon and had to force my eyes back down. The little shines began to join together to form sections of mountain ranges I had seen in summer with snow on them, the Wind River Range, the Crazy Mountains. I would look up unconsciously with the sweat running into my eyes and see a flash of a range on the horizon as clear as if I were standing just outside the tar springs in Wyoming. Then I would force my eyes back down again and resign myself to being a free swamp man.

As the summer wore on and the heat increased I constantly had to erase those mountains from the horizon, but the more I erased them, the more complete they became, the more they stretched out on the horizon. Soon I began to feel imaginary gusts of wind off a field of melting snow, remembering the coolness, the touch the wind had in the mountains. I had to push that away. Then I began to miss the elk, which I had learned to take for granted when I was out there. I missed the wild feeling that they gave to the hills, the feeling of having such a big and strong animal running free in the woods, just knowing they were there. The last elk were killed off in Minnesota before I was born. I missed the elk! That floored me. It never dawned on me when I left the mountains that I would miss the elk.

August came, in the suburbs the Moon When the Ice Cubes Tinkle. My hair started falling out and circles formed under my eyes. My spirit was dying and I knew it. The suburbs of Minneapolis stretched forever, they were growing, and they were full of bitter memories. If you didn't have their money they made you feel like you were worthless, no matter how many times you told yourself different. They stoned you, they knew how to cut through your clothes with the glance of an eye. They judged you for your shoes, your car, how much money you had; they were everywhere and it never let up. It was like a vast stage setting without any real life, a place of frustrated dreams and dirty looks, superiority born of money, false smiles, stabs in the back. It was killing my spirit because I couldn't fight back. I held on to the dismal fact that I was going to be a swamp man, and kept working.

I had to work with my back toward the west by then. Every time I turned around I saw pieces of those mountains clearly, I *felt* them. I knew where they lay, all right. The Shining Mountains were due west. Was I going to make it out of this sick and wretched place in one piece? To be a swamp man? I didn't really want to be a swamp man. Deep down I wanted to be a mountain man. But I forced that vision on the horizon away. As I worked I thought to myself: *All you have to do to live in the suburbs is let your spirit die.* That's how they thrive in it. They let some vital truth in themselves die, and with it their spirits. And so the suburbs keep growing.

THE VISION RETURNS

ONE DAY when the sun was high I was kneeling in the dirt pounding a form stake in. My hair was soaked; sweat streamed down my stomach, flew off my arm as I pounded, ran down my forehead and into my eyes. When I finished I stood up and wiped my face, and without thinking I glanced west. There they were, shimmering, only it was no longer just a section of them. It was a complete mountain range that I saw now beyond the suburban landscape, white snow in their heights, cool air in the blue sky around them. This time I didn't turn away or block them out. I felt them, I dropped my hammer and stood there looking at them in every detail as if they were real, sensing them, the beauty and the happiness that vision of them gave to me filling my soul. I knew the way out there! Out across the plains and into Wyoming, along the Sweetwater and up to Wind River, that huge and windswept country. What little salvation there was left for me lay out there, and now I knew it for a certainty. I couldn't fight the suburbs and I couldn't change them; only history could change them and someday it would. In the meantime I wasn't going to be a swamp man and I wasn't going to work in the suburbs. By thunder, I was going to be a mountain man.

The joy I felt that day seemed like the height of my life. My spirit, which had been withering like the Minnesota cornfields, began to grow, to soar, to fill with life once again. I was going back to the mountains, I would cast my fate with the mountains, I would do what I could to keep them from being ruined. I didn't have any illusions about what it was like out there now, I knew the blind rush of development that was going on, and I knew how badly the wildness was being pushed toward the edge. A true mountain man wouldn't sit around and let it happen, by Jesus, he'd fight those rich bastards the smartest way he could. He wouldn't let them turn the sky black and plow up the mountains without a fight. He wouldn't let the streams and rivers die and he wouldn't let his spirit go under; he'd keep it strong and free, like the bear. And he'd fight for the wildness and the spirit that was left in the land. The mountains and the plains of America.

In the days that followed I let all the memories come back that wanted to under that blasting suburban sun: the cool breezes on the passes, the ice-cold creek water, the chill on a lone mountainside in the evening. The clarity in the air, where the Black Sky Power Co. hadn't dug in and fired up yet. I kept on working right through many suburban moons—the Moon When the New Cars Appear, the Moon When the Theater Opens, and the Moon When Everyone Buys—building up the biggest grubstake I had yet put together. Every day on the job I dreamed about the mountains and the way they would feel now as the season was changing to the first autumn moon, the Moon When the Elk Fight. I dreamed of following the elk and the deer, the moose and the bear, into stretches of mountain that were still wild, tracking them through the seasons—that was what I wanted. I didn't really want to hunt any more, because the animals were getting blasted out of the mountains. I didn't want to live in a cabin off in the wilderness any more, because it was like trying to turn the clock back fifty years. It was a constant time warp. I didn't want to turn the clock back fifty years for the simple reason that it would only happen all over again. I wanted to live in the present, I wanted to deal with the present; like a true mountain man, I wanted to be able to fight back. Those pricks at the Black Sky Power Co. and their various banker friends couldn't get away with what they were doing forever. The Shining Mountains weren't meant to be ruined.

I got my buckskins out of the closet and laid 'em out in the sun to burn the mold off. I emeried my Hawken and greased it up, and I put an edge on my Green River that'd split a squirrel whisker. I dug down in my trunk and got out my map of the Shining Mountains, and I drew in the places I had seen coming out: the beginning of the Crow Mountains, rising over the paradisial valley of the upper Yellowstone; the Tongue, Powder, and Big Horn rivers in the plains country of eastern Montana where John Colter started his walk, on the sunrise side of the Crow Mountains. Somewhere west of the Bitterroot River I had left old Gabe behind, erased him with bitter strokes, and now he came back to life on a sunny day in late fall, sitting his horse with a strong spirit, his wool capote falling down over his buckskins, his Hawken cradled in his arms. He was heading on over the Bitterroot Mountains, where he would winter with a band of Nez Percé Indians. He was a free man, and he was in love with the earth. The wind, the stretch of the peaks in the distance, the sun blazing down out of a clear blue autumn sky—those elements were his medicine, his life force. They were what called him to the Shining Mountains and held him there to stay, to roam and to see and to live. He never tried to put his freedom over someone else's head, and when someone tried to put theirs over his head he fought, one way or another. He was his own man. I wanted to catch up with him.

TRIPS INTO THE WILD

D URING the Moon When Everyone Buys—the Moon When the Trees Pop up in the Bitterroots—I started laying plans for a series of trips into the mountains, the long and wild trips I had dreamed of all the time I had been in the West. I would travel as light as I could, trying to imitate Colter's thirty-pound survival pack, and live off what roots and small game I could find. I would pack a little flour, jerky, noodles, and dried food as staples. I would carry my Hawken and my Green River; I would go on foot and try to get back into country where there weren't backpackers or rich people on horse trips, where it felt wild, where it felt something like it must have felt for the old mountain man I called Gabe. I would try for some of the feelings he must have known in the Shining Mountains, before a hundred fifty years of profit and luxury were taken out of them. The few wild places that were left.

I planned to follow the moons through a full season of growth, spring to autumn—the High-Water Moon in spring, the summer Moon When the Bears Run Together, and the Moon When the Elk Fight in autumn. Learn what I could of the animals, what they ate and how they survived. Learn how the mountain men survived. Learn how I could survive myself if I had to.

As the storms of February gave way to the first thaws of March, I began packing up my outfit with a joy that was rising in me like the sap in the trees. I had been away from the mountains for a year and I longed for the feelings, the chilled air, the sweep of the peaks at dawn. When the day finally came to leave I stopped and burned a dollar bill on the freeway, for all the sickness and envy that lay behind me, the fashionable cancer that spilled out from Dayton's in downtown Minneapolis to the bizarre suburban fleshpots of Bloomington and Edina and Wayzata, where they crucified you for the clothes you wore or the color of your skin. I burned that dollar bill for ten years of bitterness and all the poverty and pain that lay outside the gates of their exclusive clubs, until there was nothing left but a few small ashes flittering away on the wind. And then, sweet Jesus, I lit out west across the prairie.

Thunderstorms, dark flickering cloud masses rolling across the huge landscape, the wind kicking up bits of grass and blowing them over the crests of low-lying hills, wildness of spring in the air and the mountains somewhere ahead. On through the splashing rain and wind, into the night and after the dream, across the wide Missouri. By the end of Dakota the sky had broken to moonlit clouds, dark mist centers, long and drifting, mystery of the prairie where it begins to rise toward the mountains. I started to climb a long grade into big timbered hills, and I started to feel the sky opening up and the air growing sharper.

Then, late in the night, I hit the Big Horns. Winding up into heavily timbered mountains, the sights and feelings I had been aching for, thinking of the trips and getting through that timber; and then out into a huge moonlit canyon. A canyon that must have taken ten sleeps to get horses and lodges and travois through, high rock cliffs standing in the pale moonlight, mile upon mile of vast mysterious canyon, going down, empty, the unity of the mountains stretching as far as the distant stars hazing through the clouds. And at last, cup after cup of coffee, jittery and spilling with joy, I pulled into Wind River as dawn began to break back to the east.

I went outside of town toward South Pass till I got up on a big hill, then I got out, stretched out my tarp, and laid back. The sun came up red and then gold; a snow-edged breeze stirred the dead grass stalks. Up in the sky an eagle picked up the waking wind and began to ride. I looked around the vast spaces of the hills, the light flooding back to the west, and felt it all enter into me with a joy as sweet as I have ever known. After a long and bitter year: the snow-cooled breeze, the openness of the sky, the air of freedom in those wind-sculptured hills. Home of my spirit.

I rested several days with some friends at the *High Country News*, a paper in Lander that has catalogued the depredations of the big power companies for the last ten years. Then I set to work replenishing my outfit. I bought a little spyglass so's I could sneak up on the elk and the bear without them seeing me. I bought a good rucksack, one that was double-stitched so it wouldn't come apart out in the middle of nowhere. I had to hurry, for the High-Water Moon wasn't far away. I bought me some leather and made a scabbard for my Hawken so I would have both hands free to climb. I would follow the trips through like a mountain man would have done it: up the Bitterroots for the spring hunt, up into the Swans for a summer jaunt, then over through the Yellowstone country and up into the deep Crow Mountains for the final journey of the fall hunt. They were the only mountains that I was afraid of. I kept sensing something every time I saw them; they were huge and old, and they seemed to hold some kind of mute and angry knowledge that did not take kindly to penetration. I was superstitious about the Crow Mountains; somehow I knew that my medicine lay in those mountains, that that trip might be a test of the deepest lights in me. There was something fateful about that range. I didn't know what it was, but I knew I felt the fear.

A PREDICTION

FINALLY I was packed and ready to go. I stopped at a laundromat to wash my clothes, and I was sitting in my mule waiting for them to dry when an Indian, about thirty, changed directions and walked over toward me. He leaned against the car with his back to me and we talked for a while. I asked him if he'd ever been in the Crow Mountains.

"I know them," he said without looking. "Why?"

"I'm going to make a trip in them."

He was quiet for a few moments. "You'll die on that trip."

He said it without the slightest change in tone, as if it were something he already knew. For two or three seconds I couldn't speak.

"What do you mean—how?"

He shrugged. "Maybe the wind. Maybe the rocks. Maybe your own footsteps. But you'll die on that trip."

He rattled me bad, so that I couldn't speak. Finally I regrouped, thinking that he might be playing with my head, or recalling a legend he held in general. "Not if I can help it," I mumbled.

I LEFT Lander about the time the bears were first coming out, when the high country in Yellowstone was still snowed in. The Crow Mountains were a full growing season away, and early springtime was starting to come on in the Bitterroots. I felt the long miles, all the frustrations, peeling away with the simple knowledge that at last I was taking off into the mountains. I went up to the big bend in the Yellowstone near the Crazy Mountains and rented a lodge, and quick as I could I made up a five-pound batch of jerky, drying it in the oven. I packed in some lard and honey, rice, noodles, and dried soup. I packed in wool clothes for a spring snowstorm, a signal mirror in case I broke a leg, some Ace bandages and compresses for a bear mauling or a fracture, fishhooks and line, flint and steel, a comb and a bar of soap. I wasn't going to take a sleeping bag; I figured if that trapper could go all winter in the Selway without one I could cross it in the spring without one. Instead I packed a space blanket, for heat reflection. My pack weighed forty-five pounds, fifteen pounds more than Colter's did when he set out in late fall. If I never figured out anything else about the mountain men I would figure out how John Colter went all winter with a thirty-pound pack.

The ice was moving on down the Yellowstone River. Old Gabe had already left the Nez Percé and started up the Selway River on a trail he had never tried before, on his spring hunt. I meant to catch him. The new moon had shown up in the sky, the moon of high water at last, and my heart was pounding with joy. Early in the morning I tossed my pack into old Sixties and headed for the Bitterroot Mountains.

THE
BITTERROOT
MOUNTAINS

SPRING, THE SELWAY RIVER,
APRIL 25, THE HIGH-WATER MOON

Aᴺᴰ ᵁᴾ ᴛʜᴇ Selway River in the springtime, long footsteps and a light heart, taking in the power of that river for the first time. Scattering of yellow blossoms, white foam among the boulders, thunder of the rapids in the bright sunlight. All the open hillsides greening, the air sun-drenched and the pine needles glistening, impenetrable pine forests leaning sharply beneath the ocean-blue skies, the river flowing from deeper in the wilderness. The trail empty, no one else on it this early in the year. Fingers of snow melting from the tops of the mountains; the valley below flushing to life. Birds diving around and singing as if crazed, possessed by the sun. High-water time in the mountains of Idaho. I was on my way.

The river boiled, it churned, it poured. Its sound filled the clear air, and as I made my way up the trail my eyes were constantly upon it, taking in its power, its thunder, the sunlit turbulence of its deep green waters as they rolled around a bend. It is a big river, so wide in some places that I had a hard time throwing a stone all the way across. It lies at the bottom of a deep valley whose forested mountains rise up 2,000 feet on either side, brushing the clouds on a gray day. The south-facing side of the valley, the side the trail is on, has more open areas, more sunlight, and there are big four-hundred-year-old ponderosas scattered through the openings. Yellow pine, the huge tree that thrives in open spaces and sunlight, standing like monarchs over centuries of change. The other side of the valley is steeped in white fir, a more shade-tolerant tree; that side of the river looked dense and tangled. Dead snags leaning at different angles in the dimness, thick mounds of moss on the bank, lichen-splashed boulders and small rock cliffs. Steep, densely obstructed ravines, promising a tortuous climb if you had to make it. Selway. From the Nez Percé *Selwah*, meaning "smooth water."

It is much smoother down at the lower end. Up here it was a dangerous river in the spring, impossible to ford, filled with the destructive power of all the water coming down off the mountains, winter breaking. If you fell in at the wrong place you might never come ashore. As the sun grew hotter and I started to sweat a little I measured the river in its calmer runs, thinking what it would be like to swim it. It would be an ordeal which would tax the strongest swimmer. The cold would force you to swim furiously; I guessed it would take a minute and a half to two minutes to get across, being swept downstream three hundred feet in the process. I wouldn't try it unless a life depended on it, but still it haunted me: could I make that swim if I had to?

Over and over I was impressed with the size of the Selway, such a big river coming out of the wilderness. For over a hundred miles it wound through the Idaho wilderness, picking up countless smaller creeks on its way north and then west, carrying the waters out of the wild and onward toward the Pacific Ocean. I looked at a large set of rapids, and in its immediate assault on the senses, the foam and the flashing sunlight and the sound, the beauty of the rising mountains, I began to understand one of the major drainages of the Northwest, the system of rivers which came out of the Idaho wilderness. I felt it now, rather than understanding it on paper. The Selway headwatered near the Salmon, flowed north and then westward, draining the north-central part of the wilderness. The Salmon, with its forks, flowed west, draining the Idaho Primitive Area, the central portion. It emptied into the Snake River, which flowed north, forming the boundary between Oregon and Idaho. As the Snake continued north on its thousand-mile journey, the Selway came out and joined the Lochsa (pronounced *Locksaw*), which I had driven down on Highway 12, forming the Middle Fork of the Clearwater. The four forks of the Clearwater drained the northern part of Idaho's wilderness, joining together east of Lewiston and finally flowing into the Snake. The Snake flowed through Washington into the Columbia River. The Columbia cut a massive gorge through the Cascade Mountains and flowed into the sea.

The Selway was an artery in that system. About midmorning I followed the trail down near the river and came upon a run of boulders along the shore, cedar trees standing around, the heaviest part of the current running along the other side of the river. Beneath the boulders the water was green and clear down to the bottom, five feet deep. Coils of current showed here and there, a sprig of pine needles floated past further out. The sun poured down, heating the rocks, making the river shimmer as it flowed past. I was hot and thirsty. I laid my pack against a rock and looked up and down the trail. No one, the valley was empty. I stripped down and laid my sweaty clothes out to dry, then stood on the edge of a big boulder staring into the water. The rocks on the bottom wavered about. The water looked perfectly pure; a slight breeze tickled my body where the sweat was drying. I looked down the river to where it flowed out of sight. To where it flowed into the Columbia. Then I looked back at the water, out about ten feet. I hesitated some more. I shifted my feet and took a deep breath, and continued to hesitate.

At last I dove. A great icy shock as I hit the water, and I came up dog-paddling and gasping. Amazing how cold that water feels. I forced myself to swim out a few strokes, until I felt the edge of the current starting to pull gently, and there I took a few drinks, half choking. Then I turned around and swam fast back to the boulder, propelled by the cold. When I crawled back up I sat down against a rock, covered with goose bumps. The heat in the rocks felt fine. In a few moments the sun beat into my skin, melting the goose bumps, penetrating deeper, and soon my whole body tingled with pleasure, relaxing as it hadn't in a long time. I felt remade, a christening for the journey. The heat of the sun in the rocks after an icy swim. *I respect you, Selway, and I love you for your gifts. I only want to feel your power.* I lay there until I was dry and growing hot again, then put on my clothes. My shirt was warm and dry.

On up the river. It was a horse trail, bridges over the side creeks, easy and beautiful. The further up I went, the wilder it seemed to feel. An old moose antler bleaching in the rocks, big leg bones scattered about beneath a flowering clump of arrowleaf balsamroot. High above a ridge on the other side a golden eagle sailed back and forth out of sight, a dark silhouette against the blue sky, watching for pine squirrels, grouse, feeding on the keen thrill of the wind. I was high all morning with being on the way, the river, walking into the flush of spring, under the High-Water Moon. The sights, the smells, the feelings were all around. Swarms of blue violets along the trail, yellow jackets busy rising from one to the next. Scores of delicate blue moths had sprung to life and were hanging on patches of damp ground near the trail, their wings flexing up and down as they took in the moisture, rising in swarms before my boots. Out in the river sometimes there were big hot-looking gravel bars which the current split around with powerful waves, and sometimes there were small islands spired with pines. The river wound with a big sweeping current around one bend after another, each a little closer to the wilder country which lay ahead.

As the sun got higher I stopped for a while in a deep stand of spruce overlooking a gorge, made a little fire and boiled a cup-bottomful of new pale green spruce needles, and squatted there watching the white mist rise and letting the aroma and fragrance of that brew penetrate into my head. The spruce were just starting to bud out at the ends of the branches, some of the needles loosening the husks, some of them still wrapped tightly. Earth minerals. A small seepage came down behind me, choked with alder and low brush, and in among the thick branches a male fox sparrow chased a female in a gentle and endless courtship. He whistled, she scolded, she forever eluding him even while she had already picked out the nest site. Water and cover, by a river. They flew in and out and through the thick budding branches without the least hesitation, me wondering how they could fly in that thickness without hitting something.

Just down over the edge of the cliff the river narrowed and poured through the gap, thundering into a pool with a violence that sent shining clouds of mist and spray rising slowly in the sunlight. I watched over the edge and saw two green-backed swallows winging around over that mist. They were building a nest in the rocks on my side. Every so often they would go down, pick up some mud and deposit it in a place on the cliff that I couldn't see. The rest of the time they skylarked over those rapids. They had a bright green patch on their backs that was iridescent, that shone and flashed as they swooped, and they played with those rapids, diving in close to the tremendous turbulence, winging through the mist, then heading skyward, turning, whistling. Every so often they would come back and add a dab of mud or a bit of grass to the nest, then go out and dive some more. How to Build Your Home in the Woods.

The river pulled me on, the flush of life returning to the Bitterroots everywhere you looked. Big huckleberry bushes were filled with white flowers. Butterflies dipped about on the breeze, and warblers sang out from the gloomy stillness in the dense shaded timber across the river. I came up over a rocky rise and caught a flash of movement in the river near the far bank, and several moments later I saw an otter rise playfully in the easy current on the other side, take some air, and curve back down under, fur dark and gleaming like the water. It came up like that three more times, crawled ashore at a sand wash, and crossed it waddling with its back humped in the air, then slipped back into the river and continued its journey. It swam faster than I walked; if it was a female she had young in a mud den by now; the eggs of the mergansers and geese along the river, and their young after they hatched, were on her hunting list. Her mainstay was trout.

The trail I was on would trickle with backpackers in another month. Two hundred years ago it was a Nez Percé hunting trail, used during summer migrations. Seventy years ago it was a long and tortuous pack trail for the few homesteaders who tried to settle at the junction of Moose Creek. Now sport hunters, backpackers, and fishermen found their way up it after the middle of May.

I was hoping at the end of the trip to cross over the Bitterroot Mountains and come out in Montana, and I had thought about getting in a ways and then striking off on a compass bearing. After I looked the country over I realized that kind of trip would take about two years. It was steep and very dense, and you had to work up the drainages and know where the open country was, or you would get timber sickness. Timber sickness came from climbing over deadfalls and seeing only thick steep forest for days at a time. People in the late stages of timber sickness bit their knuckles until they bled and searched for phone booths. I didn't want to put myself in for timber sickness unless I had to.

So I figured I would follow the Selway up toward the Bitterroots for twenty-five miles, until I hit the junction of Moose Creek. There the Selway turned south and ran upgrade for almost fifty miles, headwatering near the Salmon River. A lot of creeks came down off the Bitterroots and drained into the Selway along that stretch, from out of some wild country. But the divide was higher there and I wouldn't be able to get over without snowshoes. And I didn't want to carry them; I wanted to stay afoot with the elk. So I decided to follow the East Fork of Moose Creek, which wound north and east off that turn of the Selway for forty-five miles, climbing all the time until it headwatered beneath the shadow of Lost Horse Pass, about 7,000 feet high. From what I heard I had a chance of getting over that pass.

There was a ranger station at the junction of Moose Creek and there was supposed to be a couple there who stayed up on the Selway in the winter and built footbridges. I would talk to them about snow conditions and then start up Moose Creek. I figured once I got past the ranger station I would be getting into some wild country.

My pack was heavy. With my Hawken strapped on, it weighed forty-five pounds. I had tried for thirty, cutting everything I thought I could get along without. I came up fifteen pounds over with the Hawken. Once I got past the ranger station I planned to go back through it and make notes of what I wasn't using.

I walked until the sun began to slide in the west. The trail started to climb more, winding up over hundred-foot cliffs which dropped sheer down to the river. There were rattlesnakes in the lower Selway but they didn't seem to be out yet. Gradually the country was rising and opening some. The moon came up over the river up ahead, triumphant over the remoteness of mountains, a growing half-moon. I followed a wide ledge to a big open cave, twelve feet of granite hanging overhead with a good-sized wall to the west. It would have been a good place to stay if the weather looked bad, but the ground was hard and firewood was scarce. I kept going. Finally I came down to a timbered flat where a creek came in, enough firewood back in the brush, and leaned my pack against a big cedar. I had come seven or eight miles and my legs were aching, my back muscles stiff. I sat down against the tree and rested, feeling the emptiness, the loneliness of the dense pines at the end of the day. The silence that stretched for miles. The continuous sound of the river as the evening chill started to rise. Secretly I wished I had brought my sleeping bag.

Boys, I come a-bustin' up that river full of the vim and vigor of the springtime after a long winter in that deadpan fort, pret' near draggin' my mule to get him to keep up with me. Up and down over that trail I sailed, drinkin' in the river and all the critters that was comin' back in, that mule pantin' and wheezin' behind me. I made twenty-two mile the first day and woulda kept going well into the moonlight, 'ceptin' I got to a little creek and that mule just keeled over and fell into a dead sleep, didn't stir an eyelash till daybreak. Had a nice time unpackin' the sleepin' son of a bitch.

Finally I got up and started dragging firewood in from the brush. Tripped and fell a couple times. The first faint star came out and the moon grew brighter behind a tall, hundred-year-old cedar. The ground was uneven. I picked out a spot with some thick bushes sheltering it to the west and built a fire not far from a freshly spun spider web. I cooked a big kettleful of noodles, soup, and chunks of jerky. Took a swallow of honey and put some water on for coffee. I was too tired to string up the space blanket. I broke the firewood up into chunks and piled them in a two-foot stack at my head. Then I put on all my warm clothes and lay down on the sleeping pad by the fire. It wasn't real comfortable. I had walked until too late; I hadn't given myself enough time to set up a comfortable camp.

The little creek came down with a swishing sound like a soft wind pouring into the night. The sky turned midnight blue and the stars came out slowly. The moon cast faint tree shadows. Two perfectly straight snags with no branches, long dead, turned ghostly white. I lay there and listened to the Selway, brushing fire sparks off my windbreaker. The dead cedar burned quieter than the brushwood. The ground was wrong, a hump near my hip. Finally I piled some wood on the fire, pulled the space blanket over me, and turned over to go to sleep. After a while I dozed.

Sometime later I woke up; the flames seemed too bright. I

yawned, looking over my shoulder, and noticed that a large portion of my back was on fire.

I jumped up, stripped off the windbreaker, and began stomping the flames out on the ground. The moon shone quietly through the trees. Just as I got the windbreaker out I noticed that the space blanket was on fire and was burning more ravenously all the time. Before I could even think of how to put it out, it was an inferno of flames, a huge orange fireball which I feared would start the woods on fire. I grabbed a stick and raked most of it into the campfire, where it seemed to burn itself up with a tremendous delight. I stared at it as it burned, and bleakness settled into my heart.

Then I noticed that my sleeping pad was on fire. A big half circle of flames was eating toward the middle like a small prairie fire. I grabbed it up, folded it in half, and smothered out the flames. When I finally opened it again a thick cloud of smoke rose into the moonlight. The Selway River poured along in the darkness like a whisper from the universe.

I sat down amid the smoldering remains of my sleeping gear. There was a big hole in the back of my windbreaker. Half my sleeping pad near the middle was eaten away. And the space blanket was a pile of threads and ashes. I couldn't believe it.

It was true. Finally I turned the pad over and stretched out again, but I didn't sleep much. There were little burns all over my hands. The moon went all the way across the sky and dropped from sight, the chill of the night deepened and many more stars came out in tighter patterns. My mind kept turning this way and that. I tried to figure out how I could get a sleeping bag. There was no way. I had made my bed and now I could lie in it. I could get hit with a blizzard at the upper end of Moose Creek. The pack would cover the hole in the back of the windbreaker, or I could sew one of my gaiters over the hole. Sleeping was the problem. Even with cold and heavy snow, if I stayed near the timber I would be all right. The pad still functioned, and I could make shelters if I had to. I would learn a lesson.

A great idea, the space blanket. Glad I thought it up. I pulled the windbreaker over my legs and put a fire rock down by my feet. It warmed one of them. I dozed on and off, feeding the fire, not turning my back on it. I waited for the sun. The night was long, it lasted long after the moon went down. It kept getting colder. I told myself it was nothing.

When dawn finally came I looked up on the high open end of a ridge across the river and saw an elk step cautiously out into the open, half silhouetted, and sniff for a while. Then disappear into the trees on the sunny side. When the sun finally came over the mountain I got up, stiff and tired, and found my way down to where the warmth hit on the bank. I sat there soaking it in, and I didn't feel like moving. I felt now why the elk moved to where the sun was after dawn, why they bedded on east-facing hillsides. In a short time it soaked away the chill of the entire night. First night out.

The first night was pure joy, boys, a joy to be back in the wilds and under the stars once again. While that mule laid there and snored I scouted around the creek bottom and soon come upon some turkey sign on a log, and I begun sneakin' up that creek quiet as a field mouse and slow as a snake in the sun, keepin' my eyes movin' and sharp. Pretty soon I saw the head and neck of the cagey devil a-starin' off into nothingness and listenin'. Without so much sound as a feather makes I raised up my Hawken and fired. Next thing that bird knowed he was standin' there without a head. I gathered him up and brought him back into camp and roasted him on a willow spit over the fire, the fat a-sizzlin' and cracklin', and when she was hot and steamin' clear through I bit in and filled my belly up and then some. When I couldn't eat no more I hung the rest of him in a tree so the bears wouldn't be crawlin' on me, and lay back on a sweet-smellin' bed of pine and lit my pipe, and looked out upon the mountains and stars. And I knowed that they was the best thing there was in the world, the place I belonged, and them sons of bitches back in the courthouses could eat dust and make laws to suit the rich till the shit was pouring out their ears, and I was still a free mountain man, and if I warn't a fool the mountains would take care of me. I slept as peaceful as a newborn babe that night, boys, with the stars as my blanket and the earth as my bed, and the next morning I jumped up at the crack of dawn and begun to pullin' that mule to his feet so I could get on up the trail.

Old Gabe. I had a ways to go to catch up with him.

I went down to the river and stuck my head in, then shook it off. I woke up. Tenderfoot. First night out I burn up half my cover and one of my maps. Well, I'd make it through, with or without the cover.

I walked up to the fire and set about making a biscuit for the trail. I smeared a little lard around in the kettle, mixed a big lump of dough in the cup, then plopped it in the kettle and hung it over the coals with the top on. I'd never tried it before in a kettle. As the sun rose higher and warmer I stripped and rinsed my hands, face, and crotch, and while I dried I watched a red-tailed hawk hunt the high ridges over the river. I felt better.

I packed up my outfit and by the time the biscuit was done I was ready to go. It worked perfectly; the baking soda made it rise, it had a brown crust, and it didn't stick to the kettle. The only trouble was I had put too much baking soda in the mixture. The biscuit tasted like a teaspoonful of baking soda. I should have tried the mixture before I set out.

I doused the fire, throwing the bigger sticks and the blackened fire rocks in the river, and set off up the trail. The elements would scrub them clean.

I CONTINUED on up the Selway most of the day, climbing high sometimes, the afternoon hot. It was getting wilder, and Moose Creek loomed ahead in my mind, country beyond civilization. I kicked myself for making the mistake I'd made and thought seriously about not making another one. I would guard against wetness and wind, and I'd hang my food every night no matter how tired I was. It was remote country and it might be cold; if anything happened I would be stuck up there for a long time before anyone started looking for me. No foolish mistakes, no letting my pack fall off the side of the mountain, no losing anything, no burning anything. I worked at sharpening myself to be alert, to keep my mind on the trail, to be ready for the unexpected. It was always the unexpected that did you in. When I thought I had everything figured out that could happen, I made it a point to figure that I didn't.

Toward evening I got to a bigger creek with a trail branching off along the upper bank, and there I set down my pack. I was tired and sweaty; it would be another two or three days before my legs started to harden up. I walked a short way up the trail where it started to climb above the creek and it intrigued me; I wondered what kind of country it drained. Finally I decided to camp at the mouth of the creek and head up it in the morning. If it was nice I would stay up there for a while and hunt around without the pack while my legs rebuilt. Look for bears.

I drank and soaked my head, then set about making a good camp. I found a good level patch of ground, kicked out a hip hole and lined it with grass. Next to that I built a stone reflector oven three feet long and found a big slab of yellow pine to lay on top so the fire would burn steadier and hotter. Then I dragged in the firewood. I hunted thick yellow pine branches and cedar slabs so the fire wouldn't shoot sparks, and I laid in a pile of small kindling in case it died down while I slept. Then I went over to the bank and looked down the river to the west. Mostly clear, no storm clouds. I picked out a nearby spruce at the base of the hill that I would head for if it rained in the night.

I hung the kettle over the fire with rice, chunks of jerky, some lard, and a thick handful of pale new dandelion leaves that the sun hadn't turned bitter. I left it to cook and sat by the river, chewing and spitting. Dirty Black Sky Power Co. sons of bitches. I was feeling better. I knew that I had to stop early enough to make a good camp, before I got too tired.

The moon rose again, swollen a little past half full. Two different hawks were circling around it that evening, looking as if they were half playing and half hunting. They tucked into dives, but pulled out before they got down to the trees on the hillside. I suspected that they were watching for grouse through the evening.

I ate the hot stew and it melted the tension and hunger in my stomach. I was grateful for the vitamins in the leaves, and they didn't taste bad. I winked at the mountain. It gave not the slightest sign.

I slept better. I kept warm rocks down by my feet most of the night, exchanging them when they cooled, and I slept deep when the fire burned warm. The stones and the slab threw out a lot of heat, and the hip hole was about right. The old man didn't have much on me that night.

At dawn I threw the rocks and sticks in the creek and started up the side trail, walking fast to get warm. The trail climbed up fairly high above the creek and wound around hillsides thick with timber. I could hear the creek down there, seven or eight hundred feet below. Finally it broke into the open and I looked across the valley just in time to see a black bear dive for cover. It had seen me a second and a half sooner than I had seen him. He had been feeding on the grassy hillside. Too far away to follow.

It was a steep and beautiful valley with a lot of open slopes, thickets, and arrows of pine coming down the ravines. Down below, the creek was mostly whitewater, a powerful creek fifteen to twenty feet across which piled up big logjams at the bends and flowed past giant boulders. From up above it was a white-water ribbon winding back and forth, a wild-looking bottom whose muffled roar changed when the morning breeze changed. The sky was blue, a few white clouds, and the sun had already hit the top of the mountain to the west.

After an hour the trail dropped down lower and I came upon a small shadowed clearing across the creek and stopped when I caught a movement. Mule deer were feeding in there, four, five of them, lowering and raising their heads, stepping secretively in the shadows; made my heart sing. A doe with a slight bulge in her stomach and her two yearlings, still following her.

I went about five miles further up the creek, high up the side of the valley, and by the time the sun was up in the sky I came out of the timber and climbed up on a rock overhang with a good view of the valley and the country beyond. I felt a sudden rush of joy standing out there in the morning breeze; higher, more remote country to the north, with the blue sky soaring over all of it. Fish and grouse, deer; roaming with a rifle. I savored the calling, the feelings that it stirred.

I looked down to where the creek split; there was good timber there with small open grassy areas, an open hillside with a labyrinth of elk trails. I decided to stay awhile.

I made a good camp down by the creek, next to the thick spruce, and I camped there while the moon grew fuller and brighter through the evenings. Wild strawberries were blooming all around and the sun kept shining. The creek was too powerful to ford and I had to find logs to cross it. I made a long trip up the fork of the creek which led toward the snow ridge and found some bear shit that was three or four days old, but no bears. In a dense section littered with downfalls I scared up a big whitetail doe, and she went bounding away, soaring up and down, as if the deadfalls were no obstacles at all. I watched her big white tail bouncing back and forth like a flag, and I realized what a beacon it was. Mule deer like the higher, open country and they have a tail that is like the fir trees that grow up there—sparse and scrawny. Whitetail deer thrive in timbered bottoms that are dense and gloomy and their tail is like the spruce there—thick and luxuriant. It is almost a foot high on a big deer, and when they are alarmed it comes up in the air like a stalk of white cotton. Her fawns follow it when she flees. After climbing bleakly through the timber for two hours, it was a pleasure for me to stand and watch that living white tail bobbing through the gloom.

I hunted the open hillsides for bear sign and glassed them mornings and evenings, but I didn't see any. I unwound, I wandered. My legs got stronger. The High-Water Moon was growing. There were deer and elk on the hillsides, down in the meadow. There were goose eggs and duck eggs hidden along the Selway River. The coyote had her den dug and lined, for she was very close. Mayflies rose up and down in their journey up the creek in the evening. The cutthroat trout were running, leaving the deep holes in the Selway where they had spent the winter and starting up the creeks against high water, flashing up through the rapids, leaping for mayflies, on their way into the high country. The chinook salmon were coming into the wilderness from the Pacific Ocean, a journey of seven or eight hundred miles up the same river system I described earlier, to spawn and die in the springtime at the foot of the Bitterroot Mountains. Their bodies to be eaten by otters, fishers, mink, coyotes, ravens, eagles, and bears. To feed young at the very beginning of their season. Nothing wasted, everything going back into life.

The bears walk a tightrope of survival in the spring. They must weigh the increasing hunger pangs they feel against the danger of catching a high-powered bullet in the guts. When a black bear first comes out of its den it is more sleepy than hungry. Its stomach is shriveled into a tight knot, its feet are tender, and it takes several days, sometimes a week, to wake up.

Finally it heads for the lower valleys, which are turning green at the bottom and up the south-facing hillsides. There it begins to feast on greens—grass, moss, and new leaves. Its fur is still prime, thick and fairly glossy, and it still has a fair amount of fat left over from the winter. As the High-Water Moon comes on it loses fat rapidly, continuing to feast hard and fast on green things. This is salad time for the bear, perhaps because greens are easiest on its long-dormant digestive system. But its hunger is growing. And the bear hunters are after it. It feeds at night, and when its hunger comes on during the day it must try to find a place to feed where the humans can't spot it with their binoculars. It weighs that possibility against its hunger pains, and the smartest and most cautious of the bears survive the temporary onslaught of shooters.

Now the spring was growing richer, the height of flower blooming. I ran into two garter snakes, both of which the bear would have seized and eaten. I walked through small clover patches with yellow jackets in them, and those the bear would have stunned with a lightning blow of its paw, licked off the ground, and swallowed. I saw an anthill which it would have stuck its paw into, allowed the agitated ants to swarm over it, then casually lifted it to its mouth and licked them off. The beginning of insects now, snakes and mice.

I realized that a human lost in the woods without a gun, if he were to survive, would wind up feeding very much like the bear whether he knew the bear's feeding habits or not. Grasshoppers, a nestful of mice, budding willow, lodgepole cambium, alder bark, glacier lily roots, crickets, maggots, grubs, ground squirrels, shrews, frogs, rabbits, ant eggs—fat and protein in the insects, carbohydrates in the roots, vitamins and minerals in the greens. More complete protein in the small animals. All of it food which you had to gather with your hands, either snaring, hitting with a rock (the speed and force of the bear's arm), digging out with a pointed stick (its claws), or simply grabbing. I began to realize why a bear is so strong and fast compared to a human—all the digging and grubbing it did, and the constant stimulation to the reflexes in catching small quick things trying to dart away. A big black bear can break the neck of a full-grown cow with a single blow. If a 220-pound boxer had the strength and speed of a 220-pound bear, both Joe Louis and Muhammad Ali in their respective days would wake up in the dressing room and begin to think about the details of their retirement. A bear's strength is awesome. From the bear a human learns to survive with only his hands.

I started out at dawn one morning after deer and elk, moving silently and waiting for my pumping blood to warm up. There were scattered patches of frost on the ground; warblers down by the creek. The sky was yellow with the rays of the hidden sun. Up high a raven was coasting. I realized as I walked that one thing I hadn't thought to bring was a good pair of moccasins.

Through the trees ahead was the beginning of one of the meadows along the creek. I saw a flash of brown up there and I dropped down, moving a little closer. It was a cow elk feeding alone, blocked from view below the shoulders by the bulk of a big downed yellow pine. I worked closer to the right so I could see her. Her stomach was big, hanging slightly. She might be only a week away from birth. She seemed to feed hungrily, but with a very sharp vigilance. Her head disappeared behind the log for three seconds, four seconds, then suddenly it swung up again, chewing hard and steady, her eyes covering the woods left to right in one look. I started to stalk her, crawling on my hands and knees, using brush and tree trunks for cover. I took care not to crack a single twig, watching where each hand and knee went. The wind was in my favor and I was wearing a camouflaged shirt and dark pants. Every time she looked her head didn't just rise; in less than a second it was suddenly in full view, eyes wide and gleaming, open for the slightest move. I tried to catch the first blur of her ears so that I could freeze by the time her eyes arrived. The closer I got, the more I felt the tension, the weight on every move. When her head went down I picked the route to the closest tree trunk, marked the hand and knee moves where I wouldn't crack something. I waited while her head came up, sharp-eyed, chewing like a camel, and when it went down again I moved lightly and quickly, concentrating on the places I had marked, hoping I would get there before she looked. No animal in North America did what I was doing better than the mountain lion, and I felt that for a certainty as I crept closer. When I got inside thirty feet I felt tremors in my stomach, my eyes were glued on her neck and each move seemed to take a long time.

Then she sensed me. She never saw me directly, she couldn't smell me, but her head began to stay up longer, tuning in more on my general area. My muscles were getting edgy, and I made the mistake of only waiting for a minute or two before I kept going. I made two more moves. I didn't think she saw either one of them, but after the second one she stopped feeding and stood there chewing, watching the area. Her eyes never focused on me, but at length she turned and walked away, across the meadow and into the timber.

I stood up and stretched, realizing the mistakes I had made. At first I thought she had sensed me, without seeing, hearing anything, but a little later I figured that she must have caught the tail end of one of my movements. That's when I should have waited, four minutes, six minutes, as long as it took until she showed no more sign of being especially watchful. Until she had forgotten the movement. As it happened she caught a second tiny movement, and although it didn't spook her it was enough to send her walking away.

I come up on a cow elk that mornin', boys, and decided to have a little fun. I dropped back into the timber where some elk had been standin', took off my buckskins, and commenced to smearin' good fresh elk shit all over my skin. Pretty soon I was all a-colored green and yeller and brown. I looked like a walkin' patch of forest and smelt like a wapiti if ever one walked on this earth. I took up an extra button and a hunk of sinew, and I commenced to crawlin' up on that elk across the meadow, quiet and steady like hungry painter stalkin' a meal. She looked right over me more 'n once. Pretty soon I war close enough to see a wood tick a-crawlin' up her hind elbow, and I could hear her stomach growlin'. Slow like I reached up and begun sewin' that button onto her tail. Whenever she looked back I froze like a tree in the landscape, and she never once suspicioned a thing. Matter o' fact she once reached back and took a nibble at my hair, thinkin' it was asp' leaves, I reckon, but she didn't take to the taste and went back to feedin' on grass. She was close with calf, I could hear the little critter kickin' around in there for elbow room. When I got the button sewed on good I sneaked in under her legs and observed her plumbin', but she warn't yet fillin' with milk. Satisfied, I crept away into the brush, got my buckskins, and headed back toward the hot spring. She never had the slightest inklin' that I was anywhere in the valley. If any of them Nez Percé got a close look at her tail they'd a knowed that ol' Gabe was a-roamin' around in their mountains that spring.

"Painter" was what the mountain men called mountain lions. The early mountain men called grizzlies "white bears."

I was feeling good. I saw ten or twelve more elk that morning, lounging around in the sun, biting at an itch in a hind leg, peacefully licking a nose, soaking in the warming relief of the first sunlight after a cold night. It dawned on me that this was their favorite time of year. They had just come through the winter. Their favorite plants and flowers were on the bloom, and they were far away from hunting season. As I watched them I listened to a hermit thrush in a thicket singing out the soul of the season.

My legs were getting stronger and my mind was turning more and more toward Moose Creek and the country beyond. It was never far from my thoughts in the time I was spending in this valley; behind the everyday sights and experiences it was stored up and waiting—to see what the country was like, to see high water up at the height of the Bitterroots. The peaks along that part of the range ran between 8,000 and 9,000 feet, and at the climax of the snowmelt the water came down off them in falling sheets and runaway torrents, sometimes with a spectacular power. It was a dangerous time, one that swept away the uncautious, but one that had some high sights and power for the spirit, just to see.

There were also supposed to be two trappers buried near where the two forks of Moose Creek split, their graves still there according to what I had heard. I wanted to try to find them, for I knew their story.

I spent the rest of the day roaming around looking for bear sign. I didn't see any bears; only a week-old set of tracks in some mud a mile up the creek. Goldfinches and vireos were building nests in thickets along the creek. I walked under a twenty-foot rock face just off the creek, moss and a little dripping water, and was startled by a sudden commotion of flight overhead. A bunch of cliff swallows were leaving their nests, twelve, fifteen of them, circling out over the creek in a chaotic mass of flight, warning and scolding at me. Their nests looked like spattered mud gourds stuck to the side of the cliff, close together, with little entrance holes just down from the top so the rain didn't run in. The holes looked smaller than the birds, but they squeezed out of them all right. What kind of mud did they use, that a three-hour thunderstorm didn't wash those nests into the creek? I asked them but they wouldn't say.

I forgot to bring some jerky with me and later in the afternoon I got hungry. I sat on a log thinking about the feeling, the seriousness of it. The driving power of hunger. I tried to imagine what it would feel like if I didn't have my food sack hanging back at camp. There would be a deep change. The wilderness would quickly lose its charm; I would get up and set out with one intention gnawing at my mind: stop the ache in my belly. Everything I did or thought would be colored by that compulsion. Only when I was able to do it well enough to give myself free time would I begin to enjoy myself again. The food sack gave me free time.

I thought about it before I went to sleep that night. But it was my first trip; I would learn on my own. I didn't sleep well. It got cold after the moon went down, a cold that crawled up inside my pantlegs, numbed my feet. Finally I sat up and warmed my boots good, got the fire going bright. I fell into a deep, tired sleep. When I woke up the fire was down to halfhearted coals and I was chilled to the bone. I could see my breath. I shivered steadily as I laid twigs on the coals, blew them to life. A great idea, the space blanket. Slowly the warmth of the flames began to soak in again. I slept on.

The next morning I steeled myself and started out with the idea of not eating anything except that which I could hunt up. I climbed up the steep hillside behind camp, pushing to get warm, my mind on blue grouse. Early in the morning they like the sun on those ridges; they seem to congregate on the ground up there in small flocks, pruning and cleaning, enjoying the sun and getting ready for the day's feed. Knowing that I would have a hard time taking them unless I was truly hungry, that morning I just thought I would see if I could find them. I couldn't. I got to the top and walked it quite a ways, but didn't scare any up. I looked across at that big walking ridge and saw that the sun had hit earlier; it was broader with some cover and dead snags, and I had the feeling that was where I should have looked.

I went back down to the creek and ate a lot of strawberry leaves, which tasted good to me in the morning and had vitamin C; some flower heads and clover. To tell the truth, I wasn't really up for the fur on the yellow jackets, although I could have captured a couple. The greens put some roughage in my stomach, took a slight edge off the awakening hunger I felt. But they weren't satisfying. I got my Hawken and started looking for squirrels. Pine squirrels are smart; they sense when you are hunting them. When you aren't hunting them they show themselves, scold, and run from branch to branch in full view. When you are walking quietly with a rifle and looking up in the trees they hide out of sight on the upper side of big branches, waiting until you are long past. I walked for an hour and a half without getting a shot.

I went back to camp about lunchtime and sat down, getting hungrier. The woods started to seem empty, alien, a few flies buzzing around, the sun growing hot, the creek washing past like the never-ending measure of an eon. I laid my Hawken against the log and as soon as I did a pine squirrel took off across a small grass flat.

I chased it. It hopped ten feet up a tree trunk and froze there, listening. I raised and fired. The squirrel leapt off the tree, tumbled down through the air and bounced off the grass.

Bully. Turd. I walked over and saw it lying on its back frantically kicking its hind legs in the air, flexing its ears back and forth as it died. The bullet had gone through its neck. A few more seconds and it was still.

Pine squirrels had a good life up in the branches and sunlight. They made fools out of dogs, coming down far enough to work them into a frenzy and then leading them on a ridiculous chase all over the woods. They sounded off when a big animal was passing by not far away. They had to look out for hawks, martens, bobcats, and lynx. Marten were right on their tails heavy all winter.

I picked it up and carried it back to the camp, cutting it open and peeling the skin off down by the creek. Pretty pathetic when I held the carcass up. Still I was getting hungrier. A wood tick was crawling up my leg, and a raven was watching me from high in a dead yellow pine.

Fish. I would catch some fish. I got out my line and hook and started looking for bait under rocks. Finally I found a big slug and a centipede. The bank was rough and tangled and it was hard to get down to a good spot without cutting a silhouette. At a third pool right off some rapids I tossed the slug in and a few seconds later, to my surprise, something hit it. I pulled in a six-inch rainbow. It felt as if my stomach raised up its eyebrows. I kept fishing until I lost the slug, and then went up to look for more bait.

I scrounged around until I started to feel like a bear, sense like a bear. I went for the moist area, flipping rocks. I tore apart rotten stumps, growling and grunting. I found some big leg bones scattered in the grass and broke them open on a rock, searching for maggots after the marrow. The marrow was gone and there were only a few tiny ants inside, finishing off the last particle. I found a moist log and tore slabs off; straining, groaning, I dug around in hollow stumps.

After a while I felt dirty and tired. Ants were crawling on me and the sun was hot. I had found a stinkbug, more centipedes, and a weird green beetle that propelled itself by snapping away like a popcorn kernel. No maggots and no grubs, both of which are the best bait. I found a colony of big black wood ants in a hollow log. It was later in the afternoon and periodically my stomach clenched mildly, like a fist. I thought of the one small fish I had and my mouth watered. I wanted more. I went down and fished for another hour with the bugs I had but didn't get a bite.

I climbed back up the bank with my one fish. The sun was starting to settle toward the west. I felt hungry, dirty, and low. I thought of Hugh Glass crawling along with large infected gashes on his body, refusing to give up, popping worms and grasshoppers into his mouth and swallowing them to keep going.

I went over to the hollow log, sat down, and eyed the big black ants crawling around in there. Mechanical, heartless, devoid of emotion. Pinchers. Go out, ceaselessly, and relentlessly, grasp organic matter and drag it back into the colony to be devoured. Wound other bugs and drag them back squirming to be dismembered and eaten.

I didn't think those big wood ants bit you, though. Red ants bit. What if I was starving? I stuck my hand into the red loam and let several of them crawl on it, like the bear. While I was watching them they suddenly began to bite hard and effectively, and with an oath I shook them off. I pinched one, popped it in my mouth, and swallowed twice before it went down. The legs were like little steel wires. I couldn't bring myself to make a meal of them. If I was starving I would gather them on a stick, pinch them, and make a pile of them, then wash them down with water.

I started back toward camp with my fish. This was what I would be up against if I lost my pack and gun in a stream crossing. Scrounging. Digging. Gulping things down with my nose plugged. Chasing after snakes. Constant searching, constant hunger. But I knew now I could do it if I had to.

I cleaned the fish, wishing I had more. Every time I thought of its hot white meat I started to drool. Its skin was dry now. I brushed a few ants off the squirrel carcass and took them both down to the creek. I rinsed the squirrel and laid it on a rock. The water thundered. I held the fish under and started to move it back and forth. Suddenly the skin turned slimy and the fish popped out of my hand. I grabbed for it and missed. I watched it dance away down the rapids.

I stood up and looked at the mountain for quite a while. I didn't swear. Finally I nodded, picked up the squirrel, and walked back toward the camp.

The sun was setting; already early shadows had fallen over the camp. I walked up the hill until I came to scattered patches of arrowleaf balsamroot, looking like sunflowers, now in full bloom. Up and down the Bitterroots they bloom on the open hillsides as high water comes on; elk like the leaves when they first drill their way out of the ground. The whole plant is edible. Nez Percé Indians gathered them extensively as they began their spring hunting migrations, roasting the seeds. They are an important spring food if you are needy. The seeds are especially nutritious. But they take time to gather.

I sat down by one. Both the leaves and the stalks tasted highly aromatic raw, like balsam, so aromatic that it was unnerving. The roots were big and hard to get out of the ground; I hadn't brought up a good digging stick. I went around to different plants taking some flower heads, young leaves and stalks, in different places so that I didn't leave a sign of it. Enough for a meal. At last, tired and very hungry, I went back down into the gathering shadow of the valley and built up the fire. The moon was coming up, swelling, a small bright ring of haze around it. The woods were quiet and lonely.

I hung the kettle over the fire to begin simmering the plants. I put the squirrel in the other pan with a little lard and set it on some coals. Then, wishing again I had a sleeping bag, I went out and began dragging in the night's wood. The dinner I was cooking looked pretty meager. My feet felt wet and gritty.

Lordy, boys, what a celebration I had when I first come up that valley. She was a purty valley, fresh as a mornin' breeze, with snow in the high country beyond, the quakin' asp' leaves just a-comin' out that faint fresh green the way they do so early in the spring, givin' life to the hillsides. Spring was in the air and there warn't no flies out yet. First thing I spied was heavy elk trails comin down one hillside to a meadow on the other side of the creek, and I knowed that meant salt. I waded right across that deep thunderin' creek to rinse off my plumbin', but that son of a bitch mule wouldn't chance it so I had to go back and throw the bastard over to the other side. When I come ashore he was just pickin' himself to his feet, givin' me the evil eye, but I didn't pay no mind. I left him to feed.

They was Indian birthroots and yeller glacier lilies a-bloomin' away, and I stripped off my buckskins and gathered some of them bulbs for stew. The flowers of them lilies afore they unfolded was better than any beans you could get at that thievin' Fort Safeway, I'll tell ya. I took what I needed, my heart wingin' along like a sparrow, thankin' the blue sky and the mornin' breeze for feedin' a poor, brave, cunning, humble son of a bitch of a free mountain man like myself.

The sunshine was my clothin' that day, boys, and I didn't have no wants in the world. Warn't long afore I found that lick, and it was a little hot spring a-flowin' down into the creek. Elk prints everywhere. Glory, if the earth ain't a wondrous thing I don't know what is. Pretty soon I was sittin' there soakin' my feet, and thinkin' about the huntin' life.

And by the time the sun was goin' down I had me a camp up on a little bench overlookin' the valley, white grouse meat simmerin' with onion and salt, fish bakin' on a willow rack, a cup of mint tea a-brewin' at the edge of the coals. Deer and elk come out on the hillsides everywhere as the sun went down, and I seen a couple of bears wanderin' out of the woods in different places, rootin' and nosin' around as evenin' come on. It was a joy to me to be livin' amongst so many wild creatures, and as I looked out over them mountains I thought that they was so big and wild and filled with game that the day would never come when you had to worry about it gettin' scarce. I dipped a hot biscuit into that mouth-waterin' grouse stew and settled back to watch all them critters, glad that I was warm and well by my fire, and a free man.

I looked at the squirrel carcass sizzling in the pan. It was turning pale brown. It looked like a little voodoo doll without a head; its front legs stretched downward. It lay on its back and sizzled, perpetually stunned. It didn't make my mouth water.

I had enough wood in for the night. I sat down by the fire and took off my boots, letting the heat at the insides, and got out a dry pair of socks. I noticed that the skin around my toes was stained with dirt. I let the fire eat away the moisture, then put on the socks. I didn't see any bears. I didn't see a mountain lion. I didn't see any grouse.

I kept turning the squirrel over, until my hunger overcame my judgment. The moon had grown a little brighter. The pines rose up in complete stillness, no breeze, only the sound of the creek. My mouth watered then and I picked up the carcass and bit in. The meat was tough and stringy, hard to chew. Every time I went to take a bite, a picture of the creature frantically kicking its hind legs floated into my mind. The meat had a gamy, unpleasant taste. I ate it anyway. I opened the kettle and spooned up mouthfuls of greens. I ate everything, chewing and sucking the bones until they were bare. I ate the last wilted flower head. When I was finished I burped, an unpleasant burp that brought the taste of that squirrel back. I held my stomach. It wasn't full.

The fish would have done it. I made some coffee and sat there watching the flames. Dusk was settling heavy into the trees, all silent save for the tumbling of the creek. The moon stood above a tall dead pine, highlighting the ghostlike peeling of its bare branches. The moon's bright shadowed edge was growing, like the stomachs of the deer and elk I had seen, swelling over new-born porcupines, coyote pups blind in earthen den, antler velvet, bird eggs blue, green, brown, and white beginning to appear in fresh nests along the creek, up and down the mountains. That was the song this moon sang, through the days and nights, swelling toward hatching birds, down the endless run of the creeks into the rivers.

Something, I don't know what, made me look just down the trail to the right. There, where the trail came up from the creek ford, stood a big elk, her fine-looking legs and the dark fur of her belly wet and tangled, dripping water on the ground. I was spellbound by the sight. The moon shone down through the trees and cast the faintest brush of silver over the rough of her back. Her belly had a low, deep curve to it; and as her black eyes stared at me a muscle in her shoulder began to quiver. She couldn't believe that there was a human sitting up there by a fire; as she stared different muscles in her began to steel up for flight. She was so taken off balance that her pride seemed at stake, and it took several seconds for her to put it together to run. Then finally the action: a bound off to the right, shaking out the cobwebs, a longer and harder bound into the timber, then the high and graceful bounds as she disappeared slowly amid the deepening dusk of the forest.

My spirit sang for the wildness in it. It was fine to see at a time when I had been thinking about the moon: the calf she was carrying, her fur dripping from the violent waters of the creek, the silver-etched light of that night falling down around the strength of her body. She was printed in my memory. When I finally went to sleep I slept fairly sound, keeping the fire well stoked. It didn't seem so cold.

I WAS on my way back down the trail before sunup. The ache in my legs was turning into strength; my winter legs were beginning to harden up. The pack felt good, and I strode along with my back straighter, taking in the rugged sights of dawn in the mountains, using the muscles in the back of my legs more to stretch out my stride, to stop trudging with the pack and start walking with it, even upgrade. The upper country of Moose Creek lay ahead now, and I felt ready for it. I wondered about snow conditions up there, but that was why I had brought the lard. In a pinch, mixed with flour and a little salt, it would keep walking energy flowing through my blood for a week or longer. Or if I got hurt and had to wait. I took good care of it, cooling it in the creek whenever I stopped.

About midmorning I came down to the Selway, the air still pleasantly cool. I washed my hair, ate, and took stock of my provisions. I had been out six days; my rice was well down, jerky was a third down, flour was better than a third down. Less than half the honey was left. I worried for a while about the country I still had to cover and the fact that I hadn't seen any grouse. Finally I decided to save the rest of the honey for an emergency.

The morning was clear and blue, a little cooler than the day before. Good for walking. Butterflies and bugs flew about in the sunlight and the river looked lovely, shining dark green all the way across, the rapids snowy white, glistening snakes of current all over the surface. I retrieved the lard from the creek and set off up the trail. I had gotten a chip in my eye from breaking firewood the night before and it still bothered me; I looked for it with the signal mirror but couldn't find it. Every time I blinked it scratched.

The country got higher, more rugged. Rock towers rose up out of the timber at the tops of the mountains, solid chunks of granite standing against the sky. Around noon I passed through a long dense willow thicket and heard a ruffed grouse drumming in it, the first one. Serviceberry bushes, some fifteen feet high, were full of white flowers all along the banks of the upper river. They made misty white areas scattered through the green on the other bank. I saw a rust-colored bear feeding far up a hillside across the river, alone, no sign of any cubs. The country was big and wild. I passed through a stand of giant cedars close to five hundred years old. They blocked out the sky seventy feet up. A high white haze moved slowly in from the west. I pushed a good steady pace, up and down, overlooking the river. I was getting further into bear country, and I reminded myself to hang my food sack up at night. I camped under a cedar tree that night and hung it up in a high bush.

Early the next morning I came down a hill and a big river came into view, pouring into the Selway. Moose Creek. It was bigger than I thought, maybe sixty feet across, full to the top of its banks and fast-running. A big ridge separated the two waters, Moose Creek coming down from the north. A little further ahead the Selway turned south, heading down toward the Salmon River. There was a big suspension footbridge over Moose Creek.

I crossed over and kept walking, up along a hot and dry ponderosa ridge. When I came over the last rise a massive open field came into view, an air sock flying at the other end. Cabins down there were scattered through the trees. I walked across.

It was strange to see civilized structures, a time warp. I came up to a fence before the buildings and saw the long stretch of the airfield, an anemometer on a pole in the process of being hoisted up, and a log cabin with snowshoes, saw blades, different packs, and fire axes hanging beneath the front porch. As I looked it over I noticed a man walking in my general direction at a good brisk pace, his arms following his stride. He looked about as he walked. He glanced over at a rising magpie, watched it fly. He looked across to a white cloud hanging above a mountain. When he saw me he changed direction without changing his stride. As he drew closer I saw that he looked about fifty, wearing a loose old T-shirt stained from work, a faded pair of black pants with countless patches and stitches, and an old pair of jungle boots. The pants were cut off just above the tops of the boots, to allow air up his legs. His face was creased heavily at his eyes, brown leathery skin. His hands were gnarled and strong. I liked him on sight.

"Name's Keck," he said, shaking my hand with a firm crunch. His eyes were sharp and alive, questioning. "Where you headin'?"

I told him Lost Horse Pass, and asked if he thought I could get over. .

His face darkened and he looked me over. "Not many people go all the way through there," he said. "And it's pretty early in the year. What are you packin' for food?"

I told him jerky and rice.

"How long you been out?"

A week, I said.

He stared at me sharply for a few moments. "Come on with me," he said.

I followed him up to the cabin, thinking about his directness. He talked with one of the trail-crew members, who had just come in. Pretty soon they stood in front of me with a huge meat-loaf sandwich, mayonnaise dripping out. My knees suddenly felt weak at the sight of it, my head spun in the beginning of a faint. My mouth started to pour.

"Here, eat this."

No, I told them, talking through the saliva, that was all right, I was seeing how I could do on jerky, I—

"Don't be a fool! Eat the son of a bitch, you might be glad you did."

I ate it. It was like heaven. My eyes weren't seeing anything as I chewed.

He showed me on the map which way to go. He showed me a stream crossing to avoid, where to hang to the bank through a boulder field. He drew me a map of where the trappers' graves were. He told me the general lay of the canyon below the pass, in case there was snow. We talked for an hour about many different things. He told me the elk were getting shot out of the Selway by rich hunters, so badly that he didn't hunt any more. He and his wife lived largely on freeze-dried food and grains year-round. He told me to take some of his freeze-dried food and pay him back later. I told him I had enough food.

When I got ready to leave he smiled a clear beaming smile. "When you shake a man's hand," he said, "give it a good solid squeeze so he'll remember you." His eyes narrowed and he pointed a work-hardened finger at me. "You be goddamn careful up there and don't take any chances alone. Remember, there's more than one man drowned trying to save his pack. If you're in trouble in that river let the son of a bitch go. You're a fool if you haven't got enough grub and don't let Penny fix you up some. Fishing might be scarce up there this early."

I told him I had enough food. I gave him a good solid crunch of a shake and told him I'd write him when I got out. Then I was on the way.

I followed a well-worn trail several miles up Moose Creek,

thinking about the things he told me. Some rich bear hunters were coming in now, and I thought about getting shot by one. They flew in, slept in an outfitter's tent on a cot, drank a lot of beer and whiskey, ate fried chicken and steak, rode a horse out a ways, and killed a bear on a hillside with a telescoped rifle. The outfitter skinned it. The carcass was left to rot. The hunter left the skin with a taxidermist and flew back to the East. He got his rug in the mail. "I killed that bear in the Selway wilderness in Idaho." *Did the outfitter tuck you in at night?*

I went on. A white osprey came sailing past overhead, crying the clear high call of the fishing eagle. Ravens circled around far over the splashing waters. It was wide, Moose Creek was, but it didn't have the depth of the Selway. The rapids didn't have the thunder or the power. Still I wouldn't want to fall in. I pushed on to get out of the range of bear hunters. The trail was littered with fresh horse tracks.

Finally I came to a bridge and crossed over Moose Creek where it split. The graves were somewhere along the North Fork, which flowed away toward a deep, lonely-looking valley. There was a big meadow between the two forks. I hung my pack where I knew I would find it again, took a little jerky, and set off toward the upper end of the North Fork. I came into some trees, scattered patches of grass, the woods still and hot. I doubted that I would find the graves. There was at least a mile of river-front where they could be and there were no definite landmarks.

I hit the river and started hunting up the bank, through brush, over rock piles, up onto little grassy benches. No sign of them. I searched into the afternoon. Lonely white clouds floated over the mountain across the river; the river coursed clear and pretty, but the air seemed solitary and empty to me. It felt strange to be looking for those graves, for them to be in this valley. It was like stepping backward in time, a feeling of being removed from the present just knowing that they were here somewhere. They were men who had put themselves against the Selway and lost.

I lost sight of the river following a game trail, then walked across a bench back toward the bank. When I topped it I saw a big cow elk, lean-looking, standing right next to the river. She jumped when she saw me, danced a little, then turned and jumped into the river. She soon lost her footing and was swept downstream, swimming steadily with her nose forward, the water flowing over her rump. It was a pretty sight to see her swimming that river under the blue and cloudy sky, the valley broad and wild with a lonely wind wandering up over the water. She got her footing again and splashed ashore, dripping, her head turning back with a look of superiority. She trotted up a little draw and disappeared in the timber.

Lonely. I sat down in the rocks and let it sink in, the soft wind, the river, the swimming elk. I looked down to where she had been and suddenly my eye caught a rectangular slab of wood sticking up, partially hidden in some brush. I got up and moved closer. It was a grave.

A prickling eeriness hit me. I walked up quietly and moved the brush aside. There were rocks piled in a body-length mound stretched out in front of the head slab. Weeds grew up between them. The slab leaned back a little, all gray, deeply weathered and grooved. Cedar, still standing. There was another grave just like it five feet away, at a different angle. No cemetery, no fence; two bodies buried in the Idaho wilderness, by a river.

Words had been carved into the slabs. Sunlight, wind, and storms were erasing those words, but they were still plainly readable.

J P	JOHN
WHEELER	SHEAN
DIED	DIED
MAY	MAY
1898	1898

Eighty years had passed. I sat down next to the first grave, looking at the mottled rocks, the weeds. The mountain where the elk had disappeared rose up solitary against the blue sky with rain clouds coming along its front. Slow, dark clouds, trailing smoky tendrils which touched down to the timber on the mountainside. I felt the longness of that mountain, the seasons that had passed, the high water that was passing now, eighty high waters, and the mountain had not changed. I sensed the larger time span of it, a time that dwarfed me, made me draw inward like a prodded insect, with the proof of the graves right there in front of me. An insect's life span, upon the body of the mountain. As I sat there with the rain passing by, watching the darkness in the fold of the mountain, a sound came out of it which made me stop breathing. Clear and unmistakable came a sound like a dog half crying and half barking. Over and over again it came out of that dark fold in the mountain across the river, calling out in a solitary and pitiful cry, a cry which seemed directed toward the emptiness beyond the sky, the depth of the earth and rocks, the cruelty hidden at the bottom of the river. I knew there was no dog in there; I realized it had to be an elk barking. The clear pitch in the sound was that of an elk. Why? Was it caught in something? I had a vague feeling that it had something to do with my presence, but I couldn't imagine what it could be. It went on for over ten minutes, and that strange solitary sound combined with the wind and the graves, the loneliness of the valley, to produce feelings in me which left me numbed and hollow, lonely down to the roots of my being. I stayed there by the grave, listening to the cry, letting its aching loneliness wash over me. The feeling was true. It seldom surfaced.

I knew the story of the men. They had lived in the Bitterroot Valley, and had come over Lost Horse Pass early in August with fifteen horses, supplies for the winter, prospecting tools and traps. Breaking loose, a winter adventure in the Selway; they would live like mountain men and maybe make some money to boot. They had bear dogs, and everything went according to plan through the autumn. They went up to a nearby salt lick and killed enough elk for the winter, for jerky, trap meat, and dog food. They killed black bears with the dogs. They killed two grizzly cubs and got chased by a sow. They killed her. They were having a good time. Rose hips were ripening all along the river. They figured if they hadn't found any gold they would make some money trapping marten.

They built a cabin and trapped until Christmas. On the first day of January three feet of snow fell and the temperature dropped to 20 below. From then on things went from bad to worse. The winter wore on, deeper snow, colder temperatures; the horses began to starve, and they had to shoot the dogs because they were eating too much of the elk meat. They tried to move the camp to where the horses could forage better, but they had a terrible time in the deep snow and two of them got sick. The symptoms were an aching in the head and eyes, shortness of breath, limbs tender and swollen. They kept getting worse through February, one of them finally going blind. They were dying of scurvy, although none of them knew it. They didn't know what was wrong. If they would have eaten some of those shriveled rose-hip berries along the river, they probably would have survived.

Five of the fifteen horses were still alive, and they made a desperate attempt to ride out through the wet snow sometime in March. They made five miles in two days, and then one of the pack horses slipped in a steep canyon and fell to its death. Shaken, they turned back. By the time they got to the cabin one of them was dying and the other was turning delirious. The third man probably survived because he was a good deal younger. As he was digging a grave for the first to die, the second man came running out of the cabin barefoot and shirtless, his eyes wild and his hair flying, and grabbed ahold of him. "I've been traveling all night," he said. "I'm hungry. Can I stay here tonight and get something to eat?" In his mind he had just made it back to civilization, safe and alive.

He died twelve days later in a coma. The surviving turn-of-the-century mountain man dug another grave, wrapped the body in a blanket, and laid it in. The wild rosebushes along the river were budding by then. The dogs were dead. Eight horses were dead or lost. His two companions were dead. The dogtooth violets were beginning to bloom yellow and the grass was turning green. He was left with the empty cabin in the lonely valley where he had watched the men sicken and die, and with four live horses. The big mountain with the dark fold where the elk was now crying out stood silently across the river. He made it out several weeks later on foot over the crusted snow of Lost Horse Pass, leaving the horses behind.

The rain clouds had drifted on up the North Fork, passing the graves by. Dandelions were blooming about the flat. A little thunder rumbled up the North Fork, but it was going farther away. The elk still cried out, a lonely, nonhuman sound. I stood up, eyeing the graves, the ordeal of the one man who lived turning in my mind. They would have survived it if they had gathered some mountain sorrel, also known as scurvy grass, as they came over the pass, and made tea out of it through the winter. The same with dandelion leaves. All contain vitamin C, as do rose hips, which hang on the branch most of the winter. In the mountains they are vital winter survival food. But the men never thought of an invisible little thing like vitamins. They were going into the Selway to be mountain men.

I walked back toward the East Fork, sobered, looking out to where the waters stretched away into the timbered wilderness. It was dense and it was rugged. It was vast. A new respect was dawning in me for it, something having to do with its distances and the impassibility of whole stretches of it. It was easy to underestimate the Selway. To head off into it for an adventure and not take into account what difficult country it was, how far you must travel if you had to get out. I had underestimated it in a way, and the first night out it swallowed up my sleeping cover. Now my food was running down and I had been traveling steady on jerky for over a week. I wondered about my strength. I felt all right, but I remembered the weakness in my knees when I stood in front of that sandwich. The taste of the jerky and the baking-soda biscuits was getting very tiresome. But still, the jerky was keeping me going. A handful of it killed the hunger, enabled me to walk another five miles. And I had the lard. If anything happened I had the lard.

I got my pack and started up the trail. I was past the ranger station now, forty-five miles of wild country ahead to pass, no one else in it. It was what I had been waiting for. The worry about my food supply was steady in the back of my mind, but I heard grouse drumming and saw one lurking through the brush. I figured if I needed to I could get one. I held on to that new respect I felt, the new awareness of the region of wilderness which stretched out behind the Bitterroots.

I walked the rest of the day through a dim and gloomy forest, very thick, a few big cedar and ponderosa rising up, jumbled piles of deadfalls everywhere around. A couple of ravens followed me just over the timber, squawking and flapping about. They gave me a weird feeling, passing through that gloomy forest. The last of the bear hunters' horse tracks petered out: I had gone beyond their reach.

By the end of the afternoon I cut off the trail toward the creek and went down through a silent and wet bog looking for moose. Moose shit looks like malted-milk balls. There was no fresh sign. A great number of swirling green swamp plants were sprouting up, unfolding leaves glowing green and yellow in the few patches of sunlight which fell through. I couldn't identify them and wondered if they were edible. The swamp and surrounding woods seemed empty, no grouse drumming. I came to an opening on the creek and looked out on a scene that struck me deeply, so wild it looked. Down around the bend the creek came rushing over the rocks, wide and powerful, crowded in between pine banks so dim and tangled it looked as if you couldn't get through them without an ax. I felt a pang of loneliness, and at the same time a surge of freedom knowing there was no one else in it.

I went back up, crossed over a creek, and made a camp just where a big open stand of cedar was beginning. The moon came up over the mountain after dark, a pale splotch in the clouds, but looking rounder. In a while it disappeared completely. After I ate I curled close to the fire and pushed the thought of a sleeping bag out of my head. I was just drifting off to sleep when there came a huge tickling across my cheek. A daddy longlegs. I flicked it and settled back into the hip hole. Before long there was another huge tickle across my neck. This time I smashed it. Before I could even get comfortable again another one was crawling on my hand.

I sat up and stared around. By the light of the fire I saw that the camp was alive, glistening with daddy longleg spiders. Sixty of them, seventy of them, all over the woodpile, across the ground around the fire, on my knee, over my boots—spiders everywhere I looked, their bowed legs glinting as they went along.

"Why are you doing this?" I said aloud. I was tired. The glowing orange legs were everywhere. It was too dark to move camp, and I was too tired. "Go away," I said. They didn't.

I threw twenty-eight of them in the fire. They popped with a little cry of gas, and the stink of it lingered on. It was bad medicine for me to kill daddy longlegs, but I couldn't sleep. Finally I gave up. I closed my collar around my neck, tied my bandana over my face. I buried my hands in my armpits. I closed my eyes.

At last I slept. Later in the night a small amount of rain fell in my face, then stopped. There were a few spiders left. What were they doing? I went back to sleep. Before long I had a dream in which my relatives were making several phone calls, making some kind of arrangements. A little while later a National Guard plane flew over, and air-dropped me a sleeping bag.

When I woke up, I figured old Gabe was still a long way ahead of me.

THE SUN was high the next morning when I rounded a bend in the trees and saw a big black bear just ahead feeding on low green plants. It hadn't seen me and the wind was coming up between us, angling toward the bear. I slipped behind a big cedar and silently lowered my pack. Fear tingled along my back as I thought about sneaking closer; I felt defenseless, and I wished I had a .357 just in case. Still I got down on my hands and knees, and when its broad powerful rear turned toward me, showing the scrawny scrap of tail, I crawled silently to a closer tree. The wind kept swirling toward the bear, but he didn't smell me. He was feeding in a small patch, grazing away. His fur was shiny and thick enough to bury a cup in, still prime. He moved toward some low green plants and I crept quickly to another tree, trying to identify the plants, my heart tripping steady. The closer I got, the more naked I felt, the more I saw the power in his shoulder and his ass and I realized how much damage he could do in a very short amount of time. He was wild, he lived wild, his black fur made him look wild. I felt the wildness just watching him. Yet he fed relaxed and docile, all his attention tied up in the green plants. His eyes looked small and poorly focused; he picked which plant he would eat by smelling it, rather than by looking. If it was a low branch with a lot of leaves he would put the branch in his mouth and swing it to the side, stripping all the leaves at once. He chewed steadily, as if he were hungry. Once he looked directly at me for a few moments and didn't show any sign of seeing me. He kept feeding. Then a big soft whirlwind blew up and suddenly he was gone, bolting silently up through the bushes without so much as a glance in my direction. His nose knew what was close. He ran up through the undergrowth without a sound, disappearing quickly. If I had stalked more downwind I might have stayed with him longer.

I PUSHED ON with the high country on my mind, following the creek through a wide and densely timbered valley, always climbing, toward where it took its swing to the north. I saw another big black bear in a steep opening just across the creek, feeding on the greens along the bank, solitary and unmindful as it picked among the leaves. I thought that the females with cubs must be doubly careful in the spring, for I had seen four bears and none of them was with cubs—probably all males. I didn't see much other game. The open hillsides seemed deserted. I saw two ruffed grouse in a day and a half of climbing, neither of which I had a shot on.

My food sack was shrinking. The jerky was better than half gone, my soup and noodles were running down. The higher I went, the more the worry over food gnawed at me. I shot at a squirrel and missed. I wanted to know that if a big snow came or anything else happened I could get enough to eat to keep going. The weather was turning gray and colder and I couldn't tell what it was going to do.

I was entering an increasingly deeper cedar forest, dim for long stretches. I camped a night and went on. Late in the afternoon I came out to a meadow and saw that just ahead the valley and the creek with it turned sharply to the left, northward. I knew that from here the pass was about twenty-five miles further up. I had seen very little game and I was tired and strung out. I looked around and didn't find any fresh deer sign. For a while I sat at the edge of the timber mulling things over, and then I looked down to the west and saw weather coming in. The tops of the mountains down Moose Creek were being erased as a dark gray mass moved up the valley. The timber above the creek began to toss, bits of witch's hair flying off the branches, and the creek turned a dark stormy green. The ridgeline disappeared. Across the valley through a lot of open air I saw hundreds of individual sheets of rain riding in on the wind, big and lonely. I went into the thick timber and tied a dead pole to a tree trunk, letting the other end rest on the ground. I strung the poncho to it.

The wind hit the timber and planed up over the top in long

hard gusts, swirling around a little down where I was. Some rain came through in drops and little showers. The forest floor was already soaked; I dragged in a pile of firewood. I found some dry dead cedar needles at the very base of a trunk, and some bits of dry peeled bark from the underside of a log. As I worked at the fire I heard some ravens calling through the storm, and it seemed as if they were laughing at me. I got the fire going, and it took a half hour to build it up to the point where it would start eating wet wood. Finally it was roaring, big flames licking around in the wind and sizzling with raindrops. I put the kettle on and mixed in some noodle soup, a tablespoon of lard, two big tablespoons of flour, a bunch of broken jerky, and the last of the rice. My mouth watered and my stomach ached. The wind moaned through the trees and the air grew dimmer; the bright warm flames seemed the only thing that separated me from some kind of strange and lonely obliteration.

By the time the rice was done the storm was passing away. A band of light appeared in the west. As I ate I huddled close to the fire wondering about the wisdom of going higher with my food so low. My body felt tired; it seemed as if somewhere behind my muscles a trace of exhaustion lurked, something that I was hiding from myself as I pushed on. I hadn't been sleeping well. It worried me considerably that I had seen so few grouse. The higher I got, the scarcer they would be. I didn't know what I would do.

Darkness came on. Rain fell intermittently through the high canopy of cedar, shining past the fire. I had dragged in stump ends, big wet slabs of ponderosa and long poles five inches thick, which I fed into the fire from both ends as they burned. I kept a big hot bed of coals burning under the slabs, and piled the other wood close to dry. It steamed, and the force of the heat dried out my pants and boots. The heat from the big coals was steady and warm, not fluctuating so much.

I fell asleep and began to dream. I dreamed that I met a woman who was very kind and caring, and who invited me into her home. I told her that I needed a rest, that I was so tired I could barely stand. As I talked to her my eyes kept falling shut and I had trouble moving my jaw. She said that I could sleep on her couch. I lay down there, and sank into an immediate sleep, one that kept growing deeper. I felt as if my body were slowly turning into warm sand. The dream corresponded to reality. I let go down to my bones and slept without moving for two or three hours, as deep as I could sleep. I needed that sleep. The big fire worked beautifully, burning through the rain that fell. Finally I woke up in the deepest part of the night, put on more clothes and chewed some tobacco, feeling warm and secure in front of the flames. Sometimes I could just barely see where the moon lit a smudge through a thin spot in the clouds. I wanted to go on and see high water up on the divide, under a full moon. Rain fell off and on through the night. When I woke at dawn snow was falling through the tops of the cedars.

I went out in the clearing and saw that all the surrounding mountains were coated with new snow. Six inches or a foot could have fallen up on the pass. I was undecided as to what to do, but I figured I would rest a day. I drank some coffee and then went out walking with the rifle. I hunted up the creek all morning, following little streamlets up through the timber and working down along the bank of the creek. I didn't see a thing. I started to get a low gut-ache, a dull pain that stayed steady and wouldn't go away. I ate strawberry leaves. A little sun came through the clouds now and then.

When I got back to the clearing a gopher stood up and began piping at me with sharp whistles that pierced the ear. I decided to eat it. I fired at its head.

As I approached I saw it kicking, trying to get into its hole. I ran and grabbed it. It took a breath and gave a terrible scream of pain and terror, disbelief at the thing that had just happened to it. I killed it quickly with my knife, taking the carcass to the fire and cutting it up in the kettle, stewing it with lily leaves. It tasted good at first but bad toward the end, like the squirrel. I ate it all anyway.

The gut-ache persisted into the afternoon, low and steady. I didn't know what it was from, but it wouldn't go away. In the evening I came back to the clearing and saw two whitetails standing there looking at me, a doe and a yearling. The doe started to lift her tail and moved back twenty yards, but the yearling stood there staring at me, tense as spring steel. *Say, could you spare me a couple of pounds of tenderloin?* I waved my arm and the young deer exploded away, and they both went bounding off into the timber.

I went back to camp and sat down, putting a biscuit on over the coals. At least there were deer around. The ache in my stomach went on. Gopher bones were scattered outside the fire. Through a certain lethargy my mind was tripping over the food possibilities ahead—grouse doubtful, fish for certain up at Moose Lake. I still had nearly all of the lard; jerky for four or five more days. Then, straight ahead where my eyes were lost in thought, I heard a ruffed grouse begin to drum.

A sound like an old John Deere starting up, a sound that brought me instantly into the present. I rose up and sneaked into the woods with my Hawken, toward the sound. When I got in a ways I waited three or four minutes, till it drummed again. I sneaked closer, stepping very carefully. Finally I spotted it standing on a log. It spotted me. Fast I raised up and fired. A little puff of feathers flew up from its back and it took off in a big hurry, flying straight away through the woods. Scared but unscathed.

Son of a bitch. I sat down on a log and ran my fingers through my hair. I thought to myself that I should be hunting them for knowledge, rather than food. But I was very hungry.

As I sat there I heard another one drum further off in the woods, and I started out again, sneaking. The ache in my stomach steeled me; I let my instincts out, I let the hunger direct all my thoughts and senses. I became a hunter like the coyote is a hunter, with only one thought in my mind: to get some meat. This time I wouldn't miss.

But the little devil got away. It saw my shoulder move and hopped down off the log, and when I got over there not ten seconds later it had vanished. I looked all around. Then I realized that it had lurked away using cover against the point it had seen me, and was probably thirty feet away somewhere and frozen. I searched but didn't scare it up. They were experts at lurking away under cover. But when it first saw me it hesitated two or three seconds before slipping off the log. I realized that I couldn't make a sound during the stalk, and that if it saw me I had to fire immediately.

I heard another one. They were drumming all through these

woods just off the meadow as the evening grew deeper; they had come in here to drum at the end of the day. I stole along for a time, then spotted it beginning to drum again on a big two-foot log, its back toward me. There was a tree standing right in front of it. I took off my boots and used the tree for cover, going barefoot. The pine needles were wet. I took five minutes and stalked to within twenty feet, using the tree for cover. Whenever it started to turn toward me in its watchful circle I froze. I kept my Hawken close to my shoulder and moved behind a big tree. It drummed again, partially hidden behind its tree. I stepped slowly out and as my weight settled a tiny twig cracked beneath my foot. The grouse's head jerked around and peered out at me from behind the tree, surprised. Without hesitating I clamped up and fired, the picture of that bird's craning, surprised head already etched in my memory, lost in the damp gloom of the forest, the far-reaching loneliness. The grouse tumbled off the log.

I ran over and grabbed it by the neck, its wings beating on my arm. I laid it on the log and sliced its head off; blood spurted out and it beat its wings furiously, a mindless but desperate attempt to live, to survive the impossible. The blood pumped out, the wingbeats died away, the downy breast lay warm in my palm. I felt that pang of remorse, the loss of life of something wild at my hand, when the wildness was now running for its life all over America. Then it became deadened, I could see the white breast meat cooking and I could imagine Lost Horse Pass. My mouth watered.

I hunted for an hour or more and shot another one. When I got back to camp it was starting to get dark. I stripped the feathers off and cleaned them, my stomach patient and happy, my spirits high. The night was turning old, steel clouds empty of rain passing slowly overhead, holes in them. I quartered the grouse and stewed it in an inch of salted water, some violet leaves thrown in, for a half hour. When it was done I took it out in the clearing and sat down to eat.

A star showed through a hole in the clouds down the valley. The mountains looked clear and cold in the fading light, snow shining dully on a bare peak across the valley, deep banks of fog smothering the ravines, rising in wisps. I bit into one of the small drumsticks and the meat fell loose in my mouth, drawing saliva, tasting more delicious than chicken. I savored it as I chewed, letting it slide down my throat, feeling the immediate satisfaction when it hit my stomach. I felt some of the body bliss that the mountain lion felt in the middle of winter when, with an empty stomach and the temperature at 20 below, it successfully hauled down a deer, and first tasted the warm blood flowing from the open neck into the snow. By the time I finished the second drumstick the ache that had growled in my gut all day was completely gone. The new snow high in the timber, the sharp chill to the mountains and their solitude in the evening, all swam in my spirit as one clear picture, something that I was a part of, living with, living through. It no longer seemed alien and empty; instead it felt wild and spectacular, a wilderness that would sustain me if I ever needed sustenance, for any reason. My whole body began to feel good again. The muscles in my arms and legs felt relief. I drank the icy stream water from my canteen in big gulps, feeling as if the minerals in it were slipping into my blood, bringing my system to life.

I slept with a full stomach that night. The moon wandered through the passing clouds. I woke up late with the fire died down and felt a deep chill, penetrating toward the bone. The moon shone through a hole, near full. In the morning my feet were very cold, and it was cloudy. Snow was falling lightly through the trees again. I didn't care. I heated the broth and drank it down, warming my boots before the fire. Then I packed and started off up the trail.

My mind was seeded now with the high country and visions of high water near the top. As I walked I created pictures of it, turned them around, re-created them: a flooded creek pounding at a logjam, a torrent tearing rocks off the bank and rolling them along its bottom, a swollen creek plunging over a chute. The power of this time, the noise, the violence of far more water in steep places than the earth could absorb; trickling off, pouring off, catapulting down the mountain. The time of year when water seems to rise up in a rage against the failing reign of winter, to feed with ever more violence, shining relentless violence, upon the sinking heaps that once were the stoned contours of winter. A revolution in the spring. The sun coming back to power, burning down a sudden change over everything. It was in my feet now as I walked, in my head as I thought, to get up there and see it at the top. The Bitterroots turn into the sun at high water, the rising hulks of the main range somehow mingling gentleness with ruggedness as they shed water through the timber; and the higher, ruggeder country on the Idaho side spilling it off in hidden fantasies of remaining wildness, the wild side of the range. A range which seemed to have a song to sing at high water.

I kept going for two days through a high dim cedar forest, past where the creek made its final turn toward the Bitterroot Divide. I kept trying to catch glimpses of the high country ahead, but the cedars closed it out. The further up I went, the deeper the forest seemed to become, blocking out the light, creating a spell of dimness and solitude which hung over everything. I left the trail and wandered back and forth through the stillborn forest, half driven to push on through to the divide, half intrigued by the cathedral atmosphere. The trees were huge, some of them eight feet through at the trunk. They rose up a hundred feet, a forest of giants, and then branched out to form a vault of green which cut off the sunlight to infrequent shafts, leaving the floor bare except for dead branches and scattered low greens. I climbed over fallen logs covered with green moss, found a moose antler dropped a few months before, wandered through scattered patches of yellow-violet leaves. The haunting air of·the forest remained constant, like something out of Lewis Carroll.

Food pushed me on. I roasted the grouse and ate it cold as I went, and by the second morning it was bones again, gone. I had a little jerky left, most of the lard, flour, the dried soup, and the honey. Rice was gone. I didn't know how long it would take to get over the pass, or how much snow there would be. I wasn't seeing any more grouse. I started to hit big pools of snow water, a few slabs of old snow riddled with cedar needles. Snow fell through the high trees on and off, not amounting to anything, but making the forest seem gray and lonely. I found wild orchids up on the side of the valley, deep in the shade, stunning complex flowers, making a mystery out of the solitude and loneliness. Every so often I found a small earth-darkened skull, or a scattering of big leg bones.

I went on, pushing up the valley. The trail started winding up hillsides, around big slabs of rock, and the cedars gradually began to fall away. The creek crossings were becoming more difficult. I climbed up over rocks and through brush to find logs to cross on, and when the logs were wet and the distance was over a body length, I took off my boots and walked them barefoot. Once on a log eight feet off the creek with a good-sized waterfall beneath it I almost fell, and so sat down and inched the rest of the way across as if it were a saddle. I kicked myself when I got across, for I could have broken a leg.

Finally I started to climb even higher on the north side of the valley, up a thick ponderosa hillside mottled with boulders as big as cabins. I still couldn't see. I climbed up around a boulder as big as a house which was old, which had grown into the mountainside. At the top it flattened out, parts of it carpeted thickly in moss. The sun burned through a fissure in the clouds and shone weakly onto the moss. A grouse drummed close by and I spun around. I saw it move in dense greenness by a log; when I approached it burst into flight and sailed out over the moss and into the valley. I could see out there. I walked over the boulder to the edge.

The whole valley was bursting up out of the timber into the sky. Rock towers, pinnacles, cliffs soaring out of the forest: after days of gloom in the lower country the valley was in revolt, a silent and seemingly eternal revolt, against the dim and shadowy tangles of the lower drainages. Formations of rock riddled the skyline, and further up the valley they became even higher and more precipitous. There was a stillness and grandeur in it that caught in the soul, that burned into the memory. After the long and winding journey up Moose Creek it offered a sudden sense of spiritual relief, a feeling of having made it finally up to the main mass of the range, the Bitterroots; the heights at last, the clouds, the mountains where they made the sky.

I took off my pack and sat back on the moss, easing the ache in my shoulders, letting the miles fall away. It looked snowy further up the valley. I could barely see where the drainage started to swing south toward the final leg of its rise to the pass. I piled a big wad of tobacco in my mouth and sat spitting over the edge, feeling like a mountain man, covering the country with eyes and spyglass. The sun shone dully, coming out occasionally in soft floods. It was goat country. Across the valley was a set of crags called Goat Heaven Peaks, but I couldn't spot any among the rocks. The sky seemed bluer where it showed through, the air keen and alive. I looked straight up and watched the clouds roll past, and they were so close that I just stared for a while, mesmerized by the folds and the slow billowing of their expansion. They were right up there, magnified, and they passed by in a huge silence. I rested in their depths.

Finally I started up the valley again. Further up I could see whitewater in different places and I wanted to get closer to it, to move up till I found the place where the snowmelt was at its height. Boulders, lots of boulders now, bigger and more sheer cliffs, walking up and down the hillside and sometimes touching down on the creek where it came around a slow bend clear and yellow, brilliant. Then up higher again, catching shots of the snow and peaks through the pines. Feeling the spirit of the high and wild valley, its emptiness and remoteness. Finally I came out to an open slide quite a ways up the hillside, and in the woods beyond I could see that patches of snow were beginning to show up. I put down there and made a camp next to some deadfalls, building a good-sized fire and baking a biscuit, drinking coffee.

I was so tired I didn't feel like moving. Mist and fog hung around the peaks as the evening came on, and I drank soup with some lard in it and fell asleep before full darkness. The moon rose a little later, looking full, drifting through the clouds, leaving a white gauze across high faces of rock. Somewhere up above the slide water was splashing steadily over rocks. The sound of another creek up ahead funneled in and out of Moose Creek's sound as the wind changed. The moon directed the waters. I needed fresh meat, I could tell. I fell back to sleep, curling close to the fire.

When dawn came I felt better. As the light began to spread I sat up, stoked the fire, and drank coffee, watching the fog, listening to the waking sounds of the valley. An owl hooted somewhere up the slide, calling to the last of the darkness. Then came the sharp break of a stick far down the hill, maybe an adventurous bull elk; I watched but didn't see him. The fog down the valley was like rose-colored smoke, the light suffusing slowly into its depths. A pine squirrel awoke uncertainly nearby, and far down in the valley a lone grouse drummed once, then fell silent. It was high, craggy country, foggy, wild, no other humans within forty miles, and I sat there with that feeling for the first time. It was a snatch of that remote feeling I had been seeking, a deep glint of it; I savored it, I held on to it. There was no one but me, and the valley in its wildness belonged to the eagles and the bears and the elk.

A mockingbird landed at the very top of a dead tree, facing where the sun was hidden, and let go a long and astonishing medley of song, as if it were singing to the whole valley. I thought about the animals I had seen, the animals I hadn't seen, and all that was born at this time of year. The movements, the breaking loose that happened. When the High-Water Moon rises over the Selway the elk were moving to the natural salt licks scattered through the wilderness. They stay for a long time as the snow melts and the sun warms the winter out of their bones, eating fresh food, resting after six moons of cold and hunger. It is a time of relief for them, a time of animal pleasures. Inside half of them the calves are pushing toward daylight; the grass is growing higher and greener to receive them. Black bears sniff keenly from the denseness of the surrounding forest, waiting, calculating for the first taste of tender fresh meat since the snows and the big sleep. High in the peaks along the divide the mountain goats are moving toward places where they will drop their kids. A female mountain lion has just given birth to two tiny blind kits in a cave beneath a boulder, high in some rocks, and she knows where the mountain goats are. She is making short hunts now, taking whatever small prey she can find and returning to nurse. But she knew; her den was lined by choice at an elevation where there would be deer feeding under this moon. The moose, feeding all winter on twigs—willow, alder, red thorns, snow willow, and mountain ash—are turning toward the greening hillsides now for fresh grass. Their long, lazy, wandering, floating summer vacation is just beginning. Plodding now through patches of snow past eggs hidden along the middle reaches of Moose Creek, past flowers that are mating with the wind and the bees. Where was Bullwinkle now? He was lost in the spring.

The sun topped the ridge and began to burn away the fog in earnest. I took some jerky—not much left—and started climbing the slide, keeping certain landmarks in mind so I wouldn't lose the camp. The higher I went, the more water I began to see. Finally I climbed up on a broad ledge with a good view and looked around. There was a forty-foot waterfall coming over a cliff two hundred yards up the mountain. It was the one I had heard. Down the valley through a gap in the fog stood a distant cliff, as if framed in a picture, maybe a five-hundred-foot drop. It was a big, rugged valley, and the mountains rising above it were leaking, everywhere they were leaking. Little threads of whitewater came over wide knobs of granite and spilled down into the timber below. Bigger falls poured through notches and splashed into pounding basins of rock. Sometimes when the sun came out a round hill of granite on the mountain across the valley would begin to glisten, and looking at it in my spyglass I would see that the whole surface of rock was alive with water, a huge sheet trickling down, day and night, from the snow above. At the heights were deep wet areas of snow, sinking now, still heavy but collapsing, saturating the rocks with their steady melting. All of it finding its way into Moose Creek, and along Moose Creek on into the Selway, making it buck and plunge all the way down with the release of the great snowmelt.

I sat in the rocks and watched the valley spill, the clouds drifting past, the whitewater cascading from the top—winter turning rapidly into spring. It went on day and night for a week or ten days before it started to lessen; now it was near its height. All the ravines were swollen with it. There was a big loneliness in it that I hadn't expected. The valley was rugged and enormous, and the melt went on in a way that was poignantly nonhuman; it seemed to predate human feelings, to pour methodically out of a geography unchanged for 10,000 years, out of the rawness of nonrecorded history. With or without me or anyone else it was happening all by itself, beyond even the haunting songs of the mountain warblers. The ticking of the years. It happened when the sun was shining, it went on under half-cloudy skies like the sky over me now, through everything it drained away the frozen moratorium of winter, transforming it into the rise of life in the spring. One round ring in a tree.

Finally the sun came out through a big hole in the clouds and I started climbing up toward the waterfall. The light was warm and it felt good; when I got up to the waterfall the sound of the water pounding the rocks drowned out everything else, and I took off my shirt, which smelled like a dead wood rat, and let the water beat it into the rocks for a while. I did the same with my socks and pants, wrung them out to dry, then stepped under the falls. The noise filled my head and the water pummeled my skull and shoulders, making me stagger, making me groan, making my teeth chatter, freezing splashing cold. I scrubbed my pits quickly, gritting my teeth, and then jumped out. I stood there breathing hard waiting for the sun to do its work, feeling the first tantalizing rays of warmth beginning to penetrate the numbness. My front teeth were clicking away.

Then the land went dark. I looked up and saw a big cloud passing in front of the sun, one that would last a long time. I cursed. I began to shiver uncontrollably. I picked up all my clothes and ran down through the rocks, toward some timber. When I got into the trees I held a quivering match to some witch's hair and got a fire going, waited while the flames built, kept building it until finally it was giving warmth. Relief. I turned round and round, drying. I roasted my clothes dry on a stick. I felt good again, clean.

I went further up the hillside, past the falls, using them for a landmark. It was a rugged valley to bush, big boulder fields, slides, stands of timber which came down steep and angled with dead logs. A few moose tracks in patches of snow—but still no Bullwinkle. Maybe he was already up to Moose Lake. Finally I worked up a hill and came out to a huge gash in the mountainside, Dead Elk Falls, down which poured a long whitewater torrent. Dead logs were strewn along its bottom like so many toy sticks, thrown this way and that by the force of the water. The roar came up steady, haunting the trees with its noise of destruction. I went down and stood by the edge for a while, watching the spray and feeling the thunder, wondering over the force. Then I crossed on a huge yellow pine and climbed up the other side.

I got back to camp early in the evening, hungry. Food worry startled to needle me again, for if I got into a situation where I really needed some meat it would be very hard to get it up here. I went beyond the camp and found a large patch of dogtooth violets; I sharpened a stick and started to dig for some of their roots. They ran deep, five and six inches, and were extremely difficult to get out. The stems broke off easily, and the little white tubers were hidden beneath a tangle of pine roots and small rocks. In an hour's time I had only a small handful. Black bears ate many of those roots in the spring and I wished that I could come upon one digging them, to see how they did it. I guessed that they merely clawed big holes in the ground and then sniffed out the tubers. The roots were white, an inch or so long and about as wide as a pencil. I picked a bunch of leaves, brought them back into camp, and made a meager stew with bits of jerky, lard and soup, and the roots and leaves. I baked another biscuit for morning. I needed fish. I would get up to Moose Lake and catch some fish.

Later in the evening I went out lurking, looking for the big bull elk. I covered a few small clearings by the creek, finding one of his tracks in the sand, and watched the openings on the hillside. No luck. The next morning I went out again, working the borders of two different slides, big long ones with lots of grass, moving slow and quiet, staying in the cover most of the time. No luck. No moose either. In the evening I looked again for the elk but didn't see him. With what little food I had left, and the scarcity of game this high, it was time to move for the pass. My reserve strength was down; there hadn't been near as many grouse as I thought there would be. The only way I could have maintained my strength was to have taken a bunch of grouse in the vicinity of the North Fork, where I saw the most, and then carried that meat with me. Or fished more seriously. But fishing in a creek with a drop line takes a lot of time and I had preferred to keep walking. So I did. Now the water ran past me and the mountains were melting. I caught a glimpse of the moon after it got dark, and it looked full.

THE NEXT MORNING it was drizzling. The clouds were heavy and close, smothering the rim of the valley. It seemed big and lonely, an air to it that made me feel lost. The wind was damp and cold.

I packed up and started walking. Moose Lake was about five miles below the top of the pass, but that last section of the map was the one I had burned up. I calculated by the section I had that the lake was three or four miles ahead. Now I wondered how much snow there would be once the valley made its final southward swing toward the pass.

The drizzle and fog held steady. In an hour or so I began hitting regular patches of snow. There were moose tracks in the snow and a few elk tracks, none of them very fresh. The snow wasn't yet compacted and I broke most of the way through. Where the moose had stepped the snow held me up and I followed their tracks when I could. The snow was scattered in ten-foot patches, not bad yet. But it was at least eight miles to the pass and I didn't figure it would get any better. I went steady; I felt tired, worn out, and I knew there would be no grouse up this far, but I just kept walking. My only hope for fresh food was fish at Moose Lake. I imagined that the lake was open at one end and the fish were hungry.

Fog hung in the trees and grayness seemed to settle over everything. The woods were wet and dripping. I came to a roaring creek which came down over the rocks like a runaway train, tearing live trees out by the roots and lodging them against boulders. I inched across the tumult on a high log and walked on, foggy snow-soaked woods.

Late in the afternoon the snow got worse. I ate the biscuit and some jerky and kept going, wet to the knees. Only bits and ends of jerky left in the food sack. I had my gaiters on and they kept the direct cold of the snow off my legs. Mounds of snow twenty feet long stretched over the trail, and the ground between them was muddy. I started to think about the pass; I pictured the top several times, and in my mind I saw myself going over it and down the Montana side. It was forty miles back to the ranger station, only seven to the top of the pass. I set it in my mind that I was going to buck the snow any way I could and get to the top of that pass.

By the time I stopped in the evening my nerves were worn. When I took off the pack I felt a wave of dizziness, and I sat down until it passed. I wondered how my body strength was holding up, how much reserve I had left, and how difficult the rest of the climb was going to be. I had the lard; I held on to that thought. I felt a deep sense of loneliness. I knew how far in I was and I knew I was beyond help. Anything that happened I would have to take care of. No matter how weak I got I would have to work my way out, for there wouldn't be anyone over that pass for weeks. It felt as if the weather in the valley itself were turning against me, building up a subtle force that came down with increasing effectiveness the further I went. It was a spaced-out loneliness, that feeling, as if something in my chest were slowly evaporating. I told myself I could make that pass, even if I had to make it in feet and yards. I looked ahead. The valley looked bleak and wet.

I built a fire and drank a lot of hot soup and some noodles, and I felt better. There was snow scattered around; I made a bed next to the fire under a thin spruce. I figured that if the snow got bad I could travel three or four hours after first light, when it was still frozen. I figured that if the weather broke there would be plenty of moonlight and I could travel most of the night if I had to, walking on the frozen snow. The only thing I worried about was whether or not I could find my way up that pass by eyesight, by the way the land lay, for I knew the trail would be covered with snow, timbered, and I would have a hard time picking out the blazes in the moonlight. I knew there was forest nearly all the way up the pass, so I wouldn't have to worry about bad weather. I could always build a shelter and sit by a fire.

I dried out my pants and boots by the fire. It took a long time. I thought the night would be very cold, but it wasn't. The thick clouds held back the freeze. I fell asleep in a haze of weariness, barely waking to stoke the fire.

I got up at first light. It was gray and dripping; the snow was as wet as it was during the day. I sat down by the fire and warmed myself, baking another biscuit. I was sick to the teeth of that taste of baking soda in the biscuits, but it was all I had. I figured I would make the lake by noon. I would build a good camp there and rest, catch some fish. I would get as much of my strength back as I could, and then I would push for that pass. I would pace myself, not let the snow get to me.

When the bread was done I laced my gaiters up tight and

started out again. The fog drifted through the trees all morning and water dripped from the timber. I lost all sense of the country's aesthetics. It was wet and difficult, it offered no rest, and I was running out of food. Fish, I kept picturing fish lying in a snowbank by the lake. Still I saved my honey, I thought if I really got down it might give me the psychological lift I needed to get over.

By noon I was nowhere near the lake. The valley was barely beginning to swing south and I had no idea how much further ahead it was. It could be one mile, it could be four miles. The snow was up over my knees and it was one snowbank after another. I would walk a ways and then come to a drift that stretched forty feet ahead up the trail. I would rest for a few moments, breathing steady, then start in. Where the snow slid off the nearby trees I could walk on top of it, but every fourth or fifth step I would plunge to the ground. Then I would begin to plow, fighting for each step. A cord in my neck started to burn from the weight of the pack, and it burned steady from then on. Once I got through the drift I would walk along for a while feeling weak, feeling my heart pound, and then I would hit another one. I set my mind to disregard everything working against me, to forget the struggle and the weariness, and concentrate only on the progress I was making. I sighted the top of the pass in my mind and held it there.

Sometime after noon I left the trail to try the creek bank, figuring the snow would melt there with more consistency than anyplace else. It did, but it was no good. The brush was dense, there were many deadfalls, and there were potholes. And the creek wound back and forth. Finally I left it and started back for the trail. I couldn't find it. Through the snow, over the logs, back and forth. I kept steady, but inside I was strung and jittery. I felt like my heart was evaporating, like there was less and less of me and I was becoming a walking shell. As if I were losing contact with myself. For the first time I didn't feel certain that I would make it. I thought of my family and it seemed that now they were far away, in another world. I pictured my form lying in the snow three quarters of the way up the pass, done in.

I found the trail. I stopped and took off the pack, pushing the thoughts out of my head. I vowed to stop thinking those thoughts. After I had rested I climbed a tree to try to get the lay of the valley, but I couldn't see much. I caught a glimpse of the far hillside and there was very little snow there, for it got the afternoon sun. But it was steep and heavily timbered. I climbed back down, trying to decide whether or not to try it. It was at least three quarters of a mile back. I worried about climbing up there and then getting shunted on a side drainage without realizing it. I doubted if I was making a mile an hour by then. Finally I decided to stay with Moose Creek and follow it up to the lake. Just get to the lake. I ate a little jerky, shouldered the pack, and went on.

By the middle of the afternoon I was still nowhere near the lake. The drifts were up to my thighs and there was getting to be more snow than there was ground. I came down to a place where I had to ford the creek and worked up the bank for two hundred yards until I came to a little island with timber on it. I could cross to the island on a log, but I would have to wade from there. Still I figured it was the best place. The log was as slippery as butter. I got a stick and worked across inch by inch, concentrating. Then I crossed over through the brush of the island. The water looked knee deep, moving pretty good, and the bank on the other side was steep. I hesitated. How far up was the lake? I wanted to make that lake, and I wanted to get over that pass. I started across with the stick, feeling for the rocks with the bottoms of my boots. In the middle the current tugged hard and I stumbled, splashing in with one arm, submerging the bottom of the pack. I struggled up and splashed forward to the bank. When I got ahold of it I just stood there and rested. The water didn't seem to matter, the cold and the wetness didn't seem to matter. I couldn't believe that I was standing where I was, that there was so much snow, that everything was so wet. Finally I crawled up the bank.

I looked around; everything was soaked, dripping. There were deep mounds of snow up to my crotch all through the woods, and what little ground showed was submerged in running water. The air through the trees was damp and gray. I started up the trail, following it mostly by the old blazes in the trees. In a few places where it had melted through it formed a small rushing river, the snow melting from one snowbank and flowing down under the next. I climbed over the snow, through it. My boots were full of water, my pants soaked to the waist, my shirt wet with perspiration. I was hot, sweating, and it didn't seem to matter. It seemed to me as if I had left my own situation, as if with that river crossing I had penetrated behind the lines of spring into its wet and streaming innards to the trackless place where the high water came from. A place that was taboo. A region that was not geographical, that consisted of a cold and relentless process, beyond human feelings, that drenched, that soaked, that ate away at everything in its path. A process that did not want to be penetrated, that piled up increasingly exhaustive barriers in front of any form of life which attempted to trespass. Yet the moose had made it through already, the incredibly powerful moose, there were still tracks in those deep mounds of snow. It was the only sign of life I saw.

I went on until early evening. I had never felt that empty, that much like a shell. It seemed as if my willpower had turned me into a machine, almost as if I had stepped outside myself and could watch my own struggle without feeling the hardship or the difficulty of it. I could watch my body climbing over the snow and slogging through the water, and I was separated from it. I began to think about that fine line between willpower and physical exhaustion—how far could the will drive the body after it had run out of energy? Hugh Glass, abandoned, crawling. How long could the will force a body drained of strength? Did the will finally give up, or did the body cease to work even though the will desired it to keep going? I didn't know, but it seemed that if the will stayed alive the body would keep moving past all reason. I was nowhere near that point, but at the top of the pass I could be.

I didn't think of turning back. It was forty-five miles back down to the ranger station, another twenty-five back down the Selway. That was the only other way out now. I just kept going, my mind cemented to the top of the divide, wondering if I would die on the side of that pass. I kept feeling flashes of doubt, feeling the sense of evaporation in my chest, and I fought to keep my identity, to keep a sense of who I was. Every so often I would flash on the graves at the North Fork. The wetness, the wilderness, seemed to be erasing me.

All the potential firewood looked to be soaked. I kept going until I found a big pile of three dead trees which had fallen across each other, containing countless small branches. I put down there. There was a relatively dry patch of ground just under a dense little pine, although I would have to sleep at an angle. I sat down and rested, and my eyes fell shut. I heard water trickling, draining, dripping, pouring, through my head. I felt water in my body. Water was triumphant everywhere.

A deep chill hit me, and I got up shivering. I found dry needle sprigs on the lower branches of the pine, dry twigs where the downed trees sheltered a pile of branches. I got a fire going, and I built it into a blaze as big as a washtub. I put on my wool pants and they felt good. I made a stew of soup, jerky, two tablespoons of lard, and some rice that had spilled in the bottom of the food bag. One small swallow of honey. Then I started drying my clothes, boots, and socks. It must have taken three hours, for when they were dry it was well after dark. The fog remained; there was no moon or stars.

I lay there thinking. I might make the lake on foot, but no further. I began constructing a pair of snowshoes in my mind, using the rawhide and pine boughs. Take a long pine bough and loop it, tying the ends together. Then start tying a crosshatch webbing of rawhide, maybe four- or five-inch squares, dividing as much rawhide as I had between the two shoes. Tie and weave lesser pine boughs with the needles still on into the shoes, for more buoyancy. Then tie the shoes onto my boots. Maybe unbraid some of the rope and use that. But it was dubious. The rawhide would stretch with the weight and the wetness, and the wet knots would be impossible to untie. It might be very hard to repair or tighten them. They might come apart in a mile or two, or as soon as I started climbing. I would be lucky if their reliability was 50 percent.

My only other chance was that the nights turned colder and the snow froze. Then if I could see the way I could walk out in one night. How long would it be before the weather lifted? In three days I would be completely out of food except for flour and lard. There would be no rabbits up there and no grouse. No deer. Only fish.

But fish would be enough. If I caught a bunch, dried them,

and ate them with the lard I could climb for another week. Everything depended on fish. Five, maybe six miles of deep snow beyond the lake, a steep uphill grade near the end, timber all the way except maybe at the very top. I couldn't make it without staying on top of the snow one way or another. If I got halfway up the pass, or three quarters, and couldn't go on, I would be in trouble. I would be out of food and exhausted, and I would have to come back down through all the snow ten or fifteen miles before I could find meat.

It didn't look good. It was seven miles forward, seventy-five miles back. I didn't think of turning back; I only wondered if I was going to make it. I felt completely alone, and I knew that in this kind of snow willpower alone wouldn't be enough.

I fell into a deep sleep. The fire was big and hot, and I could sleep for long periods before it began to die. The night grew late, but the full moon never came out. I had wet slabs piled around the fire, and I fed them in as they steamed dry. Then at one point deep in the night I began to have a vivid dream. It was one of those dreams in which you believe you are awake and really living it. I was getting close to the lake. The snow was up to my chin and I had to dig my way along. Sometimes I climbed up and crawled along on top of it, until my stomach started to get cold. Then I went back down so just my head was sticking out. I was soaked. At last I came to the crest of a little hill, looked over, and saw the lake spread out just below. There was no water showing anywhere—it was completely frozen over, white. In the very middle of it lay a big comfortable-looking oblong box.

I woke up suddenly. The darkness was all around, the trees were dripping, the snow shone faintly in large heaps. They were still wet. I rubbed the vision of the box out of my eyes. Then, like a small avalanche, it dawned on me that I was making a serious mistake.

In a flash all the knots in me untied, and I felt a surge of release. I would make it, back down the way I had come. I had been asking for it. I had been ignoring all the factors that were working against me, not giving them the right weight, writing them off in my fixation to get over the pass. It was a classic pattern, the Donner party, every ill-fated attempt to get over a pass at the wrong time of year, or to get over when not fully prepared for the snow conditions which might be encountered. Or without enough food. A process that involves for some reason the growing mental fixation that one *must* get over the pass, one must make it through a certain way, even when the "must" part of it wasn't true. Only if it was an absolute necessity should I have tried for the top of that pass, and it wasn't. I was foolish to fight the mountain's flow for no reason.

I had been denying too much. I never thought of the lake being frozen. I didn't have a hatchet to get through the ice. I was ready to try seven miles of wet uphill snow with pine boughs on my feet. I didn't know the lay of the pass and I could have hit three or four days of fog. The snow wasn't compacted and it wasn't freezing at night. I wasn't prepared for that pass in several more ways than one.

I dozed on and off until first light, then packed up and started back down the way I had come, stepping in my old foot holes. It took until dusk, steady pushing all day, to get back down out of the snow. I felt worn to the bone, but it didn't matter; I was on my way out. I drank all the honey and ate the last of the jerky. The clouds held together and the wet fog still drifted through the trees, but the eerie feeling of snow water trickling through my veins was gone. I was back on solid ground. The further down I had gone, the more I sensed that I had made the right decision. There was some regret in it; I wanted to make that pass, to look back the way I had come from the top. But it would have been foolish. Survival, I realized, depended more upon the decisions one made, instinctive or otherwise, than it did upon willpower or the act of surviving itself. What one *sensed* about one's situation. My subconscious told me in the dream what I had been suppressing from myself.

Two and a half days later I limped across the large open meadow to the North Fork of Moose Creek, not far from the graves. I dumped my pack and eased down onto the grass. The knee was torn out of my pants. My hips were aching. The bones in the bottom of my feet hurt, and that cord in my neck had burned all the way down. I was done in. If the ranger station hadn't been there I would have hunted a deer and rested for many days. I couldn't walk any further.

The clouds still held; there had been fog most of the way down. But the drizzle had stopped, and it looked like it might finally be breaking. I looked across Moose Creek up to an open hillside and saw eight elk lazing around in the grass and rocks; maybe they knew the sun was coming. One of them was licking the rocks, and watching it through my spyglass I realized that was the salt lick where the trappers had seen a hundred elk that fall eighty years ago. There were eight up there now.

In a while I saw a blue-winged teal rise from the grass and fly out over the creek, and the stripe on its wing seemed to contain a breath of the whole season's change: a bit of summer blue, warm skies on the way. The mountains were coming back to life.

I looked back up the way I had come. It had been empty and wild, but only because I was traveling early. I remembered how wild and far it felt, knowing I was up there alone. I felt lucky to have experienced that. Soon, maybe in another three weeks, Bob Backpack and Heidi Hiking Boots would come tripping over that pass, loaded down with gleaming equipment and Nikon cameras, eighty-five-dollar hiking boots, their breezy fixation upon status making a mockery of all that the mountains meant. It would have brought a sense of ruination to see them; violence and development follow them just beyond the trees. Their moneyed questions stink for miles after they have passed on the trail. They weren't up there yet, and there was no sign of them in the melting snow. Up and down the creek the journey held an unbroken air of wildness for me. For that I was grateful.

Eighty miles up and down Moose Creek, and I didn't see a single moose. My luck.

Somewhere down under the horizon the moon was on its way up. On one of the last few nights its roundness had peaked, and now it was sliding slowly back down into darkness. The end of spring. Out of that darkness, as tiny hooves hardened in a wet womb, a thin crescent would appear in the evening sky. The Moon When Deer and Elk Are Born.

They lazed on the mountainside, scratching, munching; wandering over for a lick at the minerals in the rocks. There were a few cracks in the cloud cover, faint blue showing through. I got up slowly, lifting the pack to my shoulders, and looked in the direction of the graves. The land was quiet there, scarcely any breeze. I started out slowly and painfully, walking toward the river. As I went the words kept forming themselves in my mind: *Don't underestimate the Selway.* It was big, the biggest stretch of wilderness left in the lower forty-eight, and there was still a wildness left in it that haunted my mind, even now as I was leaving it. A wildness up there in the wet snow, down here at the graves, a wildness that I couldn't put my finger on, that I knew would pull at me after I left. An unchanged intermingling of ruggedness, high peaks, bears on hillsides, and elk swimming rivers, far and remote distances—things bound together into one feeling that caused an aching in the memory. The moon growing, the Selway River pouring and plunging with the runoff of the entire wilderness. If only it would stay wild, if only it would stay wild.

FORT HOLLYWOOD

WHEN I got back to Fort Hollywood at the big bend in the Yellowstone, I found that I had lost seven pounds. I had been out for fourteen days; one of the things that struck me about the trip was the craving I developed for civilized food after about five days. I began to have dreams about meat and gravy, potatoes, and one night a long dream about a big crisp apple. Some of that was simple taste conditioning, but I also learned from the experience that what you dream about when you are hungry is what your body needs.

In reading I found that the mountain men had a term for those who had that experience. Veteran trappers called the new men on the keelboats *mangeurs de lard*, "pork eaters." The term referred to one who was used to the diet of the settlements, and held the same connotation as "greenhorn." Someone who secretly yearned for the variations in a civilized diet. By the time they passed the mouth of the Platte River at the western border of

Nebraska their stores of salt pork, bacon, smoked ham, and dried fruits usually ran out, and it was the arduous journey up into Montana, the nightly feasts upon fire-seared elk, antelope, and buffalo, which finally changed a pork eater's tastes into those of a mountain man.

I put down the book in which I had found that with a sigh. There weren't many buffler left on the northern plains of the Yellowstone now; lots of Toyoters and Caderlacs starting to show up. And Emil Keck told me that in the Selway the elk herds had gone down 35 percent in the last eight years, and he said the influx of rich sport hunters was doing it. They too were playing mountain man, only their game was killing off the elk.

I soaked for a long time in the tub, reading the news from the States to take my mind off the way things were going. But there wasn't any meat there either. The newspaper said that the new President was going to save the country with a lot of new spirit and some backing from the Rockefellers. When I read that I threw it in the corner by the toilet, figuring to save it for hard times. I settled back and stared out the window, watching the trains pull in and out of the switching yards in Fort Hollywood, watching the $9,000 pickups with chrome CB aerials cruising up and down Main Street. It was coming to this place too. At last I got out of the tub and dried myself, toweling my skin hard. My mind began to reach for the Swan Mountains.

I walked straight on out of the fort to the Yellowstone River, following that wild feeling, and on up to where it made its big bend to the east. Beyond the new glitter that was rising in the fort. There I spent some time in the cottonwoods, and I started to feel better. I held on to my anger at what was happening to the mountains. I held on to my spirit, felt it as I watched the river. The water was green and muddy, high, shining with power. The last of the milkweed seeds were singing down over the water on a stiff summer breeze. It was a big and beautiful river, and it flowed into my spirit. Recharged, I walked back into town.

This fort by the big bend in the Yellowstone was called Fort Hollywood because an increasing number of famous actors, directors, screenwriters, and stars were beginning to colonize the valley of the upper Yellowstone just to the north, a valley which

I thought to be the most beautiful in the Rockies. The Hollywood migration began early in the seventies, and by now the old fort, sleeping for so long, was buzzing with new energy, new gossip, new trucks, and new money. Big money. The bankers, the real estate agents, and most of the merchants loved these new celluloid pioneers, and opened their doors to them with huge grins, radiating good traditional western hospitality. The people who lived and worked on the land weren't quite so convinced. Moon after moon they watched the price of land around the fort spiral up toward the sky, climbing beyond the reach of their sons and daughters. They weren't so sure that having the stars around was a good deal.

Unfortunately, soon after the stars began showing up, a severe epidemic of Brown Lip Disease swept through the fort. Symptoms of that advanced West Coast affliction, ultimately venereal in nature, include a bent lower back accompanied by a kissing sound. The bankers and the businessmen were the first to get it, and they could be seen hobbling all over the fort with bent backs and handkerchiefs held to their mouths. Oddly enough they were still smiling. When I rode into the fort the effects of the epidemic were still spreading, and there was no medicine available for it at the fort. I hoped that I wouldn't catch it. The only medicine I knew of for it was back in the mountains, and I hadn't really found it yet. But that was a factor in my hurrying the preparations to head up into the Swans.

OUTSIDE the window of my lodge the lilacs burst into bloom, filling the breezes with their silent perfume. The cottonwoods along the big intermountain rivers, the rivers that were the highways of the mountain men, were spilling their white seed to the wind, and as the birth moon passed away the big rivers began to rise with the high mountain runoff that I had seen in the Selway. In the days that followed, the Swan Range began to take hold of my imagination. It was up there under Glacier Park and it was one of the wildest ranges left. Across the valley the Mission Range was higher and more spectacular, but it was crawling with backpackers. The hope fixed in me that I could get away from people at the top of the Swans, feel my spirit break into the open, maybe catch up with Gabe. That I could find the real mountain man experience I had been searching for all the time I spent looking for that mythical cabin in the woods. It didn't depend upon having a Hawken rifle or a Green River knife. It was some kind of simple bursting open of the spirit.

And maybe up there I could find it. I would go higher, even higher than I had been in the Bitterroots. Off the trails. The scattered wildness, the little land freedom that was left at the end of the seventies was up near the top. And so the Swans began to take over in me, solitary, maybe as yet unruined, and as the birth moon died and the new bear moon began to rise I felt their lure stronger and stronger, melting away the frustrations. I dreamed of taking off up into that range.

Bears were on my mind as I got ready, the fact that I would be in grizzly country, the subconscious feeling I had that my medicine was tied in with bears. Before I left, my friend Michael Boehm, a writer and a guide, stopped in to see me. He grew up in these mountains and knew their ways better than anyone else I had met in seven years in the Rockies; he had made long solitary trips up to small nameless lakes with a burro, pursuing trout, and he had tracked elk and deer since he was five years old, all over the country I was covering. He acted as my adviser, steering me in the right direction, telling me what was important, what to watch for. He had already made the trips I was starting out on.

I talked to him about the bear feeling I had. He thought for a while, and said, "You ought to carry a pistol." He left the room and in a while he came back with his .357 Smith. He handed it over, letting its weight sink into my hand, my head. "Take it with you if you want," he said. "If you're going to be crawling around after bears, it's a good idea to carry that. Odds are you won't have to use it. Maybe a warning shot. But you never know, especially when you're alone. Bears have a mind of their own."

I decided he was right. He knew what he was talking about; he had been run up a tree by a big black bear with cubs once.

We went out and ran some rounds through it, shooting at tin cans in a gravel pit. Because the pistol had a floating firing pin he carried it with a live round under the hammer, and the first trigger-pull shot empty. He did that because he felt there was more danger in heavy brush of catching the trigger on a stick than there was of dropping the piece on the hammer ear. I thought that was a good idea.

Later in the evening we drove out of the fort and up the Yellowstone where the Crow Mountains first rise up in all their ruggedness, so big and high with dark-looking chasms and dull-gleaming peaks that they make any conversational murmurs die out in the throat. The colors of evening showered the cloud formations, and the peaks moved slowly past like tremendous barriers between the seventies—a decade which in the Rockies was finding its ultimate expression in Fort Hollywood—and something old and dark, an old spirit in the earth. Something that made me uncertain even as it called to me, because I couldn't put my finger on it. We rode along without speaking, watching them pass by, and then Michael broke the silence.

"It's like they're saying, 'I dare you.'"

That was it. He knew that old spirit. There was nothing I could add to it, and before long the night came down and closed them out.

soon the wild rosebushes burst into bloom along the big rivers, and the last of the runoff with its turbulent muddy waters headed on down toward the Missouri. The elk calves were running fast by now; I was filled with a powerful urge to get out of Fort Hollywood and away from civilization altogether, into the wild. I started packing, and on the basis of past experience I cut my pack down to the following list:

2 plastic canteens, GI, one quart each
Cutter's insect repellent
½ bar soap
small whetstone
snow goggles
8 rawhide laces
kettle
spoon
fishline
8 hooks, 1 sinker

60 matches in a small plastic bottle
zinc oxide
2 pens and paper
1 pound Skoal chewing tobacco
poncho
wool shirt and windbreaker
sleeping bag
sleeping pad
signal mirror
spyglass
extra compass
first aid: 2 Ace bandages; 15 compresses; 10 Band-Aids; 3
    feet of surgical tubing for emergency tourniquet; ½ roll
    adhesive tape; chapstick; 20 hits of Tylenol 3; 20 tabs of
    Vibramycin; a little crystal meth.
50 feet of ⅝" nylon rope
tin cup
comb
2 large sewing needles
a little extra string
2 pairs extra socks
1 ounce gun oil
2 ounces boot oil
1 snapshot of New York City

With the possibility of losing my pack in mind I carried on my person the things I would need to get out or survive an unexpected injury: 25 matches in a waterproof carrier, compass, hunting knife, bandana, surgical tubing, small flint and steel, signal mirror, 10 bullets, a plastic Jesus, Apollo 7 rocketship. The surgical tubing is a good thing to carry because you can make a slingshot out of it if you have to. The rocketship is a little bulky, but you never know when it will come in handy.

FINALLY I tuned up poor old Sixties, pouring some Stopleak into its sense of social justice and its concern for the poor and racially oppressed, rebuilding its axial awareness of world affairs. "*By God you'll make it through yet,*" I whispered in its broken wing window. By the time I added my food sack the pack weighed thirty-two pounds. Gabe was riding up the Swan River by now, hoping to meet up with the boys. On a bright dawning morning I took one last look at the Crow Mountains, then I rode on out of that fort.

THE
SWAN
RANGE

SUMMER, PYRAMID PASS,
JUNE 30, THE MOON WHEN
THE BEARS RUN TOGETHER

THE TRAIL was deserted, and the higher I climbed, the more my spirit seemed to be shedding its weight, breaking into the open. I wound up through small lush meadows where the thimbleberry bushes were blooming with white papery flowers, the grass spattered with late-blooming bluebells and buzzing with bees, and with each footstep I had the feeling all through my body that I was heading into an adventure. My pack was light and there was iron in my thighs; there was a stretch of wild country ahead of me and I was free to roam. I kept climbing higher into the range as the sun began to settle, filled with the promise that was now daring to raise its head, that I would find what I was looking for in this range.

At the top of the pass I left the trail and climbed a steep hill to the north, to get a look at the country. When I got to the top I saw a good-sized lake down below, surrounded by timber. At the head of it to the left rose a huge pyramid-shaped peak, grass-covered all the way to the top, maybe a thousand feet higher than where I stood. Again I felt that surge of hope. Tomorrow I would climb it and see if I could look up the range. If I could make it out above the other mountains I could bush it by sight, as if it were unmapped, wild.

I hunted around the top of the hill for a soft place to sleep and finally found a little grassy swale with rocks just under the surface. I dug them out and made my bed there, then cooked some soup and biscuits about fifteen yards downwind, wrapping the dough around a stick and roasting it till it was a crisp brown. I was careful not to spill any soup on my clothes, for grizzlies were on my mind and sleeping near cooking smells with them in the woods was a dangerous thing to do.

Finally I hung my food sack downwind, hoisting it quite a

ways up, and crawled in under the canopy of stars which had come out over the hilltop. I lay awake for a long time feeling the surge of excitement that came with the thought of taking off up the range. I couldn't sleep because of it, but lay there wide-eyed and watching the stars, wondering if I was going to see a big silver bear. Before I started in I talked to a wilderness ranger who told me that there was a remote basin about fifteen or twenty miles up the range called Grizzly Basin which hardly anyone got to all summer. He said I might run into one there. But he said the possibility was remote; he had seen only two in eight years of patrolling. He said nowadays it was largely a matter of fate.

As if to illuminate that thought one of those huge, rare meteors flashed into view and streaked across the sky, a burning ball of red fire, before it finally broke into glowing chunks and fell into darkness. An omen? I was starting to feel superstitious, for the Crow Mountains were the next range on the horizon.

Finally I went to sleep with my shirt over my head to keep the mosquitoes off, and a short time later it started blowing and raining. I pulled my poncho over me and dozed off and on while it rained. At last it stopped and as dawn came the sky began to clear, shot through with yellow and orange beams. By the time the first shaft of warm sunlight hit me the mosquitoes were gone and I fell into a deep, relaxed sleep.

WHEN I woke up the sun was blazing out of a blue sky and a strong wind was blowing across the top of the hill. The mountains off toward the wilderness side were bathed in morning haze, but the air around the lake was bright and sparkling with the sunlight and wind. The big peak on the other side of the lake stood like an earth giant in the sun, looking high and windswept near the top. It was a perfect morning to take off. I filled a canteen down at the wind-whipped lake and climbed up toward the base of the peak. Bear-grass stalks were flowering here and there, big rich white flowers standing waist high as I passed. Elk ate those flowers with relish, but they filled my mouth with bitterness. Maybe they were better after a few boilings. I didn't have much food this trip and I would have to gather what I could.

Finally I started up the mountain. I climbed over rock slides and zigzagged up steep expanses of grassy mountainside, bare-skinned in the big wind, the lake shrinking steadily below me. When I was halfway up I looked back across into the wilderness, and the peaks looked nondescript to me, dry weather-blasted bare tops, like huge hills, more and more of them jumbled, scarred, sandy-looking. Would I find it here, would I be able to make my way up the range once I saw it? I kept on climbing, holding on to a hope which measured itself in a hard way against my past experience, higher toward the big blue sky. Nearing the top I climbed on all fours up big shining slabs of red slate, past the last few wind-tormented fir, scrambling over the shiny rock surfaces. When at last I walked out into the full force of the wind I looked to the north and saw a line of snow-streaked peaks thrusting up into the distance, twenty-five or thirty miles north they ran, higher than any of the other surrounding mountains. The Swans. For a long time I wandered over their rugged heights with my gaze, picking out the divide, sizing the distant ridges I would have to go over, sensing the cool winds on the snowfields. I could bush it without the maps. I pulled out my compass and took a shot; the range ran about 340 degrees northwest for the next twenty-five miles, and with that as a reference I could do it by eye, picking out major landmarks as I went. I got out the map and tried to find Grizzly Basin in the distance, but the peaks were too close and jumbled up there to make it out. It lay somewhere on the west side of the divide. That was the only thing I had to keep track of.

I sat down and spent a half hour searching all the visible country with my spyglass for goats or a bear, but I didn't see anything. The wind came over the top from far across the Swan Valley in huge gusts, streaming past with a force which made me feel like yelling. Down on the lake I could see it cutting fast-curving patterns over the surface, like some form of sky-maddened energy racing crazily just under the water, then dying out. It was a big wind.

I stood up, took off all my clothes, and let go a yell at the top of my lungs, letting out all the breath and energy in me. The wind carried it away fast, dissipating it swiftly into the surrounding vastness. Finally I picked up my pack and swung it on my back, starting down off the top and out along the thin grassy spine of the divide, due north. The wind washed over my body, tickling my crotch and raising goose bumps along my back, whistling past with a force I had to brace myself against as I walked. Then it died down, and the sun grew hot on my skin, melting the goose bumps, warming my nakedness before the open sky, the surrounding mountains. Then the big wind came up again. I walked down the divide, memorizing the lay of the country ahead as I descended, my bones singing with happiness at the spirit there still was in the earth.

The goddamned skeeters like to carried me away when I first rode up into that valley, boys. Sons a bitches was around me in swarms all the time, so's I had to build smudge fires at night to get any shuteye, and if I hadn't pegged myself down afore I went to sleep I'd a probly woked up in Calcutta all white and shriveled, or wherever it is them dirty sons a bitches go when they get done lickin' their stingers. Jesus, they was thick in that country. Then if it warn't the skeeters it was the goddamn bogs, whar all of a sudden my charger'd start sinkin', high-steppin' and plungin' with white rollin' eyes, throwin' mud ever'whar, and then the mule'd start in and try to pull my arm off while I was tryin' to stay on the charger, and sure enough that iron-headed son of a bitch would manage to buck them furs off, so's when I finally gets 'em both to solid ground there's my winter's plews, scattered all over that stinkin' bog. Hell of a time it was, what with the skeeters singin' steady in the trees. If I hadn't a been on Fitz's tree blazes and didn't know him and the boys was up ahead somewhars, I would've sure enough turned around and packed it on out of there.

Tisk-tisk. Sounds like he's having a little trouble.

As the shadows started to lengthen, the wind turned colder, and just before I was ready to drop off the divide I stopped and dressed, taking a last look at the country ahead. I picked out a crescent-shaped peak along the divide as one landmark, and a big hawk-headed peak down one of the far ridges as another. That gave me the lay of the next basin. I studied it for over ten minutes, memorizing details and projecting my route again and again, for I knew how much it could change in shape and contour once I started to get down into it.

Down off the rocks, down a series of cliff-like terraces hung with gnarled roots and small grassy goat places, toward the gateway to the range. When I got to the bottom I was standing before a shadowy canyon leading back up toward the divide, and I stopped there for a while sensing its harshness. It was filled with a deep river of rubble, thousands of years of broken rock peeling off the divide in the springtime, in the summer, and clattering down into the silence of the canyon. The quiet on the other side of a past decade of violence; motionless river of evidence that the mountains were slowly crumbling while something mindless was building up. I lowered my head to the climb and sweated in the cool evening air, going around tall boulders, making lonely rock sounds with my boots, setting my mind to the long rock-strewn climb. Every so often I looked up at the shadowy rock walls on either side, jagged in the twilight, and sensed the decade I was living through in one of those fallen rocks. I was making my passage, breaking the thread for a few moments. It was a test I was looking for in the mountains, not a foolish one but a true one, a test of fate and self-knowledge. The more I thought about the Selway, the more I felt that I had passed it there, made a good decision instead of trying to force my way over the top for no real reason. Now I was on the threshold of the wildest country I had ever been in; once I was over the saddle above me I would be cut off, face to face with it, and that was what I had been looking for.

There were a few stars out when I walked over the top. Spread out below was a broad basin steeped in mountain twilight, subalpine under the peaks of the divide, caught in the stillness of the evening. Three small lakes dotted its upper reaches, dark and mirrory, draining into each other through small winding canals. It was perfect to wander in, but it seemed overwhelmed by an eerie sense of lifelessness. Nothing was out or moving all the way across.

I made my way down a long shale slide, coming out on a little tundra flat where a dark slow spring flowed. More of the stars were out and my shirt was damp and chilly. I gathered some straggling deadwood and built a fire on a boulder, so as not to burn a hole in the tundra, and cooked some freeze-dried stew. I hadn't seen any rabbits or grouse yet. I hadn't seen anything, and I didn't have much jerky. The night before I had a dream in which I flushed five grouse, grouse all around me. But I hadn't seen a one.

Some fox sparrows were chasing each other over the rocks in the last of the twilight. I crawled into my bag with chattering teeth and waited for it to warm up, listening to the small trickle of springwater in the grass. A cold wind was whistling off the top of the peaks I had just come over, and I knew I was cut off now. My only hope if I got hurt was the signal mirror.

Soon the stars were out across the sky and the only noise was the occasional empty sound of the wind in the high rocks. The awareness that I was in grizzly country always grew more heightened with the darkness, and although I tried to reason with my paranoia, as I lay there looking at the stars my senses were still alive with it. I listened keenly into the darkness for a long time before I allowed myself to sleep, and I kept a nearby tree in mind in case one came in during the early hours. I knew that grizzlies which lived in country open to hunting, as this range was, were incredibly secretive and hard to see, and that they rarely came into a camp unless all the humans were gone. I knew that my chances of even seeing one, much less getting attacked by one, were very poor. But the knowledge of their presence did something to the night, filled it with a certain menace that kept me listening hard and sleeping light. Once I asked an old-timer at Fort Fistfight how to find a grizzly; he laughed at me and said, "You don't find them, friend. They find you."

He spoke a simple truth about grizzlies. Still I thought I had a fair chance of seeing one from high on the divide, watching mornings and evenings. The ranger had told me that Grizzly Basin was hard to get to; for that reason I thought there was a fair chance I might run into one there. After that it was fate, and that was what made my scalp tingle in the darkness.

I would work the upper end of the basin in the morning. It was rugged, maybe three miles across, innumerable clefts and gorges, small lakes. See what sign there was. Keep moving up the range till I got some sign.

DAWN BROUGHT a cold gray sky, a wind that was edged with emptiness. I made a tiny progress through the ruggedness of the upper end of the basin, climbing hills of rock, passing through fringes of timber, threading around a small dead lake with sunken black logs all over the bottom. Instinctively I began to feel the grizzly and its country, sensing its range, its mastery of the terrain it covered and the loneliness it roamed through. It was the monarch of solitude in these mountains; it seemed to thrive in all the loneliness, needing nothing but food and wild spaces. Its interests and mine coincided exactly in the Swans; I felt a deep inner urge to get away altogether, to escape for a time from the least contact with people whose consciousness was centered on money and profit, and to travel wild. That was the grizzly: hiding, watching, traveling away from the humans who would kill it for status. The further I explored across that basin, the more I began to feel a deep and instinctual identification with the big bear, sensing its hunger, its solitary hunt for food, the vast and rugged country which it roamed through in its search. I was careful as I went, eyes always ahead, always aware of which way the wind was blowing.

Late in the afternoon I came to a lake high in the boulders, uncertain of where I was. There was a gap in the mountains close by but I didn't know if it was the divide or an outlying ridge spur. As I was trying to get my bearings a cloud of snow and sleet came swirling over the top of the mountain and began to rain down into the lake, turning the rocks wet and slippery. I was hungry, and as the wet gray weather closed in I felt a faltering sense of loneliness and loss of direction, one that seemed to pierce me so I could scarcely think of what I should do. I began searching halfheartedly around for a place of shelter from the wind and sleet, my jacket and my hair starting to get wet, but there seemed to be only boulders and little stunted trees, boulders and more boulders, a foundation of rock. Finally I found two dense firs growing close together, and I crawled in on the leeward side and got a little fire going. I had gathered some round hyacinth roots along the way and those I boiled in a kettle of soup. They tasted the best of any root I had yet found, but they still left me with a yearning for meat.

The hot broth made me feel better. I knew that grizzlies prized hyacinth roots and dug them wherever they found them. I also knew that although grizzlies were 80 to 90 percent vegetarian, they were eating bugs and rodents too. They were eating some grasshoppers, for I was starting to see little ones in the grass. None of that helped me much, for the thought of grass-hopper stew did not move me to the hunt.

Finally the weather blew over and the rocks began to gleam with a dull faraway light. I decided to go on, and climbed up above the lake until I saw my landmark peak ahead and off to the right. I had to stay on this side of the gap. I kept working along under the divide, careful on the slippery rocks, wondering about finding a deer in this range if I needed to. So far I hadn't seen one; it seemed strange to me with all the grass, the wild-ness. The snow was gone, the grass was green, and the grass-hoppers were out, tiny, starting to grow. But no deer.

I was walking through a long grassy channel in the rocks when I saw some reddish fur on the ground up ahead. It was marmot fur, a pile of individual mouthfuls of it with the guts lying next to it. They had been out in the sun and air for a few days, for they were blackened where they were exposed. Grizzly, I thought. But then I thought about it some more and decided finally that it was a coyote. I was fairly certain a grizzly would have eaten the whole thing, fur, guts, and all. An eagle would have carried it away. A lynx might have left a solid patch of fur. But a coyote probably would have pulled the fur off mouthful by mouthful. Or a weasel? I went on, still looking for the first telltale sign of the big bear.

The range was rising slowly, growing more rugged. I saw clearly that it had been formed by a gigantic buckling of the earth's crust, for all the major outlying rock formations were thrust at the same angle, and I began to get a feel for the two giant slabs of crust which had jammed together and thrust up-ward toward the sky over a distance of fifty miles. I was getting closer to Grizzly Basin, and the more distance I put between me and that last saddle I had climbed over, the more I felt as if I were heading into the wild, the spirit of what was left. Was it in Grizzly Basin? There was something in the name and the re-moteness of it that led me to hope it was.

I no sooner got outta them son of a bitchin' bogs when my charger stepped into a nest of ground bees and throwed me clean up into the trees, buckin' and whinnyin' while they stung

the hell outta him and the mule and me and ever' other goddamn thing in sight. I was most of the afternoon collectin' my
outfit after that swarm of devils hit, and I begun to think I'd
made a mistake comin' up to this north country after all. Jest
afore dark I kilt me a little deer and carried the hindquarters in
by the fire, fillin' my belly plumb full o' hot meat till my eyes
begun to get heavy. I put the last tobaccer I had in my pipe and
lay there by the fire smokin' and dreamin', figurin' one more
day's ride and I'd catch up with Fitz and the boys. Dozed off, I
did, plumb without thinkin', and when I woked up the fire was
down to flickers and glowin' coals, and right acrost from that
fire, like a nightmare come true, was the biggest son of a bitch of
a grizzly you ever seen.

The hair rose on my neck. A mountain of fur it was, standin'
silvery in the moonlight, head low to the ground, them close
beady eyes a-starin' right at me acrost the fire. Warn't time for
my Hawken—I took ahold of my pistol and begun slitherin'
backwards away, hardly thinkin' but jest wonderin' if'n that big
monster was gonna jump on me and tear me up. When I backed
into a tree I reached up and felt a branch, and with that I begun
climbin' quiet and slow, never takin' my eyes off'n that bar's
eyes, ready to fire down its throat, and that bar jest standin' thar
motionless, a-watchin' me. Then of a sudden when I was jest
high enough to be outta reach, it let out a growl and come at me
like a runaway wagon, so fast it put the jitters in my gut, and
went crashin' by underneath me and took a swing that fanned
the laces of my moccersin. The son of a bitch woulda tore my leg
off! Strong and fast, Lord, my leg! But by then I was gettin' mad,
since I was far enough up the tree, and I went to yellin'.

"You big furry son of a bitch! What's the idea of comin' into
my camp and runnin' me up a tree?" By thunder, I was a-gettin'
mad.

It come back around underneath, big as an ox, growlin' at me,
eyes flashin' red in the firelight. I pulled off a dead branch and
throwed it at him, and it bounced off'n his hump. With that he
reared up on his hind feet and let go a roar that shook the
cobwebs outta the night, and stood thar a-snappin' his teeth,
murder in his eyes.

I clumb a little higher.

"Why, you chickenhearted son of a bitch! Come on up here an' fight, you mountain o' lard!" And I let out a growl, barin' my teeth at him, roarin' at him jest like he was a-roarin' at me. I was a-challengin' him.

That got him true mad. He come up right underneath me on his hind feet and wantin' more 'n anything to get his claws onto me.

"You big tepee rug! You couldn't bat a fly in the middle of January! Run me outta my own camp, will ye?" I busted off a stick and took to bangin' the tree and roarin' and growlin', just a-darin' him to come up and get me. Oh Lord, he was mad. His teeth was snappin' and clickin', saliver drippin' off'n his jaws, his eyes squinty with hatred jest to get his claws on me. I roared back at him agin, yellin', "Run me outta my own camp, you great big pile of buffler shit!" And I took that long stick and cracked him square 'twixt the eyes.

It warn't nothin' I seen, but of a sudden that stick war gone from my hand and a-sailin' out through the trees like a gunshot. Lord a'mighty! It happened right in front of my eyes, and I never even seed his arm move.

That sorta took the wind outta my sails. Anything that had an arm as big around as my waist and could swing it like a bolt of lightnin', well, it warn't nothin' to fool around with, nor tease. I set back and shut up, watchin' him tear up the brush and claw at them branches, lettin' him play his anger out. I'm thinkin' that if I got him mad enough he was liable to foller me the next day and jump me somewhars, for them grizzlies got a memory in 'em. I set up thar quiet like a mouse, waitin', and finally with a few last growls he went on over to where I hung them hind-quarters, and looked back in my direction. I set still. Finally he give a low growl and dropped back down, pickin' up what was left of the meat and draggin' it off into the dark. I still had some strips laid on the rocks by the fire, enough for another bellyful, but he got most of my meat and I was gettin' low on powder. Top of that, I had to set up thar in the tree with the skeeters and lissen to him breakin' and crunchin' bones off in the brush. My meat, by cracky. And when I couldn't hear him eatin' no more I still dassn't come down from that tree, on account of I feared he might be layin' for me. I set up thar in that pine tree till dawn

come in the east, sore-boned and talkin' to the skeeters, cursing
them goddamn meat-stealin' grizzlies, and if I didn't know the
boys was only a day or so ahead I woulda packed up my outfit
and got the livin' hell outta thar.

What can I say? The life of a mountain man isn't always a bed
of roses.

I sat lost in my fire, up near the last lake at the end of the
basin. I would go over the top in the morning. The only thing
that bothered me was the rocks around the fire, which contained
strips of moss, rather than tasty fresh strips of venison. He had
me beat on the meat. I was beginning to feel that familiar yawning in my muscles that came with lots of bushing and not
enough meat. I didn't know yet what I was going to do about it;
wait and see how wild the country was up ahead. Hope for small
game. I hadn't been able to find any more good roots.

I poked a stick into the fire, sending a storm of sparks up, and
sat dreaming about the big rivers that ran for hundreds of miles
through the mountains, all the wildlife along them, meat when
you needed it, wild animals to watch when you didn't, deer
everywhere, big herds of elk and buffalo; grizzlies throughout
the thickets and river bends, among the chokecherries and
buffalo berries, lords of it all, in a way dominating even the
Indians until the mountain man came along with his flintlock
rifle. There were only about eight hundred of the big bears left
now, scattered about Glacier and Yellowstone in Montana and
Wyoming. And they were in hiding, on the run. Research was
the only real thing that could help them.

Finally I got up and carried my food bag a good distance
downwind, hanging it up in a dead tree. Then I turned in,
watching the clouds clear away from the stars, the same stars
from Taos to Wind River, up the the Swans. Tomorrow I would
be up on the divide again. I wondered how wild the country
ahead was before I had to hit a trail, and whether it would feel
right taking some meat. Maybe somewhere up ahead.

WITH the sun spilling gold to the east I set off down through the
rocks, heading for the northern rim of the basin. At the bottom I
hit a small oblong lake just under the divide with piles of rock
spilling into it all around, rippling clear green with the feeling of

glaciers, ice water, and white clouds. But dead, no fish. I hunted around the shoreline for tracks and found a few scattered elk tracks, but that was all. No big bear tracks.

I stopped near the outlet, taking off my shirt and socks and washing them with the soap bar, sudsing them up and then scrubbing them on the rocks. After I had rinsed them and wrung them out I hung them on the back of my pack to dry and scrubbed out the kettle with a handful of gravel, then packed it away. I usually alternated socks like that, and found that it worked well. When I finished I soaped up my head, submerged it in the lake, then shook the water loose like a dog. My senses came alive.

Up above the lake the morning sun had turned the upper half of the high rimrock bright yellow. I crossed over the marshy ground below the lake and there I found a well-defined pathway which led up out of the basin. I kept expecting it to fade out, but it didn't. Grizzlies sometimes formed trails like this over their range, more definite than elk trails, wearing them deeper. "Moccasin Joe," the mountain men called the grizzly. But as I followed it higher toward the sunlight at the top of the rampart I didn't find any bear shit, or tracks. After a while I figured that all the animals used this trail: deer, elk, goats, bears, and coyotes. It was the easiest place to get over the ridge, from one basin to the next, and so it was well worn.

The art and history of pathfinding was becoming clear to me: American civilization learned the trails and passes over the Rockies from the mountain men; the mountain men learned them from the Indians; and the Indians learned them from the wild animals. Humans first began to understand the lay of the land by watching the movements of wild animals.

I followed the trail up over a grass-swept saddle; as I went down the other side I caught sight of the divide again, 400 feet of rugged rock wall. I picked a route up a slide that had brush and grass most of the way and started climbing, zigzagging, up into the morning sun. When I got to the top I walked to the other side and looked over some big cliffs, 700, 800 feet down to a wasteland of rocks below. Across the nothingness another steep hillside rose up, and some sharp whistles came at me from there. Marmots whistling a warning, though I couldn't spot them. I was carrying my Hawken now when I wasn't climbing, and I wondered how those marmots tasted.

I walked up the divide in the sun and gusting wind, north up the range, and *she was a-gittin' high and mighty, boys, she was startin' to rare up like a—*

Sorry.

When the sun was straight up I came to a break in the divide, and far down to the left lay Grizzly Basin. It was remote, rimmed by low spurs of peaks breaking down off the divide. I knew its shape from the maps; I knew it when I saw it.

I sat down and glassed it for a long time. It was cut off on three sides by spurs of mountain, and the whole basin and the country beyond it looked rugged and untouched. The only way into the basin was up the creek which lay about 2,000 feet below me, or through a break in the peaks at the far upper end. That was where I would go out. I watched for a long time, taking the bullets out of the pistol and sighting it, clicking it as my gaze wandered over the basin. The map didn't show any trail coming up that creek. Would there be a big silver bear in that basin? Grizzlies usually fed in a big circuit, covering the same sixty or seventy miles again and again. A traveling male might spend a day or two in that basin. A sow with cubs might spend more time in there, because it was naturally protected from humans. I thought there was a fair chance there might be one in there. If it was a sow with cubs I couldn't make any mistakes. To stop a charging grizzly with a pistol, even a big magnum, is a feat of almost superhuman skill and nerve. Their skulls are close to an inch thick, and the frontal bones have been known to deflect high-powered rifle bullets. They charge onward at thirty-five miles an hour with their hearts blown apart, with their windpipes shattered in their throats, with their jugulars shot out, with chips of their skulls blown off their heads—they charge on toward the enemy even though they are dead on their feet. There is no animal in the mountains with the heart and guts of a grizzly.

But their nose is extraordinarily sensitive, the only point on them that is really vulnerable. More than one mountain man saved his life by directing a hard and accurate blow with a rock or a hatchet to the nose of an attacking grizzly. It is the one pain they apparently cannot stand, and they leave off, retreat, after they get hit hard in the nose.

However, I would not like to try that out to see if it worked. The more I thought about it, the more I figured the best defense I could muster was to see it before it saw me. To slow down and listen when visibility was limited, and to form the habit of proceeding as if there were always one close by. I had been forming that habit ever since I started out, and it was becoming second nature.

Finally I got up and climbed down the breaks, over crevices that were two feet wide and thirty feet deep. Whole chunks of the mountain were breaking off, over centuries, gradually making this cleft in the divide wider and deeper. When I got to the end of it I saw the start of a narrow chute winding down out of sight, looking smooth and steep. I felt a devilish lure in me. *Go ahead, give it a try.* I measured it: it was a long, long way down. Two hours? But it looked like it kept the same grade all the way, and it was the most direct shot to the entrance of the basin. Otherwise I'd have to drop down off the other side of the divide and go all the way around to the north. Finally I figured what the hell and hung my rope around my neck, starting down. The sun was straight above me in the sky, and big white clouds with dark edges were starting to come in from the west.

It soon narrowed down to about three feet, with a jagged wall on the left which offered handholds now and then. It wound back and forth, at times over smooth rock, or over stretches of loose shale, steep enough so that I was constantly aware of the feeling of breaking loose and sliding out of control. I worked slowly down on the seat of my pants, holding to rocks, digging my heels into the damp shale, sometimes turning around and climbing close to the rock over the steeper slides. Far below, the valley lay in hazy silence, a blanket of deep timber, not even the sound of the creek coming up. I was buzzing with the height, the danger of slipping, the great length of the chute which stretched out of sight below me. There were occasional stunted firs with gnarled roots, boulders caught here and there. I concentrated on each handhold, each place I set my foot, and soon I was sweating, unaware of my pack, just concentrating on keeping good contact and friction as I worked downward.

When a half hour had gone by I began to notice that for all the descending I had done the bottom didn't look any closer. Strange, I thought. But it was when I looked back up that I got the shock. The top was long gone and the way back up appeared so impossible that my mouth must have parted when I looked at it. It was such a crazy angle that I knew it was now out of the question. The only way was down.

I wiped the sweat from my face and sat there with my heart beating faster than normal, feeling a sudden and far-reaching sense of loneliness. I looked along the mountainside to the right and saw it breaking away in a series of cliffs there, big cliffs, impossible to get down. Then it occurred to me: What if there was a cliff at the bottom of the chute that was longer than my rope? I looked down for some kind of clue to the grade down there, but couldn't see a thing.

The sun had moved along the sky some; bigger fragments of cloud were coming in and scraping across the top of the mountain out of sight. I started down again, the wind whipping over the boulders in gusts, making it all seem high and devoid of life except for my laboring body. I kept going, sliding a little now and then, always looking for something below to grab on to if I broke loose. The further I went, the more I felt the enormity, the loneliness of that mountainside. There was no help, there would be none, and the top as a way out became more and more impossible as I lost its elevation. I began to feel cut off; there was nothing but the immediacy of each hold I found as I let myself down. I forced myself to concentrate only on my descent, and listened for the sound of rocks above me. Every time I took a look down at the bottom of the valley it appeared the same. It was as if I were going down on a treadmill.

Then I came to a place where the chute turned into smooth rock. It went straight down for twenty feet and wound out of sight around a boulder, something terminal in its appearance. The clouds passing overhead were bigger, dark in the center, and while I sat there hesitating over the menacing steepness a rumble of thunder sounded in the distance. The sun blinked out and the wind turned cold, a big mass of cloud passing close above, and the feeling all across the mountainside turned bleaker. Wouldn't it be something if it started raining? I thought.

I pushed off, working down the wall. I didn't look down; my pack felt as if it were filled with cotton. I wished that I was lying in a cornfield in Nebraska. I inched down for about thirty feet, the thunder slowly moving closer. When I finally hit shale and small lodged boulders again I sat and stared, sweating. I doubted if I was even halfway down yet. The thunder was closing in, and it occurred to me that if the chute got wet I might be stuck up here all night.

That gave me new energy. I looked around and noticed that there were more stunted trees now, and I remembered the rope around my neck. I got up and uncoiled it, doubling it around a small tree and throwing both ends down the chute. I started down backward, feeding the rope slowly, keeping it wound around my right wrist. It worked well. From tree to tree I went, racing the storm, trying to get down far enough to where it wouldn't stop me. Lightning was beginning to flash in the air and thunder boomed close over the rocks, the wind at the front of the storm starting to whip and lash at the branches. I hit a smooth stretch of rock and hurried down it, the air around me taking on that lethal yellow light just before lightning hits. Then I could feel it in the air, in the hair on my arms, and I was filled with a sudden and amazing rush of fear. I dropped onto my stomach and in the next few instants there came an explosion which felt as if it blew my eardrums out. I could still feel its impact in my chest as it went rolling away down the mountains, and then I heard a trickle of small rocks coming down the chute above me, and I was up and yanking the rope free, scrambling down backward, fearing a landslide. I found a big break in the wall and crawled in behind it, huddling out of the way, and a small amount of rocks and gravel came spilling and bouncing past. I looked up the chute and there was nothing else coming. A few big drops splattered off the rocks, wind came whipping up the chute with deep whistling sounds, and then out on the mountainside a spear of lightning flashed from hundreds of feet up, sizzling the air, and in the same instant that tremendous boom bounced off my body, the power of it all, and I pressed down against the rocks and hoped I wouldn't get hit. Another jag came down and struck amid a terrace of small trees, the thunder exploding and rolling away—huge, lonely power. In a short time the sky opened with rain, a downpour that splashed off the rocks with mist and fury, the spirit of the mountain talking to me, drenching me. The lightning was moving away, up the mountain. I sat back in a stupor of relief, watching the big sheets of rain ride the wind across the valley.

IT WAS evening, a soft steel light coming through the breaking clouds, when I came down onto the long boulder-strewn delta at the end of the chute. There had been no cliff at the end. Sweet-vetch flowers were blooming all over and I gathered handful after handful as I made my way down the final pitch, stuffing them in my mouth and chewing up their sweetness. I was soaked, smeared with mud and gravel, so tired that I kept turning my ankles. As soon as I felt that I was down my pack suddenly changed in weight from cotton to lead, and I had to stop and dump it off my back, rest my shoulders, before I could go on. I stumbled on down, thinking how much the human body could do when it was faced with a crisis. I pictured myself at the top of the divide—"Well, I'll just go down this little chute here." Heh-heh.

Don't underestimate the mountain.

Near the bottom I gathered a big handful of bear-grass flowers, to stew while I dried my clothes. When I got down to the creek the bottom was dense, dim and dripping, big Douglas firs two feet thick with an understory of knee-high green foliage, all of it soaked. I sat on a boulder hungry and unable to get myself going, feeling lost in the wet loneliness of that eighty-foot-high forest. It had taken me close to five hours to get down the chute, and the feeling at the bottom was far different than up on top of the divide. I could feel the big silver bear, its haunts, its hidden routes and nocturnal passage, more than at any other time on the trip. I sensed instinctively that this was where they lived, early in the season. Down here with the mosquitoes.

It started to drizzle again. I got up and went to work stringing the poncho, building a fire to dry myself and drive away the mosquitoes. I tied my rope off between two trees and made a tent of the poncho, hauling my gear underneath, and sat by the fire listening to the rain, feeling the deep loneliness, the remoteness, in that creek bottom. The trees looked big and wild; the flames alone gave comfort.

I propped a pole over the fire and hung the kettle, throwing some of the last of my jerky in with the bear-grass flowers. I drained the water out twice, hoping to boil away the bitterness, but they still had an acid taste. I ate as many as I could force down, and devoured the jerky, wondering why the elk liked those flower heads so much. As the woods grew dim a bank of fog started to come in, burying the upper half of the mountain and drifting ghostlike through the rain-soaked branches.

I cleared the brush and dead branches away between my bed and a tree I could climb about twenty feet away, and I hung the food sack high up. By the time I crawled in, the woods were pitch black, shrouded in fog, and the rain had stopped, giving way to stillness and dripping sounds. It felt so wild that all I could do was lie there and listen, sense it, let the isolation and dark chaos of that wet night sink into my bones. Any place familiar seemed a thousand miles away.

Finally my thoughts turned toward the basin ahead. The air was drifting slowly down the creek, so none of my smoke had gone into the basin. Tomorrow morning it would reverse, and instead of following the creek up I would climb the ridge above it and move into the basin across the wind, watching ahead and below me, working down from there. I would watch for digs, tracks near springs and little creeks. Torn-open logs; well-used trails and big black piles. A grizzly with cubs.

In all the surrounding darkness, the wet and cold, I began to have a new sense of the big bears, an appreciation, despite the fear I felt, for their natural adaptation to life in the wilderness: the great thick fur that no mosquitoes or flies can penetrate, the oils in it that make it shed water like canvas; the big long claws for digging and ripping and the tremendous power and speed in the forearms; the hump of brute strength in its shoulders; the keen sense of smell, and the uncanny intelligence as it watches a human pass by unaware of its presence; the totality of all those things that make it the true lord of the wilderness, able to catch a mouse from under a rock or kill a buffalo at a river crossing.

The big silver bear.

AS THE DAWN MIST began to lift I stood atop a boulder over the basin and watched the little openings, the breaks in the forest which the raising fog began to reveal. All my senses were tuned for that bear. The basin as it came into view was more rugged than it had looked from above, with many channels and hills of rock intermixed beneath the timber. The sense of remoteness that it held as the fog began flowing up the mountainside remained. It looked like a lost basin. Finally with the first hint of foggy sunlight to the east I took a compass shot and started down in, feeling as if I were heading toward an encounter with fate.

My pants were soon soaked again. In about fifteen minutes I found a well-defined trail that led along under a rock wall, and I hadn't gone more than thirty steps when I came upon a pile of bear droppings that would have filled up a plate. I stood there staring at it, then looking around me, thinking that any bear that could unload that much of a pile had to be a pretty big bear. The woods around me took on a new air.

I poked through it with a stick. Five, six days old, maybe more, full of worms and bugs. It was shot through with seeds, grass, moss, roots, a few small bone splinters, but hardly any hair at all. Ninety percent vegetative.

I started out again, each footstep silent, watching constantly from side to side as I went, covering all the woods, stopping now and then to listen. The wind was coming up across my line of travel and I knew, I sensed, that traveling the way I was, I would see it before it saw me. It relied almost completely on its nose and its ears to detect the approach of a human; I had both those senses covered, or so it seemed to me then. If it was feeding in some brush, hidden, I would hear it. Only if it was lying up, resting, would I not detect it.

Little nameless creeks came down off the divide and cut shallow gullies through the basin, overhung with leaning pines, trailing shining gravel bars here and there. On the third one I crossed I stopped in midstride; there down in the mud was a smooth hind bear print bigger than my boot. When I first laid eyes on it I felt a tingling in the back of my neck at the size of it, and again I involuntarily looked through the woods around me. It was the first clear grizzly print I'd seen, and the size of it was what sent that strange fearful thrill through me. Immediately my imagination began to paint an animal big enough to fill that track, and when it had done so and the animal stood there in front of me, with a bulk proportionate to the track, I could only stare. They were bigger than I realized. The bear that filled that track stood higher than my waist.

Gulp.

I crossed the creek and found a front track as big around as a saucer, five quarter-sized toe marks strung tightly in front of it, and five claw marks hitting well out in the mud in front of those. Then grass, no more tracks. There were no raindrops showing in the tracks, although the area was well shielded from the sky by the timber. In that kind of mud it was hard to tell how old they were, but they weren't very old.

I compared the back print with the front one, and it occurred to me that they were quite similar to the prints a human would make walking on all fours. The long hind track was shaped like a bare footprint would be in the mud, and the front track had the same proportions as my hand when I pressed my palm into the mud and let the tips of my fingers hit out where the claws would hit. If I walked on all fours the proportions would be uncannily similar to a medium-sized grizzly.

This was a big grizzly, probably a male, since there weren't any smaller tracks with it. I memorized the folds in the hind track and stood there listening for a while, watching.

The trail died out. I climbed over big piles of rock, looking into the timber below for long moments, and stepped silently over roots and through wet brush, working across the wind, across the basin. I was filled with a mixture of fear, hope, and anticipation; always my eyes were moving, searching, and my ears as I paused were keyed for the slightest break or scrape. Often I looked behind me, for once a grizzly discovers a human on its range, if the hunting pressure isn't too great, it will get behind and follow, unbeknown to the human. Most of the time it does this simply to keep track of the human, see what it is up to. Still it was an eerie thought, and I kept half hoping and half fearing to see a big mound of fur move behind a tree when I looked back.

Nearing the northern end of the basin I started to hit more clearings, areas of open grass scattered with dense thickets. I had been searching for over three hours in a state of continual vigilance, and the mosquitoes had been eating on me steady.

Timber sickness was starting to set in. I stopped at a small creek and drank my fill, splashing the water all over my head, and rested for a while. I was hungry, and I hadn't seen a rabbit or a grouse all morning. I walked on, watching the thickets, running my gaze ahead to the little openings further up, searching for that single little movement that would telegraph the presence of a feeding bear, way off in the distance.

Suddenly a thicket cracked just to my right and there out of a trembling mass of green leaves rose the head and shoulders of the biggest bear I ever saw. Grizzled and silvery, the fur flowed down off her head to her huge sloping shoulders, one arm raising up with the claws out in the air, and seeing that, a great rush of fear hit me like a splash of cold water. Her eyes were turning red with surprise and anger; her teeth gleamed into view beneath black lips forming into a snarl and she let out a roar that shook the whole thicket. Behind her one cub, two, three cubs came shinnying up out of the bushes, racing up the trunks of different trees as fast as they could, going straight for the top. Thoughts raced through my mind like meteors—run? bluff? make a stand? —and in that second or two that I decided, it seemed as if I were staring at her for the rest of my life: the sunlight giving a silvery sheen to the crest of her enormous head, her teeth gleaming with a deep growl, that great arm poised with claws as long as a man's fingers cutting the air, and the whole tremendous bulk of her body rising higher than me, overwhelming me with its might and strength.

I knew I was staring death in the face. I pulled out my pistol and my hatchet and began walking backward, slowly, never taking my eyes off hers. She let out another great roar when she saw me move, and took a swing with her arm like a sickle slicing the air. I just kept going backward, holding on to her eyes. But she wouldn't be held. She dropped down and came at me in a furious rush, a mountain of muscle and bone bearing down on me like a runaway freight train. I raised up my hatchet and let out the roar of my life: "Stop, you son of a bitch, or I'll bust your head open!" But she wouldn't stop, she was too crazy with anger at me for her cubs, and I didn't have the heart to hit her on account of she *had* cubs. So she plowed into me like a ton of bricks.

We wrestled all over that goddamn mountainside. We wrestled tooth and nail, hook and claw, the whole afternoon, bushes flyin' up in the air, trees tippin' over, boulders rattling down into the basin—me tryin' to keep them fangs and claws off me, her tryin' to dig 'em in. One hell of a wrestlin' match, it was—I might not be here today 'cept that I knew a fair amount of jujitsu. By sunset we was both tuckered out and we set there eyein' each other, taking a breather.

"Look," I said, "I'm not one of those capitalist sweathogs who has to have a grizzly-bear rug to prove he's a hunter."

"I'll bet," she said. She was still panting some.

"No, really. I could have hit you with my hatchet and I didn't."

Her eyes narrowed. "If you would have hit me with that hatchet I'd have chewed it in half and spit out the pieces."

"I don't doubt that." I thought for a moment, changing tack. "Couldn't we be friends?" I said.

She grunted. "I trust you about as far as I could throw you," she said.

"That's fairly far."

She got up and shook herself, raising a pale cloud of dust. "I have to go check on the cubs," she said.

I followed along behind her, amazed by the bulk and breadth of her back, the roll of fur over her hump of shoulder muscle, shifting loosely as she walked. She didn't seem to care that I was walking with her; she was looking toward her cubs.

"Do you mind if I feel your fur?" I said.

"Just don't get grabby."

I sunk my hand into the thick and luxuriant fur; it felt woolly underneath the long silvery guard hairs. It was summer fur, but still heavy and thick. I felt her back muscles flex as she walked.

"Scratch right there, will you?"

I did, and she stopped and arched her back, groaning with pleasure. Soon I was scratching with both hands all over her massive back, while she stretched, cringed, and grunted with satisfaction. That turned the tide for me.

"Come on," she said, "I'll introduce you to the kids."

We went back up to the clearing and she called the cubs down from the trees. They were full of joy to see her; they kept jumping toward her chest and shoulders, clawing at her fur and giving little whimpers. She lay down on her back and let them crawl up on her chest to nurse.

"Where's the old man?" I said.

"That lazy animalistic son of a bitch! He'd eat all three of them if he got the chance. If he shows up around here I'll stomp his ass into the ground, and he knows it too."

When she finished feeding them I played with them till dark, rolling all over the grass. That night I slept amid warm bundles of grizzly fur, and the next day we set out hunting, wandering together into the distant mountains. I was never heard from again. Down through the years there was a persistent rumor in the Swan Valley about a wild mountain man wearing skins and carrying a spear, traveling with a family of grizzlies, seen at odd times of year fleeing over distant gaps in the mountains, but it was never documented. Most of the townsfolk merely laughed at the story, but a few old-timers swore over the flag that on certain moonlit nights—

Sigh.

A cold band of light spread out across the western horizon, infusing the peaks there at the rim of the basin with a deep aura of loneliness. From somewhere in the coming night a chilly wind sprang up, cutting through the grass in whirlwinds, whistling off the far rocks. I was standing at the upper end of the basin, staring down at the last empty clearing I had searched through. I hadn't seen a grizzly with three cubs. I hadn't seen a grizzly with two cubs, or even one cub. In fact, the only things I saw in Grizzly Basin after all those days of anticipation were one pile of shit, three tracks, and a bunch of poison mushrooms.

A good summation of the seventies. I had searched all day, and I found nine million mosquitoes. As I climbed wearily out of the basin the back of my mind slowly, helplessly, transformed itself into a television screen. It was as if the seventies had caught up with me again, and had taken control of my subconscious there at the end of my search, and now with a high whinnying laugh over my dream of Grizzly Basin were now flashing one television commercial after another before my inner eye. Full-color images of people roaring up through the trees behind me in new jeeps, people drinking beer, people brushing their teeth, people with football flags biting into huge double

cheeseburgers, all of them happy, wonderful, smiling with sparkling teeth, swarming up the basin behind me in my imagination. It was as if there was no way I could escape it, no place
that was safe from it, no dream it couldn't touch.

I stopped and closed my fist, getting a grip on myself. I let the
loneliness of those mountains sink back into my soul. I called on
my mountain man medicine, and I kept fighting the images, the
high whinnying laugh. I'd beat those sons of bitches. And finally
the images were gone, and the laugh was gone, back beyond the
Swan Mountains, away from my mind. The light was fading. I
noticed that the wind was blowing.

I BUILT a wind-whipped fire and cooked a kettle of rice, roasting
biscuits on a stick while I waited, and after I had eaten my fill I
lay in my bag on the soft moss and listened to the wind describe
the vastness, its heights, the yawning spaces: an old dark song
about the spirit in the earth.

*I come up on the boys in the evenin', and a sight for sore eyes
it was to see 'em at the head of the lake. Fire and a big kettle,
furs piled up, and traps, buckskins movin' around, Hawkens agin
the trees and horses feedin' out in the flat. Looked like they was
close to pullin' out. I hallooed from around the lake and rode on
in, thinkin' about coffee and mebbe a little flour and mebbe a
tetch o' whiskey. There was Black Harris and old Bill Williams,
Russel and some of his boys, but I didn't yet see old Broken
Hand.*

*When I clumb down off my horse wouldn't none of 'em give
me a good steady look, they was all sorta hang-headed.*

"Whar's Broken Hand?" says I. Meanin' Fitz.

*Black Harris give me a look like a morgue. "Gone," he says in
a flat voice.*

I stopped in my tracks. "Gone under?"

*He shrugged. "Gone. After he brung in his catch he went a-
footin' it up into them mountains to the east, scoutin' fer the fall
hunt. He never come back. We been huntin' him since afore the
full moon." He dropped his eyes. "Can't wait no more, Gabe.
Gotta take these furs to rendezvous whilst thar's still fixin's left,
afore Ashley heads east."*

*I'm thinkin' he's still alive. I got the lay of the country and
whar they searched from Black Harris, a little frame outfit and a*

bunch of jerky, a coil of rope. The boys would take my plews and traps on in with 'em, git me fixin's and trade goods at the best price they could bargain. There was friendly Flatheads camped farther up the valley makin' fish, and for some whiskey that I'd carry they'd git them Indians to hold on to my charger and enough of an outfit to git me across Three Forks when I come out. Russel told me the Indians was ridin' east for buffalo with the new moon, and if I come out in time I could travel with 'em.

Next mornin' at dawn I waved my Hawken to the boys and took off up that huntin' trail whar Fitz had started in. Thick timber all the way up, but I was footin' it hard. Spent the night in the timber near the top, looked like the top anyway, tangled country and hard to keep bearin's. Next day the boys' tracks started to play out. I kept a-goin', climbin' up and down them mountains, watchin' the country below for smoke. The boys figured he was bones and wolf meat by now, that he'd a come out by this time even if he was hurt. I figured he was stuck somewhars, and still alive.

He was swinging into action. I was still ahead of him in this range, but he was starting to close the distance. The wilderness he had was vast. He lived through the beginning of it.

THE SUN was bright and warm the next morning. I hunted along the high rocky slopes under the divide for a marmot, but the few that were up there saw me coming from a long way off, whistled their warnings, and were gone by the time I got within range. They could sense that my intentions were predatory now, that I had them in mind. It felt as if they read my mind, from five hundred yards off. They weighed close to ten pounds and it looked like there would be a fair amount of meat, although I guessed that it would taste like an old gym shoe. I would have to sneak down on them from above if I was going to get one.

As the sun rose higher I passed around a shoulder of rock and came into view of the next basin. It was bigger and more remote than the last. At the far end a series of white waterfalls spilled down over the rocks in the sun. The first major trail over the range was still about ten air miles further north, and the region I was entering felt clear-aired and wild.

I took my time working across toward one of the waterfalls,

hunting for an unaware marmot, watching the open country below for animals. Sometimes I walked over the same surface of rock for three or four minutes; sometimes I dropped down into steep grassy ravines. My body energy was steadily going downhill. When the sun was high I found a bunch of wild chives growing out of a wet mossy spring, and I sat down there and ate one after another, pulling them up and stuffing them in. They tasted delicious for a while. As I chewed away I noticed two ravens descending lower in the basin, dropping toward a small hill of rock. I watched their distant black wings gleam purple in the sunlight as they dropped out of sight. Then as I chewed, another raven descended toward the same area, spiraling downward, and still another. Suddenly it dawned on me. Food.

I scrambled up and shouldered my pack, gathering a quick handful of chives and stuffing them in my pocket. When I finally got down to the edge I saw several crows and a smattering of magpies in the trees at the bottom of a timbered hillside. It was maybe three hundred feet further down. From among their perching ranks there was always one flapping down out of sight, or coming back up. A few of the ravens in the trees were pulling at chunks of something, eating. There was carrion down there, something big. And where there was something big and dead there was likely to be a bear.

All the miles of searching, the hope, the fear and wondering, suddenly all of it was pinpointed in front of me, down by the hillside. I tested the wind and found that it was coming up the drainage toward me; I lined out my approach against it, down to the left, straight through the timber along the edge of hillside. I could feel the adrenaline giving life to my muscles, sharpening my concentration; I could feel the small rivets of fear in my stomach. I knew that if there was a grizzly feeding on that carcass it would be sleeping nearby. Black bears ate their fill when they found carrion and lay around for a while sometimes, but they usually left it for other feed, coming back to it every second day or so. But once a grizzly found a carcass it took full possession of it, caching it, feeding on it, camping near it until it was completely gone. It would charge anything else big that tried to feed on it. I guessed that it would sleep downwind from the carcass, which would mean that I would pass by it on my approach. I knew that if it smelled me odds were it would get up and run, but if I surprised it out of a sleep at close range it might jump on me.

I started down, angling over the rocks, and when I finally stepped down to the bottom I caught a whiff of something rotten coming up on the wind. I stopped there with my heart beating fast and steady and unsnapped the pistol. If one came at me from close range, I would leave the pack on and drop on my stomach, lie still. If one got up and looked at me, I would start moving slowly backward and shout at it. If it took a step toward me, I would fire a warning shot. If it charged, I would activate my Apollo 7 jet pack and blast off toward Kansas.

I moved forward through the grass and scattered trees, step by step. My senses had opened wide; it was as if I could see and hear insects. As I drew closer I began to catch more of the nauseous smell, and I could see the birds moving through the trees. I watched sharp to the left, for the timbered hillside there was dense.

At last I came in sight of it. It was a dead elk, a cow, lying in a clearing, and there was nothing on it except birds. I could hear the flies buzzing around it in swarms. I stood there for a long time, listening and watching, searching all along the timbered hillside. The sun was higher in the sky, shining brightly on the clearing and the dead fur of the elk, and the sunlight and the sound of the flies lent an air of stillness and emptiness to the woods. The stench was overpowering; I had to move out of the wind from it.

I took the pistol in my hand and started walking toward it, staring ahead at the timber. When I was within ten feet of the carcass I stopped again and watched, sensing; nothing moved, nothing came out. I began to steal glances at the carcass and its immediate surroundings, still watching that densely tangled, timbered hillside. Approaching a grizzly's food cache was a very dangerous thing to do.

There were three different piles of bear shit in the grass, but none of them was very big. The grass was all matted down around the carcass for ten feet or so; it had gotten a lot of traffic. There was a small pile of sun-blackened guts a short distance away from the hooves. It looked like it had been dead for a week or ten days at least. The head was held to the body by only a single stretch of fur on the upper neck, and a big cloud of flies swarmed constantly around the raw neck opening, hundreds of them, the great buzzing sound making me wince as I stepped a little closer. A lower jawbone was separated from the head and picked clean, about ten feet away. The molars looked well worn; this elk might have died of old age. There were no signs of injury anywhere that I could see. Its anus was all torn open; they had been feeding heavily into the anus. There was another big swarm of flies around there.

Anywhere downwind the stench made me gag. I walked away from it, upwind, and sat down well inside the timber, just to get away from the endless swarming sensation of the flies and breathe some fresh air for a while. I couldn't see the carcass, but I could see most of the clearing. The birds began dropping down to it again, pecking off their unseen scraps, flying back up into the trees. The time seemed to drag past, to float stillbound in a sea of hot sunlight and buzzing flies, the stench of death and decay, the birds feeding and flying up into the trees as if nothing were amiss. I don't know how much time had passed, but when I happened to glance toward the carcass I saw something move like two ears. It must be a magpie, I thought. But then it moved again and I saw a patch of fur behind it with a silvery sheen to it.

I rose to my knees, filling with a strange buzzing energy. I saw its ears and its back as it moved around the carcass, slow and unaware, and the thought kept hitting me: *it's too small*, too small for a grizzly. Then it dawned on me. It was a grizzly cub.

Real fear came over me. For a few instants I scanned the hillside for a bigger shape, then moved instinctively away to my left, toward a rise in the rocks, keeping my eye back toward the clearing. The cub didn't see me. I began climbing up into the rocks, without much regard for the noise I was making, just climbing fast. When I got about thirty feet up I crawled onto a small flat overlook and stopped, looking back.

The cub had heard one of my rocks fall. He headed back toward the dense timber on the hillside at a walk, without much alarm or hurry, and disappeared among the trees. I kept looking for some sign of his mother, thinking it strange that she would let the cub come out alone, without first nosing around for danger herself. Then I began to think that the cub was fairly big, maybe a hundred pounds. This was the Moon When the Bears Run Together, the mating moon for bears, the moon when females leave their yearling cubs for good. This young grizzly was on his own for the first time in his life.

The more I thought about it, the more I was certain that that was it. I sat there with the fervent hope that he would come back to feed, a hope based on the slim premise that he hadn't been very alarmed when he retreated. The sun inched higher in the sky; I had water in my canteen and I drank some of it, waiting. The clearing remained still and deserted except for the birds.

It was well into the afternoon, my hope almost gone, when I looked into the woods and saw a shape with a dull sheen to it moving through the dimness. It stopped at the edge of the timber and waited there for three or four minutes, then walked out into the sunlight. The same miniature silver grizzly.

When he hit the sun he shone all over, a silvery glint that was brightest over his back and down his front shoulders, changing as he walked, shining more in one place than another, like sun-bleached hair. There was cocoa-brown fur lower in his front legs and in a line down the middle of his back; he was still immature in shape, the hump barely beginning to rise off his shoulders, but the wide triangulation in his head was already beginning to differentiate him in profile from a black bear. He was a beautiful little bear. The silvery sheen gave him a sense of something extraordinary, like a small monarch of the animal kingdom, and he walked out into the clearing with a sense of ease, a lack of wariness against attack that seemed strange to me because he was yet so small. All the fear I had felt dissolved as I watched him, and after all my conjurings of the speed, strength, and ferocity of a grizzly I was filled with a sense of the absurd at the sight of this silvery little beauty alone in the wilderness for the first time.

Without even looking around he walked up to the rear end of the carcass and pushed his nose into the hole there, in past the angry swarm of flies, into the putrid meat crawling with maggots. I felt my stomach lurch. He pawed at it a little, digging, then he left off and walked around to the front end, taking a look into the neck. He lay down there, and in a moment his head disappeared completely into the hole, past his ears. I cringed at the huge swarm of disrupted flies, the warm rotting meat, the smell of it up close. The bear seemed totally unaware of those things. Finally after thirty seconds or so he pulled out a long string of meat, and lay there chewing it up, hundreds of flies around his face. He seemed happy, oblivious to any unpleasantness. In went his head again, his body sloping forward in a relaxed position, and out came another string of gut.

Then he got up and stepped up on the carcass, standing atop it, doing nothing except shaking the flies off his head and snorting once or twice. A yearling grizzly laying claim: *This is my carcass, my meat, and I am king of it.* And he just stood there, giving quick little shakes of his head at the flies, looking about.

Then he did something that amazed me. He stepped down around the belly and began to examine the hindquarters. He wanted some of that. After a moment he stood up on his hind legs, reached over and grasped the hipbone with both paws and began rocking back and forth, tugging, trying to yank it loose. It was a movement which looked so hauntingly human, which was undertaken in such a human fashion, that I could only stare with the eerie feeling that I was looking at an animal with paws and whiskers in which somewhere the spark of a person was hidden beneath the silver fur. It was a weird, extraordinary feeling; I wanted to go down there and say, "Here, try this knife." I could hear the joints crack as he tugged time and again, but he wasn't yet strong enough to break it loose.

I knew then that there was no big grizzly on this carcass, or it would have accomplished what this one was trying to do. I also understood at an emotional level why the Indians called him Brother Bear, why they had legends of talking bears and ritualistic societies which refused to kill bears. Their subtle resemblance to human beings was mind-moving, haunting. I watched fascinated, unable to translate the feeling of it into conscious thought.

Finally he gave up. He tried chewing on the front leg for a while, but that too was unsatisfactory. So he went back to the neck hole and fed there for ten minutes, laying down sometimes, eating down into the neck, tugging, getting up and circling it, stopping for a while to pant in the growing heat of the day; shaking the flies away, licking his muzzle with a bright pink tongue. Twice more he stepped up on the carcass and stood there, resting. At last, after feeding for close to a half hour, he got up and ambled back into the timber.

I waited there while the sun shone down and the afternoon shadows grew longer, hoping he would come back, hoping for something else to show up. Late in the afternoon a coyote came out, incredibly wary, watching the timber, sniffing out each individual step it took, looking three different directions at once. It was slinking, using extreme caution; I realized that that was the way I must have looked as I approached the carcass. It grabbed the gut pile and pulled it back ten feet in one quick motion, fed on it there a little while, and then left the clearing with a chunk of it.

At the end of the day, in the last of the sunlight, the yearling grizzly came back out. As soon as I saw him again I felt a sense of completion. A part of the bear superstition I had felt, the personal sense of fate, was somehow tempered by his return. I was about to see the peaceful, solitary side of a grizzly.

It was as if, rather than feeding, the young bear was performing a ritual of possession, a rite of entry for its dawning solitary life in the wilderness. The magpies and ravens flew up into the trees at his approach; he lay down by the neck and rolled his shoulder in it, then rubbed the side of his head into it, peaceful and relaxed, as if he were taking a bath in it. He ate a little, twisting his head to get further into the neck, but he was only playing with it, not really trying for big chunks of meat. He got up and sprawled out again in different places around the carcass, licking, rolling a little, rubbing the stink into the fur of his shoulders. It was as if he possessed it totally, enjoyed everything about it, its smell, the maggots, everything. *The stink is mine, the warm meat is mine, this whole thing is mine. Life is good, I'm not hungry, and this is mine for days to come.* The lord of the wilderness, male or female, taking full possession of a pile of meat.

Then he was done, standing a little ways off from the carcass.

I started climbing down the rocks quietly and carefully, trying not to make a sound. My fear was gone. By the time I got to the bottom he was standing near the edge of the timber, doing nothing in particular, looking at nothing in particular. Slowly and silently I walked into view. It wasn't a smart thing to do with any grizzly, but I had sensed this bear all afternoon. He turned his head and looked at me, an aura of silver floating around his head. I felt his presence, I caught the wildness in him. Then he turned away and walked into the timber. When he got in among the trees he went ambling away.

I started the long climb back up, stopping at times, resting, then lowering my head and climbing higher. I looked for a marmot, hoped for a grouse; but there was nothing except rocks and stillness. Behind me somewhere were two big grizzlies, the mother of that yearling and the male she was consorting with, and the two adults were traveling together. They might be together for a day, or many days, the male following her persistently until she is ready to receive his advances, then playing, biting and licking, pawing and rubbing, as they draw closer to the actual coupling. She mates every two years; the yearling she would have fought to the death for a few days before is gone from her consciousness, driven off by the male, exiled by their adult desires. Naturalists who have seen them say they are surprisingly tender and affectionate for the short time that they travel together, sharing the same feed, touching and nuzzling. The rest of the season they might be enemies: over food, over territory, over offspring. The male bear will indeed eat his own young if he gets the chance. This first summer moon passing in the nights above me was the only period in the year when adult bears had much time for each other at all.

They were spending that time down in those long, dense, hazy bottoms leading into the Bob Marshall Wilderness. With any kind of grizzly population at all the carcass I had watched should have had a big bear on it, and the only thing I could come up with was that it was too high. When summer came on they headed out of the high country where they denned, down into the deepest and most tangled bottoms they could find. For the most part they stayed in those jungles until late summer, feeding on roots, insects, and leaves. Only in the fall did they begin to move back up into open places, as their feeding patterns changed with the season.

They were hard to find, hard to even catch a glimpse of; what few of them were left outside the two big national parks. There might be a few left in the Selway, but even in that big stretch of wilderness there had been no official sightings in years.

I clumb along them mountains for three or four days and then I run outta jerky. My feet was gittin' sore from the rocks, an' my legs was a-gittin' weak. The only thing I seed up thar was a few mountain griz, smaller than river griz, runnin' their cubs along them high open meaders down below whar they dug roots, or big lone males layin' in the snowfields sometimes a little higher up. I come up on one big snowfield and seed a track comin' a long ways down it, first I thought it war sign of Fitz, but when I got closer I seed griz hair in the snow along it, and a lot of griz tracks in the mud alongside the snowfield runnin' up toward the top o' the slide track.

It war a mystery to me what they war doin'. Looked like they got up thar to the top and then slipped. I kept on a-goin', an' later on I chanced to look back from another rise. Lo an' behold, there was a griz and a big cub a-climbin' up that path to the top o' the snowfield. What I seed next wouldn't nobody believe 'cept Judas. When she got up to the top o' that slide she set down in the snow, grabbed ahold of her hind legs so's they was up in the air, an' took to slidin' down that snowfield. Snow flyin', just a-whizzin' on down lick'ty split to the bottom. Havin' a high time, she war, jest slidin' fer fun. The cub he follered her down, and then they clumb back up and done it again. I wouldn't believe it less'n I seed it, but thar they was, two griz slidin' down in the snow fer the fun o' it, jest like me an' Fitz done sometimes over in Pierre's Hole, whilst we war waitin' fer the drifts to go down so's we could head out on the spring hunt.

I didn't see no sign of him atall, no smoke, nothin' but them furry groundhogs, an' a ball from my Hawken woulda blowed 'em to pieces. Another day o' climbin', another freezin' night, an' I knowed I was comin' onto starvin' times. A little voice started up inside me, "Forgit it, Gabe, Fitz is gone, nothin' but bones under the stars now. Go on back down to the country you know." An' I'd fight it back, sayin' go on you devil son of a bitch,

Fitz is alive, I know he's alive an' I'm gonna find him. But then I'd doubt myself, that damned voice kept comin' back, mebbe he is gone under, I'd think. An' I'd fight it some more. Stumblin' sometimes, eatin' on flowers 'n' roots. Them mountains seemed more 'n' more crazy to me, lost an' lonely as anywhars I'd set foot. No elk, no deer, an' another big son of a bitch of a ridge ahead to climb.

In the early evening I reached the northern crest of the basin, looking down to a table with a small, lost green lake. As I rested my mind turned from one vision of wild food to another: a grouse bursting from some brush, a marmot standing up straight, a rabbit racing across a flat, a deer down in the lower country. But in a pinch I was only two days away from civilization. I hadn't seen a single grouse, or a rabbit. Fish. But all the lakes so far had been dead, too shallow. This lake looked dead. A hungry range all right. I was getting too weak and tired to climb safely; I was starting to feel careless, light-headed. The vision of a fire and a big leg bone laden with meat kept floating into mind.

Finally I got up and began searching for a way down off the ridge cliff, wanting to get to the lake before dark. All along its edge it was too steep to slide down without falling, but scattered with trees with nearby tops at eye level. Finally I found a trail, and I got out the rope and began letting myself down the steeper pitches, thinking that it could only have been a mountain-goat trail. But then I saw an old elk track. As I worked down it seemed impossible that they could get up it; there were places where a greyhound couldn't jump up. I imagined what a sight it would be to see an elk going up it in a hurry.

When I got to the bottom the steepness fanned out into a long rock slide, and I began picking my way down that. Clouds were building in the west. The lake in the evening gave mirrory reflections of the harsh peaks and snowfields which fed it, immersed beneath the heights of its surroundings; it felt so far-removed and wild beyond the crags of the divide that I walked downward looking about with a dazed feeling, as if I had entered another realm, another era.

But as any good mountain man knows, you don't walk along thinking faraway thoughts when you are hungry and in need of meat. I was brought to my senses by a sharp piping whistle in the rocks down to my right. A long shot away I spotted a marmot rising up on a rock, looking in my direction. It had already seen me and I knew I only had a few seconds. I dropped the rope and raised up my Hawken, steadying the wavering in the sight that the pack caused; it was that situation in the days of the mountain man when a sudden and rare opportunity presents itself to a lone hunter with a hungry stomach, calling for sharp reflexes, and the split-second concentration of a cougar before it leaps.

I missed. Stumbling at times, I made my way down the slide, to the area of boulders and stretches of green grass where it had disappeared. I climbed up into the rocks well above there and sat down, hoping for another shot. While I waited I dusted off my old map for Captain Clark and sketched in the location of this high table I had discovered. I called it Lost Marmot Lake.

From low in the west the sun came out of the clouds, beaming across, making the snowfield shine, lighting up the ragged peaks on the far side of the lake. The lake itself shone clear green, with a chunk of white ice floating near the snowfield. I waited there till the sun went down and the wind turned cold, hoping to roast some meat that night, but the whole colony of them knew I was up there and they just lay low and waited for me to leave. They talked to each other with whistles, asking now and then from afar if I was still there; no answer meant yep, he's right above me. I tried answering with a sharp whistle, and got one to answer back several times, but then it became suspicious and fell silent. Finally I left off and went on down toward the lake.

I found a grassy aisle in the rocks up from the lake, sheltered on the west side by a six-foot wall. More clouds were building and it looked like a storm might hit. I let my eye wander quickly over the area, checking for certain characteristics in what by now had become an unconscious process in the way I chose a campsite: it was low enough not to take a direct lightning hit; there was nothing, neither sliding rocks nor dead trees, that would fall on me while I slept; it was not a natural depression in the ground that would fill with water during a heavy night rain; and it had the six-foot wall for protection against a screaming west wind. I dumped my pack against the wall, always aware of that wind, and started a cooking fire close to the rocks. While I waited for the rice to start boiling I got out the nylon flour sack I carried and dug out a little depression in the flour, then poured some water into it. As the clouds came overhead I stirred the water around in the flour with my finger until it formed the right-sized lump of dough. That dough I stretched out and wrapped around the end of a sharpened stick in a spiral, then stuck the sharp end into the ground so the dough was hanging over the coals to bake. I made two more and set them to baking. While I was waiting I sliced up some chives and hyacinth roots and tossed them in with the rice. When the rice was close to done I broke up the last jerky in the sack bottom and put it into the stew, along with a packet of dried gravy.

I ate with a watering mouth while the clouds grew darker, licking the kettle clean with my finger. When I finished I dug a good hip hole and lined it with moss from the rocks. I was tired, worn out, and I needed sleep. I didn't think a grizzly would be up here at night; too high, too open. In the last of the light I lay there and listened to the incessant sound of the water pouring into the lake from the snowfield, watched the clouds float past a short distance overhead, and felt the high loneliness of it, the cold peaks, the growing might of the range. I told myself I had to concentrate the next day when I climbed down off this table.

Long after midnight I dreamed that a big avalanche of boulders was coming down toward me, rumbling louder and louder as it came closer. I couldn't get away, and it was almost on top of me. At the last moment I woke up suddenly, sweating, breathing hard.

A high wind was lashing the rocks. For a few seconds I looked around to figure out where I was, and then when I realized it the wild loneliness in it all seemed to pierce me for a moment. A dark storm mass was coming in overhead, and the wind that it spawned streamed over the rock wall, bent the stunted over-hanging branches, and careened toward the lake. I unfolded my poncho and tucked it in around me. When the first drops hit it was sleet and blowing snow, and I felt a great sense of relief. I lay with my face covered up and listened to the wet snow swish over the poncho, the hiss of the wind in the high rocks, and drifted back toward sleep. If it stayed frozen I wouldn't get wet.

It did. At dawn there was mist hanging off the peaks, wet snow all around the lake. I got up, dressed, and sneaked up on the slide, hoping for a mormot to come out. I waited hidden in some trees for a long time, but none of them showed, or whistled. Finally I packed up my outfit and made lonely tracks around the edge of the lake, feeling lost in a way, feeling the hunger in it all.

Come to the ridge and I seed birds circlin' down below. My heart took a drop. War it old Fitz, wolf meat now, bones under the stars? I went on down and it war a dead black bear, a young'un, with four or five bear shits on top him. They warn't eatin' on him; why they was a-shittin' on him I don't know. I went back up, my knees hurtin' now from all them freezin' creeks I set my traps in up and down the mountains, an' I'm thinkin' lonely thoughts, mebbe my time was come. Mebbe the north country buried Fitz, and mebbe it'll bury old Gabe. Them rivers in my bones, the Marias, the Yellerstone sparklin' in the summer sun, the Big Horn east of the Crows, and the cottonwoods turnin' yellow along the Missoura on the fall hunt— mebbe they was jest mem'ries locked inside me now. I dreamed of a buffler feast along the Marias, me an' Fitz eatin' boudins an' hump ribs till we couldn't eat no more. Seemed like my spirit was down in my moccersins, and they war gittin' holes in 'em from the rocks. When I hit the bottom of that ridge I looked up and the top was out of sight, looked like it ended in the clouds. The thought hit me, I can't do 'er, I'm done. But I started in. I put one foot ahead of t'other and I started in climbin', not thinkin' of nothin' 'ceptin' my feet. Lost track o' time. It war like I was climbin' my past, climbin' back into my past. My bones was near empty, but I kept 'em movin', step after step. All I knowed was to keep plantin' my feet. In my mind I seed them rivers.

When I looked over the edge of the table there was a cliff of several hundred feet, a thin waterfall spilling over the edge. Down below lay a huge and deep lake, a long one, set lengthwise away from the divide. I started down, walking the terraces which angled down from the cliff, the bottom of the drainage close to a thousand feet away. It was steep and rugged, harrowing in some places. When I was about halfway down I got to a place where I needed the rope. I reached back onto my pack for it, and it wasn't there.

My mind jumped back to my camp, and from there back to the shot at the marmot. I had left it there, the night before. It was at least three hours away.

My heart sank, giving way to a numb feeling. I was halfway down, and anywhere from here on down I could get stuck. I sat down and stopped thinking, staring out across the valley toward the massive ridge on the other side. My body energy was low, I didn't have the spirit to deal with what faced me. I just blanked it out and sat there looking at the top of the far ridge. It was while I was doing that that I saw one of the tiny white rocks up there move.

I pulled out my spyglass, and through it I began to see mountain goats, two, four, several young ones, more adults, fourteen, maybe sixteen in all. When I saw that my mouth began to water.

I didn't know if I would do it, but I had new energy. I got out the handful of rawhide laces I carried and began tying them together with square knots, forming a cord about twenty feet long. I'd get down this son of a bitch all right, and when I did I'd cross the bottom of the drainage and see if I could get up above those goats.

Steep ledges and scraggly timber: lowering my pack down with the cord and then climbing down big cracks in the rock, jumping down into a ten-foot snowdrift and walking the crest; sliding down a steep shale drainage which opened up toward another chute. Two hours of it and I stumbled down into the bottom, amazed to see that the huge lake was now hidden seven hundred feet above me in a nearly vertical climb, itself on a massive table, another thin waterfall spilling over the edge. It was a wild drainage; there were no human signs, no sign of a trail that I could see.

The bottom, which looked open and inviting from above, turned out to be a tortuous maze of snowbrush and thick wet bushes. I fell halfway into a pouring little creek and pulled myself up into the snowbrush on the other side. The rocks were all wet and slick. The brush was over my head at times, tangles of two-inch branches which wound in and out of each other in patterns that seemed increasingly fiendish, as if they were trying to get me. By the time I got across to where the other ridge began to rise I was soaked to the chest and breathing hard, sweating, my nerves jangled by the wet and clinging brush. But I had stayed out of sight of the goats.

I started up after I got my wind back, angling to my right. It was a climb. I couldn't see the goats but I had picked out a rock tower as a bearing point, and I used that as I worked across and up. But then I had to angle through dense timber for a long time, using the compass, and I lost sight of it. It was hard; the cords in my neck were burning and I was seeing stars sometimes when I stopped. But this was my dream, the calling I had felt, the heart of what I had been hoping for in these trips. To travel wild, to eat wild, to go into it with a gun and a knife and survive on my own, hunt if I was hungry, live off the wild. And up ahead were the goats. I kept on climbing, not knowing what I was going to do.

The sun was sinking into the west by the time I made the top. I was a half mile down the ridge from the tower, but the wind was in my favor. I started up toward it, the ridge massive, walking quietly, still unsure of what I was going to do; just going on the instinct to get close to them, fairly certain that they hadn't seen me. When I got up to the tower I crept up to the edge and looked over, but they weren't there. I drew back out of sight and went another ten minutes up the ridge, looking again. No goats. I walked up some more, my spirit beginning to fade, and took another look.

They were grazing another two hundred yards up, spread out so that I couldn't see all of them, not far off the top. I pulled back and picked out a rock formation directly above them, and began sneaking along the top. I made certain that I didn't turn any rocks as I walked, didn't crunch any gravel. The wind was still good. When I reached the rock pile I lowered my pack to the ground and went down on my stomach, crawling slowly over the gravel with my Hawken. When I neared the edge I slowed down so that my head was close to the gravel.

When I finally saw them none of them was looking in my direction; they were about two hundred feet down and grazing gradually up the ridge to my right. A lone goat, maybe a billy, stopped to chew and look down the mountainside, into the wild valley below. The young played like lambs, butting clumsily, romping in absurd little leaps. There was a sense of calmness and peace in the adults, as if they were safe in their own element and knew it. They knew that hunting season was closed.

And I knew that I had come as close to the myth as my feelings about the seventies would allow.

I clumb to my feet atop that ridge and looked up into the blue, and when I done that I seed a swarm o' stars up thar in the daylight like the Milky Way, so's I war gonna topple over. I grabbed ahold of a rock and looked down again to the other side to steady my eyes, and what I seed there stopped me in my tracks.

Thar was a white-furred, four-legged creature with black horns standin' there lookin' at me!

I never seed anything like it. I didn't know if I war in a dream, or if it war a spirit, or if I was already a-dyin' and on my way down to the coal pits, an' it'd come to show me the way. It stood thar with long silky hair, them black spiked horns, an' dark brown eyes that was gentle and curious-like. It didn't show no fear atall; it jest stood there lookin' straight at me with them friendly eyes, like it wanted to know what I was. I couldn't stop lookin' at them eyes, nor feelin' its friendliness.

It warn't me, Gabe, that cocked my Hawken, for I war a-caught in them eyes. It warn't me neither that raised up and froze that front sight in behind the shoulder, for I was lost in its friendliness. Mebbe it was my belly, mebbe it was fourteen years a-huntin' in the Shinin' Mountains. I didn't think it out, nor will it, nor plan it fast like that, and it warn't me that tetched off the charge when I knowed I had it dead. But it was me when the smoke come out the barrel.

The ball hit square on, knocked it over into the dirt. A look o' terror come into its eyes then, and it give a squeal and begun to kickin' lightnin' fast, trying to run. It was done for and it knowed it; there was fear o' death in them eyes now, friendship changed to terror, and its whole life was makin' a last run through its body. Somethin' broke in me seein' it, I didn't want to kill it, I didn't even know what it war. Then its lungs was fillin' with blood, blood was comin' out its mouth, and it was all finished. The life drained out'n its eyes till they was glazed, and it lay there like a rock, the wind blowin' through its fur.

Don't know what it was nor what I felt, but I set down next to it and the tears spilled onto my pants. Mebbe the hunger, the damned loneliness o' them mountains. Mebbe it war tradin' its life for mine, when it war a friendly creature, when it wanted to live jest as bad as I did. I dunno. Mebbe it war the wind blowin' through its fur. I wished I could borrer some meat off'n it and put it back up on its feet and have it run off.

Thar was a bunch more of 'em with young that scattered down below when I fired the shot. They was gone now. This one had long silky hair, big as a sheep but leaner, hooves like a deer. I never seed the like of it. Whatever it was, it warn't a spirit.

Old Gabe warn't on his way to the coal pits yet, by thunder! He'd see them rivers agin.

I opened it up and pulled the guts out on the ground—same workin's as a deer. Warm an' steamy, blood on my arms. I cut little chunks off'n the liver and dipped 'em in the bile sack—bile was greener than buffler bile—an' et 'em warm whilst I was skinnin', and my stomach turned over an' growled and begun to wake up. I cut off a wisp o' that fur and put it in my medicine sack, and I cut off a scrap o' hide to carry with me. Didn't eat the heart o' that creature this time; put it up on a rock whar an eagle might carry it away. After I cut a hind leg loose I built a big fire right up thar on top o' that ridge, Injuns be damned, and nestled the leg bone into the flames. Soon it war a-sizzlin' and drippin', and I war tearin' it off with my teeth. Tasted strange, but it was fresh meat.

Sun went down, the sky turned green and the first couple stars come out, and I war still eatin' away, jerkin' strips to cure on the rocks when I warn't cuttin' a mouthful. I felt the spirit of life comin' back into my bones, and it war good. I felt a myst'ry that evenin', the same myst'ry them Injuns smoked their pipes to. It war in that green sky with a star or two over the mountains, the stillness settlin' in on the horizon, and it war in the evenin' wind comin' from afar. It war in the wood cracklin' and burnin' in the fire, the grass bendin' gentle on the last breezes of the day, and it war in the hot juices drippin' into my beard and a-warmin' my stomach. Couldn't put a name on it, but it was thar in all I could see that night, a spirit that I knowed war good. I didn't try to dig into it or figger it out; I jest set thar eatin', a-feelin' it. And while I was a-feelin' it, I happened to look down the valley, an' way down, jest over the timber, I seed a smudge o' blue smoke, hangin' thar in the quiet of the evenin'.

It war Fitz. I jumped up, hopped over the fire, tore off my hat, and give a yell at the top of my lungs. "Fitzpatrick, you flint-boned son of a bitch! I'm a-comin'! Aye, I'm a-comin'!" Tears come to my eyes, I knowed it war him. He war eight mile down the valley but I yelled to him anyway, runnin' down that ridge and a-wavin' my hat. "Aye, it's me, Gabe! Hold on, I'll git to ye!"

Didn't sleep much that night; packed up the meat and tended the fire, dozed now and then, woke up and ate some more. Hoped he warn't tore up bad. Old Fitz had hickory in him, hickory and flint. He'd make 'er through all right.

Come light enough to see I marked whar he was and hit off down the ridge. Thar were new muscle in my legs and I was a-clippin'. I figgered to git to him afore the day war out. Spirit o' that meat war in my bones.

THE FIRST STARS were out, and the sky was turning green. I watched the goats feed gradually uphill away from me; it looked like they would bed somewhere near the top about a thousand yards further up. All the adults had horns; some of them still had patches of winter fur on the rear end. The kids were very small, about a third the size of their mothers, and life was new and easy to them, a constant round of small explorations. They would sniff around here and there, nibble at something, give a meaningless leap; then hang around some, butt heads, and look stuporously at their surroundings. Every so often one of them would realize that its mother had grazed a good distance away from it, and it would give a bleat and break into a headlong run to catch up with her.

They had been born about the same time as the elk, and under much the same pattern: the female leaving her yearling and withdrawing to a secluded and remote birth place. The kids were on their legs and nibbling green things by the time they were four or five days old, although at that age they walked directly underneath the mother whenever she moved. Golden eagles tried to knock them off high ledges when they strayed far enough away from her protection, and coyotes stood up on high vantage points early in the birth moon and scanned the country for a goat herd.

They ran well now, although with an exaggerated sense of urgency which made them look a little ridiculous. When they caught up to their mothers they settled down immediately, their alarm vanishing, and once again began sniffing and exploring, nibbling; their hair fuzzy, snowy, as fresh-looking as the white clouds of the deepening summer. Baby goats under the first summer moon, drifting toward the second; the hyacinths were blooming under their hooves now, yarrow was just starting to flower, thimbleberry bushes were flowering, spirea bushes were pushing out soft pink sprays, mountain bluebells coming with the strengthening legs of elk calves. Sweet vetch blooming red, and mountain ash just breaking into clusters of tiny white flowers, future berries high in carbohydrates: for elk, grouse, birds, and people. Bears. The Moon When the Bears Run Together. When new plants were full of smells.

The spirit running through it all, like a taste of honey, like an underground spring; the beauty in the earth, life rising from it. A leg of goat roasting on the fire, and a feeling of mystery in the stars up and down the mountains, from Taos to Wind River, up to the Crows.

It was true that Gabe had never seen a mountain goat before, indicative of how rarely the mountain men got up into the high mountains. The existence of mountain goats was like a rumor or a myth to them. His story about the grizzly sliding down the snowfield was also true; many naturalists and hunters have seen it and recorded it down through the years. Again in that act there is the haunting hint of human intelligence, human feelings. The mildness and curiosity in the mountain goat was also a true characteristic of that animal. I had one look at me like that in the Bitterroots once.

It was wild meat that made a mountain man. Big game. I knew that now in a way that I never could have known without feeling the hunger. Wild meat put wind in their sails, steam in their boilers; it put the breeze into their boasts, the glint into their far visions, the courage into their hearts. I had felt it through all the miles. They killed big game when they were hungry, carried what they thought they'd need and left the rest behind. The wolves and bears cleaned the remains down to the bones. And I had felt why that was necessary. A human traveling in the wilderness for extended periods had to rely on big game; there wasn't enough fat or bulk in plants or small game to keep up with the steady drain of energy that came with exposure, fear, loneliness, and exertion. It took big infusions of meat to keep up with it, face it day after day.

Buffler. The mountain men, like the Indians, lived off buffalo. It was a complete diet in itself; no scurvy after months of straight buffler. They ate the tongue, the heart, the liver, the fat, the intestines, the kidneys, the bile, and the marrow as well as all the meat. They ate elk, deer, moose, or antelope to vary their diet, or as the country they were in dictated, but they lived mainly off of buffler. They found them following the big rivers. Once in a great while, in a fix that was far away and high, one of them killed a mountain goat.

I got up from my hiding place and stretched my aching muscles. The goats didn't see me; dusk was closing down on them from a deep mirror-green sky. Mountain goats don't have much oil in their hair, and so are very vulnerable to freezing rainstorms. They take shelter in caves whenever they can. Old-time forest rangers used to be able to tell when the storm was coming by whether or not a certain band of goats disappeared from a mountaintop. These goats were bedding high tonight and the sky was clear; a few bright stars were shining over the Swan Mountains.

I built a fire, baked a biscuit, and made stew with what I had. As the darkness became complete a dense forest of stars came out over the ridgetop, the brightest of the whole trip. I sat up and watched the sky, tending the fire and drinking coffee. It was high and open up on that ridge, the heavens were close. Shooting stars streaked across now and then. The Milky Way was a great soft cloud winding down the sky, as if the darkness were throbbing with its light. What other worlds, what structures, what movements were hidden in that soft, brilliant maze of lights? Atoms were like solar systems, molecules were like galaxies. What came next? Down here the beating heart came next. What was the drift, the flow, in the stars? What kind of rivers, what kind of veins?

The next century would be it—the end of the earth, or the beginning of space exploration. Worldwide cooperation and pooling of resources to launch a technological Columbus into the sea of space; nuclear power for fuel into space; colonies, new resources, new solar systems to inhabit. A nice dream. New mountains, a steamboat full of jerky.

The exploration of the stars.

Only the mountain goats survived the holocaust, and continued to live in their mild and curious manner, at an altitude above the contamination.

Bridger. The exploration of the spine of the North American continent. Fuel of the mountain men.

A mildly beating heart. Curious.

What was up thar, amongst the stars?

Old Gabe, and the spirit of the mountains.

The timber in that bottom was bad 'nough to scare the fleas off'n a greenhorn, but I jest took my time and climbed right on down through it. When I come out to whar the creek emptied into a north-flowin' creek I seed the smoke ahead through the trees and I got light-headed, gittin' so close.

I moved up slow so's he wouldn't blow me to hell thinkin' I war an Injun, but when I come into view of it I seed the smoke war comin' out'n a hole in the ground with a bunch of bushes around it. Like a big crack in the ground it war, like somethin' in the Yellerstone country. But it war blue wood smoke comin' out. I crep' up on it, not knowin' what I war gonna see. When I peeked over the edge there sat Fitzpatrick, twenty feet down. One of his pantlegs was missin' clear up to his hip, that bare leg skinny, his arms skinny, sittin' thar a-starin' at the rock wall across from him without no movement 'cept his breathin'. His cheeks was all drawed in around his skull, his eyes was dim, an' he jest set there a-holdin' on to one arm, lookin' into the rock. Lookin' at his death he war, an' still a-holdin' on, and he'd been that way for two or three days now. He war as close to death on this day as a man ever wanted to come.

I says quiet-like, "Aye, Fitz, it's me, Gabe. I come to pull ye out."

For a time he didn't move. Then his head come up slow, and he looked at me without seein', squintin' his eyes. They begun to focus, an' he recognized me, a little spark showed in his eyes. His mouth come open and he gasped somethin'. He looked up with that burnin' glint comin' back into his eyes, the old glint o' life that I knowed, and says to me in a croakin' voice: "What took ye so goddamn long?"

It war Fitz, an' he war a mountain man down to the flint in his bones. Give me joy.

I tied my rope off and clumb on down to him with some of the roasted meat, and when he seed that tears come to his eyes, he held it in front of his face like he couldn't believe he war seein' it agin. Then he begun to eatin', not sayin' a word but jest chewin' and swallowin', his throat makin' animal sounds. I cut him small chunks so's he wouldn't be heavin' it up right off. He was favorin' his hatchet-throwin' arm; broke mebbe when he fell.

One look around an' I knowed the story. He'd come through them bushes a little careless from buckin' all that deep timber and fell square into it. He hit bottom plenty hard, cracked that arm and maybe some ribs. It war like a big crack in the rock, only too wide to bridge acrost, and too steep to climb with a bad arm. There was an underground spring flowin' up out'n the rock at the bottom, or he'd a died o' thirst. He'd et up most of the moss off the rocks that he could reach, and near all the greenery growin' down at the bottom. Thar was a deep layer o' needles and sech that he'd set to smolderin', and most o' that was burned up. He'd cut his pantleg up into strips an' made a rope, tied a rock onto the end of it. The devil only knowed how many times he'd throwed that up and out, tryin' to catch it on a root. Reckon if'n he did catch it he war goin' to pull hisself up out'n thar with his teeth. He'd scritched the days he spent down thar into the rocks, an' thar was more scritches than I care to think about.

When he got done eatin' I pulled him out. Evenin' come and I kilt a deer down by the creek, built a big fire, and he et some more, liver an' heart, some kidney fat. He war a-comin' back all the time, lookin' around at the light and the trees, an' he took to cussin' that hole out steady as he ate. He cussed that hole till after the sun went down, fillin' it up. Then he set by the fire feelin' better. His arm was broke all right—he heard the bone crack when he hit, but it didn't need settin' and it war a-healin' already. We talked about gittin' horses out o' them Flatheads. Hoped my charger was still there.

Come dark an' he's startin' to feel like his old self. Stars come out over the trees, an' he looked at me with that long glint in his eyes and pointed off to the east. "Thar's a big river in thar."

I perked up. "How so?"

"Big as the Yellerstone! She's big an' wild, she shines, an' the timber's so God-awful high ya break your neck lookin' up at the top of it. I war the first white man ever to lay eyes on that river, ain' nobody else ever seed it!" His eyes was shinin' like meteors.

"An' beaver?"

"Beaver shines plenty. We can git horses in thar, not the way I come in but another way. I larnt it from the Flatheads." He give me a nod. Then he pointed off to the northeast, stickin' me with his gaze. "Yon lies the headwaters o' the Marias."

"Bullshit."

"Sartin! Eight days, Injun trail to the buffler country. We can git horses through thar. I got the route all in my head."

Be damned. I always wondered what country lay to the west o' the Marias. Now I war in it.

An' that war Fitz. Away he'd go off on his own, an' when he come back thar'd be a stretch o' new country to look into, a body could bet on it.

We set up an' talked most of the night, him roastin' chunks o' fat on a stick, tellin' me what it war like down in the hole. He tole me he knowed I was comin', all them days he knowed I was comin'. I tole him I always knowed he war alive. I asked him what he made of it, an' he jest shrugged an' said somethin' about good medicine an' the Shinin' Mountains.

We slept the next day, et some more, an' the day after that we started out. It war five days up to the camp o' the Flatheads what with Fitz's sore arm, an' another two days o' dickerin' an' wavin' that whiskey flask around afore we got the horses. I got my charger back, some new moccersins, and Fitz got him a set of old leggin's. We figgered between the two of us we had enough powder to git down to the Yellerstone an' beyond, if'n we didn't have to fight no Blackfeet. We set off with the new moon, a few days ahead o' them Injuns. Figgered we could drop back if'n we had to. Fitz war full o' fire over the new country we

*was seein', takin' it in keen. Me, I war a-dreamin' of the Marias,
the open country lower down, buffler fleece spittin' into a fire.
The open plains an' snowy mountains stretchin' down to the
Yellowstone. An' the mighty Crow Mountains, that turned a body
back jest by the sight o' 'em. They was a-callin' to me come fall, I
could feel it in my bones.*

AND I WAS on the way out, with that lesson about wild meat
under my belt. I followed Shaw Creek north for about ten miles,
seeing some more big grizzly tracks, and then hit off up a deep
valley to the west, toward the top of the Swans and civilization.
I was thinking about the Selway, remembering its beauty, feeling the ache of it. Feeling the coming of the eighties. And something Emil Keck told me, who had lived in it for eight years,
summer and winter, and carried seventy-pound loads on his
back wherever he went. "They ought to keep the goddamned
horses out of here. They tear up the trails, they do more damage
than ten people on foot. They bring in luxuries, and then the
garbage winds up along the trails. People don't understand what
this kind of country means when they come in on a horse with
beds and stoves and all the comforts of home. They ought to
walk it. The only horses they ought to let in here are for people
who are handicapped or too old to carry a load."

He was close to sixty. He was right; the few wild areas left
were too fragile for the freighter traffic of the horse associations
and outfitters. The high lakes were much too fragile. There were
too many people now, and the impact of horses was too great.
But the horse lobby was a powerful political lobby, and traditionally horses were a way of life in the West. The mountain
men explored the Rockies on horseback. And so the last of the
wild mountain trails were filling up with cigarette butts and gum
wrappers. Meanwhile the Forest Service was busy counting pine
beetles for the big timber corporations.

The peaks of the Swan divide scissored up into the green
evening sea where the sun had gone, aged, mountains of the
moon spilling moon sand, summer snowfields, windswept, rising
like earth gods against the indifference of the evening sky. I saw
the saddle I would go over. I wondered if a grizzly would get
me in my last night in the Swans. Up at the top of the Swans

there was a hint of the infinite. One of the peaks looked like the back of a dinosaur.

A grizzly didn't get me. The next day I climbed up to the top through the morning, over the snowfields, and up there I felt that hint of the ages, the triumph of the Swans, the hunger that forced me down off the top, mountains of pure green skies, mountains of emptiness, where there were no trails. The top of the Swans would survive the eighties, and the nineties. Somehow they were like mountains of the moon.

I found my way down the other side through a yawning gap that spilled centuries of gravel, a river of rubble, into the next valley. It looked wild and remote, but there were no wild animals in it. I kept watching the far hillside, glassing it, but I didn't see anything except the trail leading back toward the seventies.

Then come the beginnin's of the Marias River, sunshine an' hills and plains stretchin' away as fur as the eye could see. My heart was singin' to see that river. Thar was big eagles fishin' over it in the distance, thar was buffler on the horizon, herds of elk, an' it led a long way down toward the country I loved. It war somethin' to think o' that river reachin' from the Missoura all the way up to the north country o' the Shinin' Mountains—them moon mountains standin' over country that war deep an' wet with big timber an' skeeters—that river a-windin' all the way up to it under a sky that seemed so big an' never-endin', that stretched over a land you couldn't imagine whar the end of it was. It war a feelin' in my heart.

Me an' old Broken Hand, we started out in good weather an' we rode the Marias till we lost track o' the days, eatin' fish sometimes an' a-watchin' the eagles agin the blue sky, feastin' on buffler, splashin' around in the river in the heat of the day, watchin' for griz an' Injun smoke, seein' the hawks in the afternoon sky, jest a-ridin' out over that big country in the sun and the wind. It war some stretch o' country, and thar war a spirit in that river that run all the way through it, tied it all together somehow, give it all life. The river war the blood vein o' that country, an' by it you knowed whar you was.

We rode on an' on. Sometimes we'd git skunky with each

other and split up about a buffler run apart, whatever war safe for the country we war in, an' ride that way without sayin' much, even while we ate, jest a-stayin' to our own thoughts. Then we'd come back together to kill a buffler or somethin', an' git to talkin' about one perticular thing, an' we'd talk that to death, right through the day, by the fire an' on under the stars, an' mebbe into the next day. Heaven and hell usually, what happened when you went under, what hell war gonna be like, smokin' coal pits and the devil pokin' you in the arse with that pitchfork, shovelin' that coal day and night with no rest and no water. We both figured once all the mountain men got down thar we'd git together with the Blackfeet and bust out of the goddamn place, mebbe pile up a mountain of coal till we could get up to the bottom of heaven and git ahold of them boiler pipes and climb up through the floor. Neither one of us wanted to spend eturnity shovelin' coal with some spark-eyed son of a bitch pokin' us in the arse with a pitchfork ever' time we turned around. Fitz had a notion that he was gonna come back as an elk somehow, and once we got up thar he could run free like a big old buck as long as he wanted to, and he'd give us signals so's we wouldn't shoot him. He didn't have much Bible lairnin', and I tried to set him straight about people's souls floatin' around and playin' harps and sech, but he wouldn't have none of it—he war comin' back as an elk and that was that. Pretty soon we'd get skunky over it and he'd ride on ahead, and thar we'd be alone agin for a day or so, our own thinkin' again, alone with that river.

But Lord, I loved it. We rode the Marias on blue sunny days an' days o' far lonely winds, an' it seemed like a country that could never end. They was days when the water sparkled an' the sight o' that river flowin' as fur as you could see into the horizon made a man's heart swim. Old Broken Hand, he loved the Marias too, he war full of a far spirit when he was a-ridin' it. We rode it in the rain, we set under big cottonwoods and watched them blue summer storms come in the afternoon, full o' lightnin' an' thunder. Ever'day I held on to it an' the feelin's it give me. Heaven or hell, the Shinin' Mountains war fine by me. If'n I had any choice about it I'd spend eturnity in the Yellerstone country, roamin' up an' down them mighty blue peaks o' the Crow Mountains, jest a-seein' what I could see. I couldn't imagine heaven bein' better than that.

Struck me along the Marias River that if you took them two notions o' heaven an' hell and put 'em together so's you had one thing, 'twould be a person ridin' on this here earth. Sure enough, 'twould be a person on this old earth.

FORT HOLLYWOOD

THE STREETS was a-glitterin' when I got back in. Shines of chrome and roaring engines and honks and waves and squealing tires, a new gun shop, a new fashion store, more people thronging the sidewalks at the noon hour, giving you those dirty looks. *Hey, turd, are you rich? Well, I am.*

By Jesus, it was starting to get on my nerves.

I ate a big beefsteak and a bunch of ice cream, soaked in the tub, and read the news from the States. That new President had a smile like a chipmunk in a butter factory. Every other page he was grinning out at you like he knew something special, like it was going to start raining quarters out of the sky any day now. Nights he got on the phone to the Rockefellers and found out how they wanted it, and the next day he got in front of the cameras and told people all about his new plan. Sometimes his smile was like that of an angel.

Dark skies over the Shining Mountains, and the eighties were coming on. The son of a bitch was like an ant smiling down from the top of a runaway tank.

I took a lot of time unpacking my pack, looking over each smoke-stained article, smelling the body stink in the back of the pack, the filthy socks; feeling the caked grit and sweat in my shirt after I had put on a clean one. It all stunk like hell. Mountain men must have stunk to a phenomenal degree. All year they must have stunk, but especially toward the end of winter.

It had been about a thirty-pound pack and I had gone hungry. The truth of Colter's thirty-pound winter pack was coming in on me. It was a pack that depended upon a steady intake of rare bloody meat and juicy fat. The few survival tools he carried related directly to that, or its preparation: flint and steel, hatchet, skinning knife, powder, extra shot. I doubted if he even carried a kettle, for even a small brass kettle must have weighed close to five pounds, maybe more.

Night after night he speared his meat on a sharpened stick and roasted it over the fire. Wild meat. It kept him from freezing to death, from giving up and dying somewhere out in the cold winds. It nourished his spirit, refueled his urge to explore, gave him the courage to go further, and further yet, into an unexplored mountain wilderness.

At first I had thought that he made that five-hundred-mile trip completely on his own. Now I realized that that wasn't true, that it was wintering big game that determined his route. Wild meat. He was looking for Indians to inform them about the new cottonwood log fort at the mouth of the Big Horn; Indians wintered where big game wintered. He followed after the big-game herds all winter.

I would start into the Crows when the elk began their rut; I had some time before then, so I got in my mule and drove east along the Yellowstone, toward the country where Colter started his journey. I rode for two hours—close to three days' ride on a horse—along the head of the Crow Range, and I began to get a feel for its depth. It was not only a long range, it was fifty miles wide, scattered all the way through with 10,000- and 11,000-foot peaks. The Beartooths swung down into it and joined it, but from what I saw I couldn't get the lay of their separate formations. The two ranges merged in a rugged landmass of peaks. He crossed it in January or February.

Once past the head of the range I swung down into the Big Horn Basin, an ancient seabed about sixty miles across, running a hundred miles down into Wyoming. Badland country; sage, endless waves of barren-looking hills. The front of the Crow Range formed its western border. Colter climbed up into the Pryor Mountains to the northeast and looked a hundred miles down this huge windswept basin, picking out landmarks like Heart Mountain, memorizing the lay of its bordering mountains, looking for smoke, looking for herds of buffalo, noting rivers and creeks, picking out possible routes. Taking time to memorize it all. Way down to the south he saw the Owl Creek Mountains, a low-lying spur range. That was where he would finally leave the basin.

Coming off the Pryors he worked his way down and across the basin, the first white American from the East to make an extended penetration into Wyoming. On the western side the Indians were camped in the sheltered canyons which led out of the basin and up into the Crow Mountains; buffalo, elk, and antelope roamed out where the sweet grass stood thickest and the cottonwoods along the rivers offered bark and bedding places. He worked his way from one winter encampment to another like a traveling salesman, showing the Indians Manuel Lisa's trading goods and telling them where his fort was, resting in their tepees, maybe getting pemmican from them, hot stew, seedcakes.

But he was also getting the lay of the Wind River country ahead of him from those Indians. They drew him maps on old skins, on the earthen floors of their tepees. They told him whether or not he would find buffalo, and where he might find other Indians. They mapped out his route for him as he went.

When he hit the place where the Shoshone River comes out of the Crow Mountains—now the city of Cody, Wyoming—he found hot springs and geysers. He had no idea what they were or what caused them; his early-nineteenth-century mind was fully open to the superstition they held, and he was emotionally shaken by them. In all the windswept immensity and loneliness of that vast basin he felt as if he had stumbled onto the back door of hell. When he finally returned he told the other trappers about it in such awestruck terms that his descriptions were passed on almost verbatim, and later picked up by Washington Irving and recorded in his book *The Rocky Mountains*. "This last mentioned place was first discovered by Colter," Irving wrote, "a hunter belonging to Lewis and Clark's exploring party, who came upon it in the course of his lonely wanderings, and gave such an account of its gloomy terrors, its hidden fires, smoking pits, noxious streams, and the all-pervading 'smell of brimstone,' that it received, and has ever since retained among the trappers, the name of 'Colter's Hell'!"

Thus the real Colter's Hell was about sixty miles east of Yellowstone Park, at Cody, Wyoming. It was the historical backdrop of the trip I was about to take. I looked over the edge of the canyon outside town and saw some bubbles rising up in the green water of the river. That and the sulphur smell were the only evidence of thermal activity now; the geysers were extinct.

There was a stadium nearby, and the town was famous for a mighty buffalo and Indian killer.

Buffalo meat fueled Colter's spirit when he got to the end of the basin and the Owl Creek Mountains, and the Indians told him the way to go. At that point his "job" was finished; even Manuel Lisa's financially oriented heartstrings would have called him to return and patted him on the back for a job well done. He had covered enough cold country, visited enough Indians. But Colter had enough meat, he had been eating large and regular quantities of buffler, and the Indians had told him that if he crossed the Owl Creeks he would find a good-sized river that led a long way up, to three huge spirit mountains, and there he might find other wintering Indians. He was well fed so far, and in his spirit was the historical thrill, the *lure*, of standing before country that no white man he knew of had yet set foot in. Vast and wild mountains, the winds and the Crows, stood shining before him in the winter sun.

So he took off, over the Owl Creeks, and up the long grade of Wind River toward Jackson Hole and the Tetons. He might have killed a moose while he was snowshoeing the hundred miles he traveled up that river, maybe in the willow flats which began to open up as he neared the top. Maybe a moose somewhere along the upper end of that river made the difference between his going on or turning back. Whatever happened, Colter went on. When he finally topped the pass he looked across and saw the three biggest and most spectacular mountains he had ever seen in his life.

Spirit peaks. Looking so high and wild, so beautifully triumphant with a few wispy clouds in all the winter remoteness, that it was as if he had discovered the hidden soul of the Rockies. A place like no other he had ever seen, or would see. That was another part of the legacy I was starting in after, the region I was entering. It was the heart of the Rockies, a place like no other.

By then he was 250, 300 miles away from his home base. He had been living out in the open for a month and a half, carefully measuring out his powder and shot. And at that point, my friend, would you or I, if we were standing in Colter's winter moccasins, alone in the middle of that winter, would you or I have decided to snowshoe over the top of those great mountains, just to see what was on the other side? Even if we saw the distant plumes of smoke that signaled the winter encampment of the Crow Nation—would we have dared to go on and cross over the Tetons?

It is a question which haunts. John Colter did it, over one of the passes where a highway is now and down into Pierre's Hole, then back over the Tetons and straight up through the heart of Yellowstone Park. That was perhaps the most amazing part of his journey; how he managed to find his way up through the seventy-mile maze of the park with six or eight feet of snow on the ground, keeping himself in meat, and then back out through the Crow Mountains and into the Big Horn Basin again.

And finally to walk back into the little cottonwood log fort, with spring coming on, and stun Manuel Lisa and the boys with his return from the dead.

It was the kind of trip I had dreamed of making ever since I came to the Rockies. I drove up through Yellowstone Park to the northern end, then turned east, the way he had gone, along the Lamar River and on to Soda Butte Creek. It was high plains country, open and rolling, burnt to the color of wheat in the last of the summer's heat, the Crow Mountains beginning to rise slowly just to the north. I decided that this was where I would start, leaving off from the last leg of Colter's trail and heading north up the range toward its beginning, sixty miles away. Gabe was starting in up there; for some reason we were traveling in opposite directions. When I looked up that way I felt a tingling in the back of my neck, fear starting to rise. I had my own superstitions, and my time in the Crows was drawing near.

Old Sixties was starting to cough and stumble, so I headed back toward Fort Hollywood. By the time I rode in it was wheezing pretty bad, so I put it out by the shed and put a blanket over its headlights. I tied it down with a good strong rope; damn mule had a tendency to jump up on bandwagons when they come through town, and now it was paying hell for it. Its coat was all chipped up with the wounds of the seventies; everywhere I went people was catcalling and jeering at old Sixties now. It even went so far that the wife of an Exxon executive visiting Fort Hollywood threw an empty champagne bottle at it and busted one of the side windows. Seemed to me that jumping on bandwagons was an understandable crime, since everyone was conditioned to do it since the first grade. Mule mighta jumped on bandwagons, but it had other qualities that kept me riding it, courage, a concern for the future, good qualities that it seemed like people was erasing. By God, there was something to believe in with that mule. The way things was going now there wasn't jack shit to believe in. Ruination.

"*Hold on, old friend*," I whispered in the wing window, tightening its resolve nuts, spraying some starting ether into its awareness of the Third World. "*You'll make it through.*"

IN THE DAYS that followed, the Crow Mountains started to take hold of me. I packed slowly, a little each day, measuring things, preparing in a preoccupied sort of way. I was coming closer to facing it, what the Crow Mountains meant to me, and the closer it got, the more uneasy I became.

A spirit in those mountains? *Something that wasn't human, something which dark clouds and lightning bolts and grizzly claws were only imperfect attempts to symbolize, to offer a hint of its feeling.* Something dark and formless, something irrational. Something I couldn't pin down.

As the days of going drew closer I began to tighten up inside, to feel that fear. I looked around my lodge with hungry eyes, seeing things in a different light. I didn't know if I was going to come back out. I began to cast about irrationally for someone to go in with me, to ward it off. I kept reaching for that way out. But underneath it I understood I couldn't do that. I knew I had to face it.

Then one morning around the time the first frosts were starting to come down I got word that the elk were starting to bugle. I spent the rest of the day looking around my lodge, at pictures, letters, familiar things. In the evening I borrowed my cousin's motorcycle and rode up the Yellowstone along the front of the Crows, up the valley of paradise. It was the valley of the Hollywood stars now. The mountains rose up huge and strange dark blue against the evening sky, dwarfing everything, and I rode along through the washing air feeling numb in spirit. I took them in without any conscious thoughts, but with a deep feeling of humility, almost supplication. They humbled me to numbness that night, beyond thought. *I only wanted to pass through them.*

The next day I caught a ride down toward Yellowstone. It had frosted again. The elk had just begun to bugle, to roam restlessly in the dawning heat of their mating fever. With that, the summer was gone.

I said goodbye to Fitz at the big bend in the Yellerstone. We'd hit the tail end o' Rendezvous, romanced and drunk ourselfs blind, and now he war takin' a good-sized bunch to try Three Forks for the fall hunt. I had my mule packed with coffee and flour, ax, salt, traps, tradin' goods, plenty o' powder an' lead—enough fixin's to get me right on through the winter if need be.

Fitz pulled in his horse and squinted at me. "Whar ye bound for?"

I give a shrug. Hard to tell him my heart warn't in trappin' this fall, nor the funny feelin' I had. Finally I says, " 'Sarkee, I reckon. Crows."

"Be ye winterin' thar?"

"Mebbe. And ye?"

He pushed his wolverin' fur back on his head and scritched his hair a little. "Pierre's Hole. Down the Snake, I reckon. Mebbe through that big hole in the mountains. Ain't sure yet."

"I rode the big hole when the elk was droppin'."

"How was she?"

"Clear and shinin'. Tetch o' huntin' sign was all, no big war parties."

He nodded. We was both a-lookin' at the Yellerstone as she flowed past, sparklin' with waves and whitewater and sunlight, forever flowin' away outta that valley o' paradise. A blue breeze come upriver, bendin' through the willer leaves, sendin' one or two of them first frost-spotted ones into the river. An' on down toward the Missoura whar I first come up fourteen year ago. Sun war a-burnin' gold, but lower down in the sky. Fall war a lonely time for a mountain man, a time when he had to do some thinkin'. We both set there for a spell, not sayin' nothin', watchin' the river goin' past. I could feel that river in my knees.

Finally I says, "An' come spring?"

"*Down the Wind and up the Bighorn. East side, I reckon, higher up in the mountains.*"

I knowed that country all right. Reckoned I could find him.

We set a while longer. Horses was gittin' restless, an' thar warn't much else to say. Fitz pulled that fur down on his head.

"*Might see ya along the Bighorn, come spring,*" *he says.*

I nodded. "*Watch your topknot over whar you're goin'.*"

"*Yep.*"

And him and the boys rode on out to the west. The way I war a-feelin' I wanted to look back and catch another glimpse o' Fitz, but it never did for a mountain man to look back. I kept on a-goin', settin' my eyes east toward the Crows.

THE
CROW
MOUNTÁINS

FALL, SLOUGH CREEK, SEPTEMBER 8, THE MOON WHEN THE ELK FIGHT

A DAWNING RED SKY, earth light; crossing the creek amid rushing pink waters, bed rocks forever glimmering, climbing up the bank with dripping pants, sneaking slowly into the hushed gray stillness which lay over the woods. A lone pine squirrel rustled somewhere in the leaves; everything else seemed captured in silence, still sleeping behind the bars of early dawn. I moved slowly, looking about from a certain hunger in my psyche, sensing, trying to catch a hint of the mysterious feeling that had haunted me for so long. The first thing I felt was mildness.

It was in the scattered trees, big spiring spruce which were spaced at far intervals, a few lodgepoles mixed among them, and it was in the grass, the open stretches of thick tall grass which lay everywhere through the trees. There were rosebushes scattered along the creek, and the berries were soft red, almost ripe. I nibbled at a few as I went along. Low plants were turning red along the forest floor, others showing splashes of yellow here and there. And it was all filled with a feeling of mildness.

Slowly my confidence began to come back. There was a growing red light in the sky, mildness and openness in the woods all around, and it felt good to me, I felt at home in it, moving silently, sniffing the air now and then, keeping my eyes moving back and forth as I went ahead. I felt for the first time that I belonged to it, belonged to the wild. *It didn't belong to me.* I belonged to it.

And the spirit that the years of the seventies had beaten down wasn't gone; it was still there, and it was rising in me. At last I felt it coming back.

I went higher along the side of the hill till I found an elk trail, and began to follow it. The woods became a little deeper, more shadowy. There was dew in the bear grass; the first bright shafts of sunlight were slicing through the tops of the trees, but it was still quiet and subdued except for the birds. There were grizzlies in these woods, and the awareness of them was constant inside me. I had been feeling a fear of them before I started in, but now I began challenging that feeling, feeling my spirit again, calling it up and telling myself that I believed in myself, that I could deal with my own fate. I would survive. If fate had a bear in store for me, I would survive.

HIGH WINDS began to blow after the sun was well up, strong high winds which made the big spiring spruce sway strangely back and forth against the long blue of the sky. Sometimes I stopped and listened, hearing small branches break away in the trees, the rattling of the withered balsamroot leaves along the ground, the general restlessness of noise that those winds brought to the woods. I understood why horses, deer, and elk got restless in a strong wind. It narrowed down their sense of smell, and it made defense by hearing next to impossible. Easy for something to sneak up on them in a strong wind. I shifted along easily, listening and sensing, keeping my eyes moving all the time, feeling the far hints of change, the slow breaking of a season that seemed to be coming as those winds seethed through the heights of the trees. I felt as if a decade was coming to an end with that wind.

I came upon a small sage-covered hill, and saw where a bear had come over the top flipping rocks as it went, fifteen or twenty of them as it traveled in a straight line across the top of the hill. The indentations where they had lain were still damp, but there were no tracks. I guessed by the size of the rocks it chose that it was a black bear.

I went into the woods again, wind blowing, trees waving back and forth, and kept moving north, up the drainage. The further I went, the fresher the elk sign became. I saw an opening off to the right and when I walked down to it I found a small cliff overlooking the valley. I sat in the needles near the edge for a while, catching the warm pine smell on certain wind eddies, working on my knife. The scrape of steel on whetstone rose into the heat around me and I worked the edge diligently, first one side and then the other, endless circling of my hand, forcing the angle steeper and steeper until it was too sharp to touch with any sort of pressure. I honed the point until it pricked like a needle, so the whole blade would slip into flesh like butter, and then slipped it into its case.

I glassed the valley below. There was a trail across on the other side, a mile or so away, and before long I spotted a small group on horses; two fishermen on foot, and two more fishing down along the creek. So the drainage was heavily used on the trail side. So far I hadn't seen any human sign on this side, outside of some old horse tracks down near the bottom.

The valley was very broad, open and grassy all the way across, with the creek winding back and forth in big loops, leaving white sandbars which shone in the sun. Again I was taken aback at its mild and beautiful air. It was so much the opposite of what I had been expecting that it furthered the sense of mystery I felt for the range. It was a region of mildness and sunlight and glowing color just outside the fires of Yellowstone, hemmed in by dark and forbidding peaks; hidden mildness, grass and sun, as if the dark ruggedness in the exterior of the range were meant to hide its central heartland. I knew the country to the north, where I was headed, was darker, more rugged. What I wanted to know as I sat there and looked at that valley was whether it would let me pass; whether I would pass that spirit I sensed, or whether it would erase me. That was what I was wondering down at the bottom. There seemed to be a spirit in the Crow Mountains.

Don't know what war a-pullin' me, but somethin' in them mountains was a-drawin' me in like a magnet. Rode two days along the Yellerstone till I come near to the mouth of that big river I seed twice before, that come out of 'em flowin' to the south. Big and dark they was, darkness in 'em. Didn't know what the callin' war, but I war a-comin' to it.

Come up over a hill an' I seed Injuns down along the river, packin' up. Looked like Crows; women and children with 'em, as like they was peaceable. I watched for a spell and then of a sudden I recarnized that it war old White Grass and his bunch, who was my friends. They war loadin' meat on their horses and tyin' in their travois, gittin' ready to pull out. I rode down the hill with my Hawken raised up givin' the sign of peace, till they knowed me.

"Runs Like Wind!" they said amongst themselves.

I rode in and we greeted and smoked the pipe, an' I et some fresh elk loin, and we set thar cross-legged talkin' about plews an' whiskey an' the elk hunt he'd jest made. One of his daughters was my favorite woman in all the mountains, Lord knows we had some fun all right, and I was a-flirtin' with her out'n the corner o' my eye an' hopin' we could sneak off somewhars. I give White Grass a mirror an' some flints, for he war a good friend, an' I give that woman some blue beads, an' they all give her hell for it, laughin' an' carryin' on. She didn't care; her face lit up like a candle when she seen 'em. Mountain Lamb was her name, an' pretty she war. Had one busted front tooth whar a brave clubbed her for sassin' off. She warn't rightly named, for she warn't no lamb. I called her Mountain Lion. Take me nigh two packs' worth o' fixin's to buy her from him, the old devil, and I couldn't never seem to get two packs ahead. So we seed each other when the winds blowed.

I asked old White Grass how fur he'd been up the river we was on. He drawed me a map in the river sand, two sleeps' journey, some of the creeks comin' in, the country gittin' higher all the time, an' the big ridge whar they set up racks to dry meat. Then he drawed a lightnin' bolt across the trail from east to west.

"What's that?" I says.

A look of fear come into his eyes. He made a rumbling sound in his throat. He made the sign for a big evil spirit. He shook his hand like the ground was shakin'. His eyes got wild and he made the sign for fire and lightnin', an' he rattled the grizzly claws around his neck. Then he dropped the stick he war holdin' into the river, and made the sign for death. His face turned to stone again.

"I'm a-goin' thar," I said in Crow.

He shook his head quick-like. "You no go there."

"I'm a-goin' thar, an' see."

His eyes turned bright. "You die!"

"I won't die. I'm jest gonna see."

His face turned stony again. "You die."

He got up then, and went to his horse, diggin' around in his war bag for somethin'. The rest of 'em had all been lissenin', and they was standin' around sorta hushed, starin' at me like I war *already laid out on a block o' ice. Mountain Lamb Lion turns her back on me. Begun to give me the jitters, though I didn't let on.*

White Grass come back with an old bone-handled knife. It war sacred to him, a part o' his medicine. He give it to me with both hands, slow-like. "You good friend of White Grass, you never lie to him. Take this knife with you. Even though White Grass not there to bury Runs Like Wind, even though your bones turn white under the stars, I will see you in the hunting grounds beyond the sky."

Didn't say another word. Mountain Lamb Lion give me a look o' anger, like I war a fool, an' hurt in it, but it warn't her place to say nothin'.

They all mounted up, an' with dogs yappin' and travois draggin' in the dirt they trailed on out toward the Yellerstone. One little kid looked back, but his mother give him a slap upside the head an' he turned back around. Finally when they was far away I seed Mountain Lion sneak a look back, but I couldn't make out no expression on her face. Then she turned and rode on, and I knowed the ache of it.

Left me feelin' empty. Damn Injuns. I clumb on my charger and started out, up that strange river, trailin' my pack mule. Reckoned I'd show 'em. If'n there was a spirit up thar an' the son of a bitch was callin' to me, well I'd jest go on up thar and see what it wanted.

The river he was riding didn't have a white-given name when he started up it. It was the Boulder River drainage, the rugged center of the range, forming a valley over 2,000 feet deep. Realistically it was the way he would have explored the range. He was coming in from the north, and I was coming up from the south, heading toward that river. I wondered if our paths would cross.

I picked up another elk trail and followed it into a dense stretch of woods. Before long I heard the trickle of a spring down a ravine up ahead, overhung with foliage, looking cool and green. Instinctively I slowed down and began searching among the leaves, and soon spotted a deer's head, staring toward me. It was a doe, her fawn partially hidden behind her. She shifted and another head broke into view with a movement, the antlered head of a buck, further back. They hadn't mated yet, too early, but he was already hanging around her. I raised up and squeezed off a fake shot at the fawn. At that move she turned nervously and walked down the ravine, the fawn following. The buck took off separately from them, trotting and jumping downhill.

Coolness, water, comfort; waiting out the brightest hours of the day in hiding. Green hiding, trickling of water.

I drank at the ravine, then went higher on another elk trail. Soon I saw a wet spot in the dirt, and when I picked up a pinch of it, it smelled sharply of urine.

Soon after that I began seeing fresh wallows in the swampy ground, muddy beds dug out violently with hoof and horn, partially filled with water. The sign lying around was green and fresh. The bulls were making these wallows, to cool themselves in the heat of their mating fever and scent themselves, urinating in them and rolling in it. They were just starting now; all the signs were days fresh. Some of the little saplings had long fresh knife slices in them, where they had scored them with the tips of their antlers. Thrashing, cutting, rubbing: they were on the move. A movement precisely timed to the turning point of a season.

A fingernail of the new moon, going down just after the sun. A few yellow willow leaves tumbling along in the Yellowstone River, a hundred and fifty years ago. Sparrows, snow birds beginning to fly together in small flocks. Geese feeding in the northern marshes, nights of frost, clear bright stars. Bear fur turning thick and shiny.

Off in the distance I heard a strange whistle. I stopped and listened, and when I heard it again I knew it was an elk. I set off toward it with the wind in mind, hearing it again and hearing an answering bugle further up the mountain; hurrying quietly through a thick stretch of woods with the wind coming up from below. When I finally climbed up to the crest of an open hillside I heard a fluting scream which went up the scale rapidly, echoing off the hills, then trailed off to a series of rough grunts. It came from just across the hillside and down a ways. I took off my pack and crawled out through the grass, watching down below as I went. When I was halfway across I saw something move and froze where I was.

A cow elk came out in the open about fifty feet below and began walking across. She had a small calf with her, and as soon as they cleared the timber it burst into flight and ran sixty feet full speed, as if there were something after it. Then, just as quixotically, it slowed to a walk and nibbled at some grass, continuing on in line ahead of her. Behind both of them a big gleaming pair of antlers emerged from the woods.

He stood there looking about for a few moments, the glands in his lower neck swollen up bigger than a softball. Then he started across behind the other two, each plodding footstep telling of the power in his chest and shoulders, the flashing power of intimidation in the spread of his antlers. Four feet across, six points on a side; mountains and streams, ancient coal beds and wild forests were in those antlers: white ivory tips, rough bark-brown stalks; computerized hunters were after them, to hang them somewhere above the ashes and smoke back where they came from. Legendary hunters from the East were after them, Hollywood stars from the West were after them. After the spirit in the mountains. What was left of it.

Halfway across the hill he tilted his antlers back, raised his upper lip to the sky, and let out a screaming bellow, followed by three crying grunts, nodding his head with each grunt. From far up the mountain came an answer, but he didn't pay much attention to it. He followed on into the woods at a walk, behind the cow and the calf, his antlers glinting in the sun. He was huge, brown of bark and loam, growing careless of danger. Far across the valley, beyond his lingering image, was a clear view of the ridge that formed the other side of the drainage, a long and hazy behemoth, big three-hundred-foot cliffs breaking out of the timber, all of it that I could see looking deep and remote. Grizzly country. The last of it.

I MADE a bed under a spruce that night, a thick spruce where nothing could get to me without waking me up. Frost fell that night and the next, but the days were sunny and mild, with warm restless winds. I worked slowly up beneath the top of the ridge in that area, seeing a lot of elk, hearing their bugles and then sneaking up on them downwind. Most of the lone bulls, the younger bulls, were down in the spruce-fir thickets where the springs made little swamps, rolling in their wallows so their hooves flashed in the air, bugling at other elk without really going after a fight. It seemed as if they were warming up for it, sizing up other bulls by the sound of their bugles, picking out potential opponents and slowly psyching up for battle. The bigger and older they were, the deeper the bass note at the end of the bugle. They moved after every scream, but they were circling each other, staying at least a hundred yards apart, screaming and then thrashing the brush with their antlers, pawing the earth, moving on around each, unseen, in a big tangled circle. They weren't quite ready to fight yet. They just stood up near the border of the forest under the ridgetop and bugled into the evening, solitary, intent to the point of foolishness, and the cows hid about in the timber and gave little cries, like strange whining birdcalls, commenting back and forth. I had never heard those cries before.

Late in the afternoon I climbed a steep hill, leaving the thick forests behind, breaking into the grassy, scattered timber country under the top of the ridge. The wind was running ahead of me and soon I heard the thunder of hooves about a hundred yards up, and saw a herd of about ten elk streaming through the timber, a big set of antlers flashing with them. They headed down toward the forests I had just come up from. It seemed as if the more experienced bulls kept their groups of cows up near the more open country, where it was easier to herd them and keep track of them. Yet it also seemed as if the cows were leading the bulls now, going where they pleased while the bulls bugled and tried to follow and keep track of them. I guessed that as the rut grew more intense the bulls would become more possessive, using their antlers more and more to intimidate them and herd them up.

I WALKED on into the afternoon, higher up toward the top of the ridge, through lonely frost-burned meadows, ragged fringes of timber. It wasn't so much a ridge as it was a huge landmass of hills between the two drainages, for even though it flattened out near the top I still couldn't make out the Buffalo Fork drainage to the west—just irregular masses of hills off in that direction. But it was rising all the time, up above 9,000 feet now, and I knew it must be narrowing too. Soon I would get a view. I came to a still pond with trees all around about seventy-five feet across, and found a set of big black bear tracks in the mud along the edge, but they were several days old, with pine needles in them. I splashed some of the water on my head, and as I walked on out into the meadow I spotted three ruffed grouse lurking near an island of brush. I debated for a few seconds, then decided to take one, to keep my strength up in case anything happened. I shot the biggest and it flopped into the grass; the other two fanned out their tails and ran into the brush, where they remained, whistling continuously, a quavering whistle which started high and fell down the scale. I skinned it out by the pond and washed the blood off my hands and knife, wondering if those two were its late-season offspring.

In the evening I came to a steep overlook, with a wild-looking basin about six hundred feet below. It was flat down there, and there was an open meadow with a dark little creek winding through it. It spilled off into even darker-looking timber. It seemed perfect for elk, but I listened for a while and it remained silent, lifeless. I hadn't heard any other elk all day, or seen any fresh sign. It occurred to me that the bunch I had seen were hanging near the park boundary, and as soon as early bull season opened they would slip down into the park to safety. I had covered six or seven miles beyond where they had been, and hadn't heard a single other bugle. The rest of the country I had covered seemed pretty well shot out.

I made a camp overlooking the basin, hoping to see a big bear down there as the evening deepened. I dug a bed between two pines and dragged in deadfalls at my head and feet, so I was surrounded by a noise barrier. A strong wind was coming down from the north, but the sky was clear. Out in the meadow behind me there was a little spring creek, and at its edge the wind had blown over three spiring pines whose roots were interlocked, forming a solid wall of dirt and rock sticking ten feet up in the air. I built a fire behind that out of the wind and roasted the grouse, eating the whole thing in one sitting, wolfing it down. Then, feeling better, I doused the fire and scattered the coals into the creek.

There was a sharply rising hill off to the right, and I figured I could get a view from the top of it. I leaned into the rocks and climbed the short but precipitous pitch, the wind whistling through the few scattered pines, raining down handfuls of dead needles. Just as I stepped over the top a grouse exploded into flight down from my feet, making me jump, and sailed away down toward the dark timber below. I had a view all around, and it was an overwhelming sight.

A land of peaks, as far as I could see in any direction, a violent land of peaks. They stretched all the way north into the haze; they stretched in irregular rock ridges off to the west toward the setting sun. For a few seconds I felt lost, weightless, in the midst of a sea of mountains. The hard wind whistled over the rocks; as I looked at it all, I sensed immediately that I was looking at the wildest landmass left, knew it from its height and its depth and its awesome ruggedness, knew it from the countless dark and myriad drainages it held. And all its great distances. I didn't see a building or a road anywhere. I had sensed the wildness in this landmass from the outside, many times, wherever I saw it, and now I was looking into its interior. It was an awesome sight.

A sparrow hawk flew in and hovered about fifteen feet over-head, staring at me, making a chirping noise as it held on the wind. I sat down with my back against a rock and began to go over the country with the spyglass, feeling an uncanny sense of fulfillment. All the miles, the dreams and myths I had been pursuing, had led me into this, to see it and feel it, to cast my fate into it. And now I was a speck, a grain of consciousness, on its threshold.

The sun was close to the peaks in the west; the wind seemed to be making a last attempt to hurl something away before the sun went down. It came in great blasts, sending pine cones dancing over the rocks, making whipping sounds before it trailed off; it came from high and far, a maddened wind uncon-nected to any storm, but streaming over the mountains with a wild force that bent the trees and sent sprays of old needles flying. *Maybe the wind.* I looked up and saw that there were two sparrow hawks now, a mated pair, and they had let go of their feeding time to fly up and play on that big wind. The mountains stretched into the distance; the two of them were up above it all, riding the blasts like miniature kites. As I watched them I became more and more taken at the extraordinary way they were making light of that wind, the fact that they had left off everything to go up into it and take on its challenge, play with its force. It filled me with yearning, but at the same time it landed in me, the imagery and power in it, some medicine, the first of the trip. They seemed to be masters of that wind. They looped and dove in it; they rode against it in one place like a kite, holding, then suddenly shot upward sixty feet in two seconds, in the blink of an eye, and held up there for a while. Then without warning one of them would peel over and let the wind throw it two hundred feet down toward the mountain, and the other would follow, and they would both pull out twenty or thirty feet above the trees, soaring on up to try it again. And when they were finally finished, and the big wind began to die with the setting of the sun, I was left uplifted, left with a sense of amazement at their spiritual acrobatics. A vision of the simple delight there was in the forces of the earth.

I walked back down the hill feeling that it was beginning now, the medicine of the trip was starting to take over, beginning to touch me. I watched the basin below until dark, but neither the big bear nor anything else came out. It was still and lifeless, like a painting, no bugling elk anywhere within hearing. Finally I slept, and slept well. Sometime just before dawn I awoke to something big crawling up over my shoulder. Slowly I opened one eye and saw a pine squirrel six inches away from my nose, staring at me intently in the first light of dawn.

"Boo!" I said.

It jumped into the air like a spring and its legs were running before it even hit the ground. It disappeared in a frantic rustle of leaves.

FROST WAS in the grass, and wrinkles of ice had formed at the edges of the dark little spring creek which wound its way across the tundra-like flat. The ridge was growing sharper and more distinct above me and I knew I would soon get a look across into the Buffalo Fork drainage. I walked along in the frosted grass looking out over the mountains to the east as the yellowness grew brighter, two ravens rising at my approach out of a grassy cleft in the hillside up ahead, everything caught in the brightening stillness. I felt the spirit of the range, its medicine, taking me over.

As I climbed toward the top of the ridge I kept remembering

the sparrow hawks in the wind, the deep way they had struck me, the way they performed for the sheer joy in it, so far away from the realm of self-consciousness that it seemed miraculous to me. Simple impulses of delight; playing with the high of the wind. It triggered something in me, something I had drawn from all the wild animals I had seen: whatever they did, they did it only for the sake of doing it. Like very small children, they didn't know what it meant to do something for its impression upon others; they had no self-consciousness. There was a part of that that I could use, that struck directly into my inner twists with money and status, the glittering emptiness of the decade: even though I had to live with it all around I could still try to grasp that, doing what I felt simply for myself. Learn to hold it in my consciousness, draw power from it.

If I got back out.

The experience had struck me in such a way that it made me think that the spirit I had sensed was starting to take hold, that I was opening to it at a level that I hadn't reached before. Two hawks had touched me, and the range was stealing over my spirit. I was ready for its medicine.

Come up to whar them Injuns turned off to go up to their meat racks, an' I seed a dead tree up ahead with a bunch of skulls tied to it. Eagle skulls, bear skulls, elk and deer; they was all tied into crooks in that tree, some of 'em older than others, and it war a ghostly-lookin' sight. I tied my animals off and went on up to look, an' when I got close I seed whar they jest got done tyin' off little bundles of elk fur, an' bunches of hooves, an' hung 'em from the dead branches. They was showin' them spirits that they used up ever' part o' them elk 'ceptin' the hooves and the hair. I knowed then that this was the place whar old White Grass drawed that lightnin' bolt. They never went any further than this.

Went back, got my animals, an' started on in. When I rode past that skull tree I felt a tinglin' in my backside; I turned around but there warn't nothin' thar 'cept them bones. Bones under the stars, sure enough. Spirits this, spirits that, they had a spirit for ever' time you went to take a piss. Somethin' bad happened, it war a spirit. Somethin' good happened, that war a spirit too. *A spirit in the river, a spirit in the rain, spirits in the trees, bad spirits in the Yellerstone country. It war a wonder you didn't trip over 'em comin' and goin'. I didn't believe in no spirits, but to tell ye the truth, I war feelin' a tetch strange ridin' along in thar. It war too quiet somehow. I reckoned if there was any place in all the Shinin' Mountains whar spirits did live, 'twould be up among these peaks, risin' up dark-like into the sky. Seemed like there was somethin' behind 'em, somethin' that knowed you was comin' in. Somethin' big, an' dark, that you couldn't understand.*

Old White Grass didn't help none. The son of a bitch had a look in his eye like he knowed somethin' I didn't, put the jitters in me. I knowed whar he was gonna hunt buffler come late fall afore the big snows, an' I wondered if I'd git to 'em. I wondered if I'd see that sweet devil of a Crow woman again, Mountain Lamb Lion.

High them mountains, Jesus, high and strange and lonely. It war the deepest valley I ever rode through, and I didn't have no idee whar this river went to. Up into the land of the spirits, I reckoned. As I rode higher up it toward a dark-lookin' forest I was wonderin' if old Gabe was gonna see them wild waters o' spring one more time, come agin to the Shinin' Mountains when the fish start up the rivers.

WHEN I got up to the top of the ridge I could see most of the upper end of the Buffalo Fork drainage. I sat down and spent time memorizing certain of the peaks, studying the lay of the country to the north, where I was headed. The country rose in increasingly rugged waves as far as I could see. Names came off the map at me, telling the early history of the range: Breakneck Ridge, Froze-to-Death Mountain, Lightning Creek, Meatrack Creek, Lost Creek, Wounded Man Creek, Cathedral Peak, Monument Peak. The Needles. Deep and rugged country, dangerous in the fall. A tremendous high landmass. For the first time, more than on any other range, I felt close to what Colter felt, looking out upon the tremendous size, the wildness, and deciding which way he was going to go into it. That came to me strongly again and again up that ridge; at last I had a taste of what Colter felt, in some of the same region. All the vast country, feeling like a speck in it, yet holding on to his confidence and the will to make it through.

I started down toward the bottom of the Buffalo Fork Valley, a long and difficult descent. When I was halfway down I sat down and glassed it, and soon picked out a handful of horses loose in the willows. That meant that there was an outfitter setting up down there for early bull season. Before long I spotted a string of about twelve horses and riders trailing down the other side of the valley, heading south. So this drainage too was heavily trafficked, heavily outfitted. It was the same in character as Slough Creek, the same flat and open bottom country, but smaller and narrower.

I got down to the bottom in late afternoon, hot and tired, and sat by the creek for a long time, staring into the cool rushing waters. Finally I cooked a big jerky stew and ate till I was more than full. Jerky every day, no matter how tired I got of it, enough strength in it to keep going, keep climbing. I was beginning to feel that was my substitute for wild meat, the alternative in my feelings to the bounty and fuel of the mountain men, the lesson I had learned in the Swans. I accepted it, made it a part of the experience, a legacy of all I had learned. Wild animals were disappearing fast enough in this decade.

I started out again through the sparse and grassy lodgepoles, hitting the trail where I had seen the horses. It was all torn up, and my spirit was low as I walked it. Soon I saw the white tents of the outfitter through the trees up ahead, and I cut up into the timber to the right to sneak around the camp. I felt like a bear as I circled, and I felt like a bear as I watched one of them through the maze of trees, walking along with an ax.

I circled the rest of the camp in hiding and started up through a wet marshy opening to pass it by. But before long I saw another man up ahead, fooling around with a coil of wire. I stalked him for a while, but then I couldn't resist talking to him, because I knew he would know about the usage of this country and the game populations.

He was nice enough; he had worked for outfitters in this country for the past eight years. He told me that it was badly shot out and he thought they ought to close it down for several years and let the big game come back. He said that it used to be one of the

most legendary big-game areas in the West—these three moun-
tainous ridges that climbed fifteen miles up out of Yellowstone to
the north, with their flat open bottoms and looping creeks, their
countless grassy mountainsides. Now, he said, there were only
little remnant pockets of elk, scattered deer, a few wandering
moose, and a few grizzlies that scarcely anyone saw all summer.
It wasn't hardly worth hunting any more, he said.

Spirit of the seventies.

THE NEXT MORNING another clear dawn lit up the sky. I watched
sharply over the bottom as I walked along, the grass bowed with
frost and crunching softly underfoot, the vapor of my breath
following me as I walked, the chill of the autumn dawn on my
hands. The sun was just breaking over the ridge of the valley,
but the bottom was still lost in blue haze, stillness. The willows
there were hoary with frost, their still masses of leaves burnt to
the color of pumpkin. A small amount of white vapor was rising
off the ridgetop. I didn't see anything move, not a deer.

When I got to the small timbered delta of the ravine I climbed
up the hillside a little way and sat there watching, glassing. The
creek wound around dull white sandbars, its bank water amber
with turning leaves. There was nothing moving out of the timber
on the far side. Finally the sun spilled over and touched some of
the willows, and almost immediately the frost on them began to
steam. Soon it melted into beads and diamonds began to glitter
in the early-morning sunlight, deep flashes of blue, red fire. Out
near the middle, at the limits of the sunlight, a big pair of yellow
antlers rose lazily into view through the willows, followed by a
jet-black back. Bullwinkle. He was getting up to feed.

He had been lying hidden in the willows till the sun touched
his back. I felt an unaccountable sense of relief, a sense of the
spiritual power that still remained. I looked at the flashing
diamonds of water in the willows, the glowing sunlight, his shining black back, and I breathed easier, I felt belief coming back
into my veins. Here was Bullwinkle, rising for breakfast in the
backyard of a hunting camp.

I watched him feed for over an hour, sleek, glossy black, his
antlers turning slowly in the sun. He stood up to his neck in the
willows, picking, nibbling, reaching, his odd head was high

sometimes—so at one with his surroundings, so filled with the peace in it all, that he seemed to embody everything that was solid and good in that glittering morning, in the earth itself. His great physical strength was as relaxed as the sunlight; his spirit seemed to flow with the glistening waterdrops, the deep sense of peace among the morning willows. It was that combination of physical strength and a deep and peaceful spirit that was dawning on me about him, parting the veil to his political medicine, breaking through out of the medicine of the Crows. A trophy of knowledge to take back from the wild. Someday, America. Someday you will know the harmony that flows between great strength and a peaceful spirit.

He was feeding gradually closer as I watched, and I realized that he was probably headed for the same ravine I was. I crossed the little creek so as to be downwind from him, then waited and watched. He lay down again for a while, so I could only see the tips of his antlers whenever he moved his head, hidden from any passers-by. Then he got up and fed around onto the bank and began plodding toward me, his great palm-shaped antlers swinging a little. He stopped at a bush and ran them through it a few times, then rubbed them hard against a little sapling, as if they itched. The rut was beginning to yawn in him, later than the elk, just beginning to glimmer now. He walked on, giving a little groan with every fourth step as he plodded uphill, as if he were so relaxed that even the act of walking uphill contained some small and mysterious pleasure. Finally he passed by abreast, thirty feet away, and I felt the instincts in his closeness: the black sheen to his rolling back muscles, the big hump over his shoulders like a grizzly, a silvery fringe of hair at the back of his legs. His one brown, veined eye. When he was just past me I stepped out into the open.

"Say, buddy, how's it going?"

He stopped. The great head swung around and he looked at me steadily with that slow brown eye. It registered neither alarm nor fright; just the dawning realization that I wasn't supposed to be there, and he didn't like it either. He didn't like the sound of my voice. He was huge and powerful, and his gears moved slowly. I noted the location of some nearby trees.

"They'll shoot you if you stay around here," I said.

He gave a soft snort and stood where he was, staring at me. Bullwinkle didn't move for unarmed humans in his way. They moved for him.

I took a step closer. He snorted and swung around more so that he was half facing me. I took a step backward.

"Just kidding," I said.

He stood there and stared at me, at the audacious stick-like turd who had dared take a step on him, dared to stir the fathomless pool where his anger slept. When his anger woke up it was huge and violent, a tornado.

I backed away, and left him to get my pack. When I came back he was gone; I couldn't see him anywhere. I started up the creek, dodging deadfalls, remembering his powerful image.

I was climbing into the wild again; spots of sunlight flickered over the clear falling waters as they tumbled over one set of boulders after another. Clear cold water. It was cool in that ravine, tangled, hypnotic with dancing sunlight, the deepening fall colors glowing through the woods so that it seemed as if I were climbing up into an autumn dream. Further toward its medicine. The mildness, the coolness seemed to be leading me on. Climbing over a jam of trees, I came upon a slice of petrified tree resting on a big boulder, where the spring waters had hurled it and left it to rest. I counted forty-two rings. A tree so old that it had turned to rock; standing rock trees in the Crow Mountains. Further up I found a gravel bar with lava boulders in it, boulders made of countless rocks cemented together by lava. Scattered through the wet gravel were incredible colored rocks, fire rocks so colorful I got down on my hands and knees to examine them. Green quartz, blue quartz melted into bubbles and drips, white bubbled quartz with sparkling pockets of diamond-like glitter. Burnt-red jasper with little rivers of green jade running through it. All the rest of the rocks looked dirty and boring, and then those colored fire jewels scattered among them. Jewels of the Crow Mountains' fiery beginnings. I gathered a bunch of the small ones and put them in my possibles sack, hanging it around my neck, feeling a spirit that seemed so old and yet glittering with beauty, as if long ago the fires and dark violence had given birth to something mild and beautiful, something that still sparkled in the sun today. I couldn't get over those rocks; I kept stopping to look at them, turn them over in my hand, as I worked higher up that ravine. Then looking back up and wondering what lay ahead.

The creek was a wild cataclysm in the spring. Parts of the bank were torn away, big live trees were torn out by the roots, other standing live trees had huge scrapes in the bark and there were periodic jams of tangled logs. I could see big boulders and live trees tumbling down it in the spring. Now the water was way down, clear and amber-colored, and sometimes I climbed right up the middle.

It was a long, tangled climb. Late in the afternoon, while I was thinking about something else, I looked up ahead and saw a small black bear bolt up the hill on my right and into the trees. There was another, bigger bear resting in the shady grass with its back toward me, and it lifted its nose straight up into the air and began sniffing backward. Suddenly it jumped up and ran up after the other one without even looking down toward me.

I listened for a while, looking down behind me. The bigger bear had been too small to be the mother; they were a yearling and a two- or three-year-old, hanging out together for mutual security. Young moose did that too. I went up to where they had been but didn't find anything interesting. They had simply been lying up in the coolness of the ravine.

Early in the evening the ravine began to level out and the timber began to open. The sky was still clear; the air had turned quiet. I was walking along through a leafy, spring-trickling woods when I glanced off to the right and saw that familiar black fur, felt again that shot of excitement that comes with spotting a black bear loose in the woods. It was the same two bears again. They were both feeding on green plants, wandering slowly, easily, looking preoccupied with the plants and the evening air. Even though I had walked into full view neither of them looked at me, and at first I thought they hadn't seen me. But soon after I showed up they both began feeding gradually away from me, maybe three hundred feet apart. I began to get the distinct sense that they knew I was there, and were pretending not to see me. It was as if something passed through the air between us; on my part that I wouldn't hurt them, on theirs that they sensed that, and while it saved them from having to bolt they still had to mask their retreat by pretending not to see me. I was sure that that was what happened.

I walked on, wondering over the extrasensory nature of it, something passing through the air, their ability to sense my intent toward them. I realized that that was true of many other animals I had seen, birds, squirrels, moose. They could pick up on my intentions. With these two bears the gap of the wild had been narrowed to an extent that I had never before reached. Something passed between us. Thoughts of my medicine swam around in my head.

By the time I reached a level place with a little spring creek I was exhausted. I drank cold water and sat for a long time, enervated, unable to get myself to make a camp. After the sun set a cold wind began to blow, and I raised myself and made a bed inside some thick pines, then cooked jerky and soup. Loco weed was growing all around. Loco weed is wild peas; they tasted good and I put a big handful of them in with the soup. Loco weed sometimes absorbs selenium from the soil, which makes horses go crazy, and turns human pubic hair orange, or something like that, I couldn't remember what it did. But I didn't care. I was hungry and tired and they tasted good.

Just at dusk a ruffed grouse flew into the trees close by, and I stalked it and shot it. I figured to eat it for breakfast to get my strength back, and after I skinned it I stuck it up in the crotch of a tree far from where I slept. Finally I turned in.

After dark a fierce wind began to blow. It came in long growing gusts that drowned out the noise of the creek and rained down debris and needles where I lay. It was so strong I worried about my pack tumbling away outside the tree. Again I reminded myself that I was in high and unpredictable country. Bits of ice came through the pine, but after midnight it trailed off and I fell asleep. I began to have strange nightmares about a bear that was stalking me, weird hopscotching dreams that would flash me awake with beating heart and sweat on my forehead. Dreams that kept deviling my mind.

When finally I saw that first splotch of light off to the east I felt a great relief. I got up and built a fire, and sat there barefoot by the flames cutting up the grouse and dropping it in to stew, adding some more peas, throwing in some salt and pepper. The earth all around was completely still, not a breath of air, all the way up to the high rimrock vaguely visible over the trees. Just the crackling of the fire, and the perfect stillness in the sky as the clear yellow light spread further across it. The dreams and fear of the night before seemed foolish to me in that light, but it had been very potent while it was happening.

A breeze had come up with the sun, moving my smoke back down the ravine, which was strange because the air nearly always came up the water in the morning. The grouse meat had turned white by then and my mouth was watering. I began eating with my fingers, salting the meat as I ate, slurping up the hot broth and mushing the peas. Not bad. Figured if them damn peas turned my pubic hairs orange that was all right too. When I finished I poured the last of the broth on the fire and sat in the sun for a while and let it sink in: meat, stomach, intestines, bloodstream. Energy. Climbing strength. The will to survive.

Finally I got my boots and sat down in the grass to put them on. I was lacing up the second one when I heard a noise in the grass behind me. I glanced over my shoulder and there stood a bear, ten feet away.

I rose to my feet with a prickling sensation in my arms. It was a black bear, one of the two I had seen yesterday, maybe a hundred fifty pounds. In the first instant my mind flashed to the pistol, which was in my pack, and I knew that was beyond reach as defense. I was so dumbfounded at seeing it right in front of me that in the first few seconds I couldn't move or speak, I could only stand there with wide eyes and an open mouth, staring at it, searching instinctively in fractions of a second for its intent. And in four or five seconds its intent was clear to me. He didn't mean any harm.

He stood there, his head hung way down, looking up at me with deep, sheepish, yellow eyes. He kept looking up at me and then averting his gaze, shifting his weight back and forth from one paw to another, glancing at me with a look that was both sheepish and pleading, then looking down. A single drool of saliva hung from the corner of his mouth. He was standing sideways, ready to bolt, but still staying on, daring to stay and look me in the face and ask me the one question that he had come to ask. I could feel him asking me that question with a directness that stunned me.

He wanted to know if he could have some of the grouse.

I was blown away. I stood there unable to move, teetering between the fear I had felt, the apprehension, and the melting sense of those sheepish eyes, the completely harmless way he was offering himself, silently pleading. I couldn't believe it.

Finally I found my voice, and murmured instinctively, "It's all right." Very slowly I sat down in the grass, facing him, and began saying soft and reassuring things to him, telling him I wouldn't hurt him. He kept looking at me, his shining black fur glinting like a mirror when he moved his feet. Cautiously I reached for one of the leg bones, and gave it a little toss so it landed close to his head. One whiff and he took the bone up into his mouth and began breaking it up, raising his head and chewing hard and fast. I was in a state of disbelief; it was such a sudden and unexpected contact with the animal that was my favorite, top of my medicine, that I could hardly believe it was happening, or keep up with the feelings that spun off from it. I kept tossing the bones closer and closer, till he was chewing them up almost at arm's length, always keeping an eye on me, with looks that told me he didn't want to fight. I could sense that. I knew that we understood each other, and I could have made a pet out of him. He took the last of the carcass and backed away a few steps, sheepish yellow eyes still on me, and began crunching it up, holding it between his front feet, throwing more trusting glances at me.

I had no way to keep him. It would take a cabin off in the mountains somewhere, wild mountains, far from the trophy-hunting consciousness, to have a pet bear without getting it killed. This was the seventies, the demise of that dream in America, except for the rich. Any way you cut it, the bear would wind up paying the ticket.

And then, watching him eat the last of the carcass, I knew what I had to do. A lot of the rich men that came in with the outfitters had their eyes out for a cub or a small bear. They liked to have them stuffed standing up and holding a candy dish, so they could put them by the fireplace to thrill their children. A lot of them would shoot this bear without thinking twice.

I stood up and pointed off toward the wilderness of the ravine. He looked up at me and blinked, for he sensed a change in me, a change he didn't understand. He was wondering what the matter was.

I spoke in a low, mean voice. "Go on."

He understood. He took a few steps away from me with a hurt air, then turned around and looked at me again, pained yellow eyes that wrung me, that understood what I meant. A wild bear, looking up into my eyes.

I spoke louder, meaner. "Go on!"

With that he knew it was over. He turned and walked away in a shuffling gait, without looking back. As I watched him going away I felt a piercing sense of loss, as if the soul of the wild that I had been trekking after all spring and summer and fall was slipping away from me in the form of that black bear, the shining wild fur, all I could learn from him, into the woods. Back into the wild that was so hard to know, so hard to find. But I knew what was best, I knew the history I was living through. I went over to the pack and pulled the pistol out, clicking past the empty cylinder, and aimed a few yards to his right. When that fearsome explosion slammed into the mountains and the bullet hissed through the grass near his feet, he jumped up in the air and bolted into a full run, bolted for his life. In a few seconds he was gone from sight.

I was left with the breeze in the grass. I sat down, watching the place where he had disappeared, flooded with sensations that were already memory. When that feeling had passed through the air between us the night before, that was what had cleared the way for him to come in. The wild gap had been narrowed; it had sensed that this particular human meant no harm. Then this morning the smell of that stewing grouse had flooded down into the ravine, and it had begun drooling, following its nose. When it first saw me it must have stood there for a while, torn between its hunger and what its mother had taught it. But it remembered the outcome of the previous encounter, got up its courage, and walked on in. It was a young bear, maybe a two-year-old, and it hadn't been shot at yet or it wouldn't have come in.

Medicine. My connection to the earth. If that connection were true and direct, my fate would be flowing as it should. I had touched it with that bear, closed the wild gap that I had been following after all season. Positive medicine. I wondered if the other side of the bear's medicine, the dark side, lay somewhere ahead. Bears were not all sunlight and sheepish looks. They could be devastating animals if you struck them wrong.

I lifted my pack up and hoisted it to my back, starting up through the grass and trees. Somewhere off on the other side of the ridge a small bunch of coyotes had broken into their morning howl, sending up a wild rising chorus of yips and yaps toward the blue morning sky. Everything else was still.

A quiet air in that forest. I rode along quiet-like, lookin' all around. There was big tall trees cuttin' out the sunlight and givin' it a dark air, like a big old empty church late in the evenin'. Didn't see nary a deer. Ever' so often I'd see a big boulder that had a bunch of rocks sprinkled all through it, like they'd been stuck into it with some kind o' ash rock. It was like there'd been a fire in here that war hot enough to melt rocks, by Jesus. A thought of the devil popped into my mind, but I pushed the bastard out. Then up ahead I seed some dead tree trunks standin' around that looked like they was made o' stone. I rode on up thar and got off my horse, and Jesus, when I tapped one of 'em with my hatchet the son of a bitch was pure rock! It was shaped like a tree, it had roots goin' into the ground like a tree, goddamnit it war a tree, but it was made outta solid rock! It war like a putrified forest, somethin' haunted about it, like it war as old as Methoozala, older than anyone what ever lived could recall, somewhars beyond history books. It war a mystery to me, and it left me standin' thar in my buckskins feelin' small, somethin' like a child, like a damn small child. That's jest what I felt like.

Damn it to hell, I warn't no green young willow, I war a mountain man. I went over to my saddle and untied the deer leg I had stowed there, brushed the fly eggs off, and took to eatin'. Git some of that meat in my belly. I war a mountain man and thar warn't nothin' I was ascairt of, an' thar warn't no place I couldn't go. Them Injuns was crazy. Thar warn't no sech thing as spirits.

About that time I noticed my charger. He was standin' thar tight as a drum, starin' off into the woods. His ears was up, his eyes was white, an' ever' muscle in him was ready to bust loose. He give a soft snort, and stood thar like he was froze, turned to stone. Like he was seein' a ghost.

And thar warn't nothin' thar.

Well, about then that voice in me come up and says, "Gabe, reckon you've gone far enough. Turn around now and head on back out. Snow's comin'. Time to git dug in for the winter. Enough of these mountains; you made your medicine. Go on back out now, Gabe."

"No, I ain't," I says aloud, and I took to quietin' my charger. Inside I war a-turnin' around and headin' back out for the country I knowed, but outside I was lookin' ahead. I hadn't seen no spirits yet, even if that goddamned horse was startin' to see 'em. Reckoned I'd go further on.

I rode on through that forest, and I war afeared, an' under its spell. Big dark clouds come and went overhead; warn't scarce any sunlight come down through the trees, jest them rock trees risin' up like monuments to somethin' old, somethin' in the shadows, in the ash an' rocks. Horse was jumpy, an' that didn't ease my mind none. Talked to it quiet-like, for there was a feelin' in the air that made me keep my voice down. Warn't no deer that I see. I didn't understand the air in that forest; it war makin' me feel small. I jest kept on a-goin'.

I WENT up over the top of the ridge into the sun, and down the other side, searching the small grassy basins down off the top for griz sign, walking a ways along the game trails that came out of the beginning of the timber. At one point I climbed up onto a big boulder in the sun and took off my boots, working more oil into the cracks and seams with the corner of my bandana. I wore Redwing moccasin-style boots, which I preferred because they gave me more feeling in my feet for climbing rocks and crossing slippery logs. But they weren't real warm, and I had to carry extra wool socks for them in the fall.

I didn't see a deer all day, even into the evening, and I didn't find any griz sign. Just that huge ridge, growing grassy and mild, a walking ridge, higher and mightier all the time. Before dark I dropped down into an open grassy basin scattered with islands of timber, and searched from one of them to the next until I found one that would be good for a bed. Hung my food sack from a dead tree further down and turned in, to watch the twilight. No deer, no elk, nothing. Finally I went to sleep.

When I opened my eyes there was something in the air that called me awake and made me watch, listen. The pines along the eastern skyline were black silhouettes in front of a long streak of light; everything else was dark, shadowy. It was so hushed that there seemed to be something which held it, some energy behind it that I couldn't define. Whatever it was, it brought me wide awake. I dressed quickly, packed up, and started walking up through the grass toward the top of the ridge. It was utterly still, and there were no deer. Frost in the grass here and there, shadowy darkness.

When I reached the top of the ridge there was nothing down the other side. Dawn was just beginning to break over the mountains, and I stood there looking out, feeling the slow coming of light. It was all a jagged ocean of peaks, and now the rising sun was beginning to transform it. The ridges beneath it turned deep purple, and then a short flood of rays streamed through a gap in the Beartooths and disappeared into the atmosphere. It felt as if the earth were turning under my feet. The grass stems stood completely motionless; the blue in the atmosphere was growing, filling with a feeling of openness, as if a curtain were being pulled away. Then it happened. The molten gold came spilling over the raw dark peaks, flashing suddenly in my eye so I had to turn away. I looked back and saw dusky gold light hit the pines behind me, hit the frost in the dirt, and suddenly the colors became extraordinary. The frost turned purple. The pine trees turned a strange bluish violet, a color that made my mouth drop open. The grass was touched with a weird purple-blue. Everything I could see was transformed into strange and vibrant ultraviolet color, and I was overwhelmed by it. It only lasted for thirty seconds, and then the formless gold gleamed a little higher, the colors brightened to their normal shades, and the spirit passed. At that moment the grass, motionless since I woke up, began to waver a little, with the first air moving ahead of the heat. The morning breeze, coming on.

I started walking up the ridge, watching the sun take form off the peaks. It seemed like a display of something, a lesson. I had wanted to get down to the depth of my feeling about the land, and somehow I had managed to get up to that ridgetop just in time to see the world turn ultraviolet for a few moments. Finally as the sun lifted off the peaks I accepted it into my medicine. It had left me with the feeling that the earth was extraordinary, sacred, that there was a spirit in it that had briefly demonstrated its essence, and I would take that feeling into my time. That even though the history of the seventies, a ten-year cover-up of the sixties, was a history of its desecration, I wouldn't stop believing in it, or believing that someday its spirit would triumph. That I would never call that desecration "progress," or accept it in my spirit, and that I would hold on to my anger.

I realized as the sun grew higher and brighter that my anger was the truest thing in my life, the truest expression of what I was. *Don't give it up*, the sun seemed to be telling me. I thought back over the history of the decade; the progression; an anger which finds no resolution turns into bitterness; a bitterness which finds no relief turns into despair. After the sixties, that was the truth behind the seventies. I had been close to that edge. Now I would fight my way back. I would pull the egotism out of that anger and keep it to myself, a private feeling, a part of my life. *The pure anger I felt at what they were doing to the land.* I'd keep it all right. Maybe now I couldn't do anything about it, but I'd keep that anger, protect it. For I realized, under the blue sky of that morning, that if I were to lose my anger, I'd have lost my spirit.

I WENT higher along the ridge, toward a big dome-shaped mountain standing up ahead in the blue, and the ridge was growing beneath me, rising with swales and hills, saddles and hanging grassy basins, up past 10,000 feet. It was a spiritual day, and a spiritual passage toward that mountain, and I believed for the first time that it was the spirit of the Crow Mountains, a spirit that had begun with the sunrise and continued through that day. It felt as if I had slipped back a hundred fifty years, to a time when the instinctual human reaction to it among its natives was that it was all sacred. Soul of the American Indian.

I came to the mountain, a giant irregular dome rising toward the sun, and walked around the right side. Later in the afternoon I came to a small spring flowing out of a rocky cleft in the grass. I sat down and drank, watching the water that was forced out of the depths of that mountain, looking for an arrowhead. The sun, the big mountain, and the flowing spring all seemed connected, a final symbol of the day's experience, of the entire mild region that I had just come through, discovered by accident while I had been trailing John Colter. The grassy heartland of the Crow Mountains.

AROUND THE BACK SIDE of the mountain it broke into cliffs and rugged slides, and the mildness came to an end. I climbed up onto a grassy spine ridge leading north from the mountain and followed it as the sun settled into the western blue. for a half mile or so, until it dipped into a small triangular basin. As it came over a small rise I heard a sharp whistle below me, and saw a marmot drop down and disappear into his den among the rocks. I sat down with my Hawken and waited, sighting in on the spot where he disappeared. I wanted a charge of fresh meat, for I was coming upon rugged country.

I watched for ten minutes, then guessed that he was waiting for my sounds to pass by. I picked up some round stones and tossed them one after another further past the den, to make it sound like I was making my way down through the rocks. Then I sighted in again, making my rear end comfortable amid the pebbles, and waited.

Two minutes later his head appeared up to his eyes. Very slowly, like a clock hand, I moved the sight in on him and waited. I was about seventy feet away; I wanted the shot to be true, so he didn't crawl back down into his den to die. I held for seven or eight minutes, the wind turning my hands numb in the shadows, a muscle aching in my forearm. He inched up another five inches and held there; I waited another five minutes, motionless. At last he climbed up on the rock. I sighted down through his shoulder out his neck, concentrated, and squeezed. There was a split-second hesitation in him after the gun went off, then he went off the rock toward his hole.

I hurried down and found him lying dead just inside his hole.

His den had a deep musty smell; there were a few tiny bugs in his fur. I took him down to a grassy flat below the rocks where a tiny spring flowed, and cleaned him out. Acorn-sized bladder on the liver; dark green bile, clear; green mulch in the stomach. Big front teeth like a beaver. I guessed that if you sat and watched the plants a marmot ate, then ate them yourself, you would be doing all right. There were layers of pure white fat in the guts, just as if it were a part of the internal organs. I knew then why grizzlies spent so much energy digging them out in the fall. From the accounts of various naturalists who have seen them, the holes they dig look like the work of a bulldozer. It was for the fat the grizzlies worked so hard, for sometimes there were several marmots in one den.

I dug out a pit in the moist ground and built a big fire in it, putting the fat in the kettle near the flames. Soon it was melting, sizzling. When there was a hot bed of coals I laced the marmot shut with a green twig, wishing I had some wild onions to put inside it, and laid it on the coals. The smell of burning hair filled the air. I covered it up with loose dirt until no more smoke came out.

I waited while the sun sank lower, almost two hours, and then unearthed it. The hair wasn't all burned off, and it wasn't done all over. I should have built up more hot coals, and left it for only an hour or less.

I carried it over to a rock and pulled the twig out; blood-red juice trickled out and it smelled good. Where it was cooked the skin peeled off easily, revealing a hard white layer of gristle fat all over the back. Most of the meat was cool, hairs scattered over it, burnt charcoal; I almost gagged once at the coldness in one part of it. But I ate it anyway, and when I had finished I picked the crispy pieces of fat out of the kettle and ate them. They tasted good, and I ate them and gnawed on the carcass until I was full. Next time I figured I would quarter it and fry it in its own fat. The meat had a truly good taste to it, contrary to what I had expected, and I realized that these furry rock chucks were prime survival fare in the high country, as numerous as they were. It was something I hadn't expected.

When I had packed up I walked to the cliffs at the northern edge of the basin and looked over. They fell three hundred feet in a series of dark rock walls—the kind of cliffs you instinctively shrink back from. They were huge and dark, with deep clefts in them like caverns that trickled water all the way down. I tossed a rock over and counted the silence before it clattered. It was the end of the mildness.

I went back to the spur ridge and spent a long time picking my route out. I could see the Boulder River drainage maybe twenty miles up, a deep cleft in the mountains winding to the north. I made out the complete outline of the head of the Hell-roaring drainage, a circling rim of peaks. I would bush down into the head of that drainage, climb out of it over the trail, which looked like the only way out, and then try to bush north along the divide which formed the western heights of the Boulder River. As I looked at the cleft of that river I felt a surge of longing. It was the way out, the last of the sunlight shone off its rock faces, and deep in me, with all the fate-ridden country ahead, I wondered if I was going to make it. If I was going to make it out with that river.

Finally, on a steep spine, I started down off the ridge.

Rode higher in that strange rock-treed forest, lookin' this way an' that, lookin' behind me, my charger seein' spooks. Too damn quiet, an' too dark and dim. I never seed nor felt the like of the strangeness in the air.

Come late afternoon I seed somethin' move off in the woods, and I pulled in and squinted. It war a griz, a little griz, jest a wanderin' around an' eatin' plants. I knowed the son of a bitch seed me, but it never looked, jest kept pokin' around an' eatin', like it war the prince of that whole strange forest an' warn't nothin' could tetch it. I clumb down off'n my charger an' raised up my Hawken to put it under, so's the animals wouldn't hit the trees, an' about the time I cocked, a big shaft o' sunlight broke down through the gloom an' hit the forest floor, glowin' in all the dimness. It war jest like a spirit had done it! The hair rose on my arms. I uncocked my Hawken and let it sink, feelin' like a mouse caught out in the open. My fingers was a-tremblin', an' I jest stood thar a-lookin' at that silver-furred little griz like mebbe it war a spirit. Felt like thar was somethin' a-watchin' ever' move I made. I didn't know what to do.

Finally I done what an Injun woulda done. Warn't much left on that deer leg an' it war a-gittin' ripe, so I untied the son of a bitch and throwed it out thar to whar that bar was, hopin' that would please whatever it war. Griz took a sniff an' grabbed it up and begun to chewin' on it, lookin' pleased to git it. Quiet-like I got back up on my charger an' rode ahead, sorta whistlin' along under my breath, keepin' an eye on it as I passed. I felt like I was in further than I knowed.

Come a space of ridin' and it war gone, and I said to myself, "Goddamnit, Gabe, thar ain't no sech thing as spirits!" Tried to tell myself that, but it warn't what I felt. Felt like mebbe my time was comin'.

My knees was goin' bad and I knowed it. Thar'd be more 'n one Injun that would beat old Gabe in a footrace next year, an' they wouldn't be callin' me Runs Like Wind no more. They'd be thinkin' about my scalp. I knowed what happened to elk when their knees went bad. Wolves picked 'em out right off and begun follerin' 'em through the moons, till the right time come to pull 'em down. Warn't too many more years an' them streams would freeze up my knees good. This fall it felt like them spirit wolves was on my trail.

Mebbe that war the callin' I felt. Mebbe thar was a bad spirit in these mountains, and it knowed my knees was goin' bad, and it war gonna take me. Mebbe it'd called me in here, an' I warn't gonna come out.

The son of a bitch! Like hell I warn't. My knees might be gittin' stiff, but I warn't goin' down without a fight. If it war a-callin' me, why, I'd jest take it on. If I had anything to say about it I'd see them waters o' spring agin, by thunder.

I never knowed a bad spirit in the earth. I've known a parcel o' bad luck, but I never knowed no bad spirit. I've seed these mountains kill fools, quick as you'd squash an ant, I've seed their bones bleachin' under the sun, but I never knowed no bad spirit in it all. All I knowed was a good spirit. Thar was a feelin' in them big rivers that I could feel in my bones, thar was a feelin' in all the stretch o' the country that was in my heart, that done me good an' was always with me. Old Gabe war a friend of the big rivers, he war a friend of the snowy peaks an' the high plains, the gold of the risin' sun and the blue sky—he loved it all, sure enough he loved it all. He war a friend of the stars over the sky at night. Truth was, I always felt like all them things of the earth was with me, was in my bones an' heart, an' when I got in a tight spot I'd call on 'em with my spirit. 'Lo, sun, 'lo, rivers, old Gabe's in a fix an' he needs your medicine. An' they'd always come through for me, by thunder, they'd always come through. I always felt like they was with me.

And now I'm wonderin', times of fall comin' to the Crow Mountains, if that medicine was still thar. I'm wonderin' what new spirit that I never knowed afore was on the trail.

THE NEXT DAY the weather turned bad, and when I bushed down into the head of Hellroaring I ran into a phalanx of hunters, an incoming stream. The decade was upon me again. Mebbe it was a coincidence, but the day that I hit the end of that mild region of the spirit was the day before hunting season opened, the day when the skies, clear and sunny for eight days up that whole high grassy country, began to turn dark. Groups on horseback came in, and I could see bright orange spots crawling up into the mountains on both sides as the clouds rolled in. A big red-tailed hawk jumped out of a tree right next to me and flew away through the trees. I tried to make the top of the pass, so I didn't have to listen to the volley of shots that would come with the dawn, but darkness found me still below the rim. I made a slanting bed under some trees and lay there watching the fog coming in, watching the last of the dull steel light where it held off upon a high grassy shelf away to the south. A group on horseback passed by in the near darkness, talking about killing a moose. They had a permit, and I saw the image of that black shiny bull among the willows at dawn, one drainage to the east. I didn't want to hear that volley of shots at dawn; the thought of it filled me with a helpless anger. Elk falling. It wasn't that I was against hunting. It was just that I knew that it was far too heavy for the animals that were left. And the consciousness behind it, the capitalistic consciousness. Great hunters, rich mountain men of the seventies. Converging until the spirit was gone.

When there was one last smudge of light over that distant shelf in the mountains to the south, I began to hear something in the wind, something pleasing. It was a woman singing, humming far away. Her voice came from just under the wind, just under the clouds, from the direction of that shelf off in the twilight. It was the last thing in the landscape that held any light, back toward the country I had just come through, and the singing came from underneath the wind that was bringing the fog in, a pretty voice, no words or familiar melody to it, traveling up and down the scale with no two notes the same, but somehow singing of the same thing. It was like a woman singing out her thoughts as she washed her hair. I felt a single strong urge to get up and follow it, but I sensed that would be a mistake. It went on and on for a long time after dark, soothing, beautiful to listen to. I had never heard anything like it before, in all the times that I had been alone in the mountains. I could hear her voice perfectly, on and on, soothing, relaxing, singing its way into my spirit. At last I fell asleep to it.

And the next morning at dawn there were no shots. A heavy fog had come in that night, filling up the valley so that visibility was cut to about twenty feet. I waited for quite a while, listening, watching the fog roll past, but I didn't hear a single report. None of the hunters could see past the trees directly in front of them, and even those were shrouded in fog.

It was beyond me.

I BUSHED NORTH for two days, up and down, and made only twelve exhausting miles, trying to stay up to the west of that dirt road along the Boulder River where the seventies were coming in. I saw two goats high on a cloud-streaked cliff at the head of a drainage, and another morning when it was still black and foggy two elk fought near where I lay, squealing and grunting and smashing their antlers together in the predawn blackness. I could hear the cows giving their little birdlike cries, and then they all ran off at the same time with a thunder of hooves. But nowhere in that country did I find sign of a grizzly. I kept wondering if I would run into one.

Finally I got down into a deep ravine-like valley that I was too tired to climb back out of. I began following it down, and it was steep right down to the creek, going through small canyons in the rock that I had to climb up and over. I slept down there that night, dark thunderstorms coming and going, feeling a deep grizzly fear. The next morning I continued down the ravine and didn't see any tracks. By the time the sun came up I hit the Boulder River and the dirt road.

The road was wet and filled with fresh truck tracks. I felt the devil of the seventies in my soul. I felt the gleaming trucks and the dead elk, the sprawling subdivisions and eroded hillsides, the new Black Sky smokestacks and the big rivers getting smaller and warmer, the hordes of people, the fish dwindling from the creeks, the flashy new ski resorts, the grizzlies disappearing. I felt it all hit me as I walked down that road. I had hoped I wouldn't see any people. Not only did I see people, but I was going to see trucks.

I walked up the road, fog hanging off the high and awesome mountains that formed the valley. I thought with a strong irony that at last I had crossed paths with Gabe, for this was the way he had come into the range. These were the very mountains he looked up at, riding up the Boulder River, strange and dark blue near the top. He was already long past, riding up the East Fork of the Boulder River toward the headwaters of Slough Creek, although he didn't know it. He didn't know where he was. I did, by a long shot, and I felt further away from him than I ever did before.

Up ahead I began to see metallic gleams through the trees. It was the parking area for the hunters. When I came up from the mist along the river I saw thirty, thirty-five trucks and horse trailers scattered about a grassy clearing, like a touch of Safeway in the wilderness. There was no one around; they had all gone hunting. I dropped my pack and stood there numbed. I didn't feel like a mountain man any more. I felt dirty, tired, stinking, ravenously hungry, and leg-sore. I felt like I was a fool to have ever dreamed I could find it.

While I was thinking that, a black giant of a bull moose came walking out among the trucks, right in front of me, sniffing them as he passed.

Bullwinkle?

Bullwinkle. I was floored.

Salvation of spirit; medicine of the wild. Survival in the seventies.

There were the great hunters hurrying off at dawn, climbing up into the fog; here was Bullwinkle at midmorning, strolling among their trucks, checking them out.

It was strong medicine all right.

I continued to stare at him as if I were seeing an apparition, watching him make his way among the trailers, raising and lowering his great antlered head at the strange scents; long silver-fringed legs, brute black strength in his upper body, wild nonchalance, morning curiosity. A peaceful spirit inside a huge and strong body. Far and wide. From peak to shining peak.

He passed through the middle of all the trucks, smelling every one that he came near to. When he got to the end of them he stopped at a puddle and took a brief drink, looking back at them. Then he turned and walked on down the road, the way I had come.

I started after him, trying to run him off the road before a hunter came along. He looked once or twice, but didn't pay much attention to me. It was as if an unusually large fly was buzzing along behind him. Finally I got a little too close, and he swung around and gave me the evil eye. The look he aimed at me said that I was starting to piss him off, and if I came any closer he was going to stomp me.

I got out the pistol and aimed at a tree to his left. When the boom hit and the bark went flying he jumped a foot in the air, all four feet off the ground at once, and trotted off the road and up into the woods.

He had survived the despair that was in my mind. The ideological hunger of the seventies.

I went back, got my pack, and followed his tracks the way he had come. He had traveled that road for over two miles before he hit the trucks, at a walk. It just happened that no one with a moose permit came along. It seemed uncanny to me, the way he had walked into the middle of my despair, sniffed at the devils of the seventies. It hit me strong, maybe the most potent medicine yet: somehow I had to stop that glitter from eating away at my spirit.

Where his tracks finally left the road there was a trail leading up into the mountains to the west. The drainage looked huge, tangled and dark. I looked down the road and felt the longing of it, the longing to go now and make it out. I looked up the trail and felt all the fear and uncertainty, the darkness of the Crows, the instinctual feeling I had that there was something bad in them for me. Yet I didn't have to think long; I knew I would go up that trail. It was the whole point of the trip. I wanted to find out what it was. I wanted to test myself against it. As I looked at it I vowed that whatever it was, it wouldn't get me without a fight.

I swallowed my fear and started in. It was a huge drainage, a quarter of a mile across, so deep and tangled it appeared impossible to bush off the trail. Soon a fine rain began to fall, and I felt as if I were walking directly into the realm that had haunted me. In a half hour's time the woods were wet, dripping from boughs and leaning dead trees, and the sky rolled with fog. I began to get the feeling of a grizzly. It was in the wetness, the dripping tangles of foliage, the impenetrable maze of deadfalls sloping away toward the lost bottom. I tried to reason where that feeling was coming from, and I thought it was coming from the Swan trip, for this drainage had exactly the same characteristics as the ones in that range where I had seen fresh grizzly sign. I told myself the feeling was coming from that experience. But no sooner had the feeling settled in me than I saw a huge green pile of grizzly shit in the middle of the trail, with a fresh set of tracks leading along for thirty feet and then going uphill. A day old? A night old? There was a big grizzly in here.

The sense of the woods changed; my instincts began tingling. I was struck with fear. It seemed as if I had walked directly into my premonition, as if the rain and cold and dark clouds and the tracks were all saying that my premonition had been right, and I was going to get it. I didn't know then if I was going to come out alive.

I fought it off. I told myself I was going to make it, and I took out the pistol and checked it. I told myself that if I didn't have time to get up a tree I would make any shot that I had to make, even if it were a one-in-a-million shot. I kept reaching deeper into myself for that confidence, that medicine that I wondered if I still had, and I found some of it, and then some more of it started to flow up, and I let it fill my spirit again, let it run down into my right hand. Confidence of spirit. I would do it exactly right, by instinct. I would do anything I had to do to survive, and I would do it right.

I started on again. Everything seemed to be hanging in a state of suspended tension, and my eyes were constantly searching, my ears listening in every direction. The woods no longer felt empty; they were hiding a beast of great power and intelligence, one that was in deep hiding from the seventies. And it was something in the seventies that had called me into the Crow Mountains. I began to sense in some way that those three things were coming together in me—the grizzly, the seventies, and the sense of my own fate, the sense of something that was going to get me—but I couldn't yet put it together. I only knew that in some vague way they were starting to connect.

After about fifteen minutes I stopped under a tree when it began to rain harder, and crouched there eating jerky. I decided to make some soup, and I was laying tiny twigs on a pile of dead pine needles when there came a deep roar that shot me to my feet. It came from two hundred yards away, back down the trail; I stood there with a racing heart, looking back and forth for it to come bursting out of the trees and at the same time searching with fast glances behind me for a tree to climb. I knew as soon as I heard it that it was a big bear. It had bounced in my chest, shot me to my feet like an electric shock. It sounded like a deep roar of anger.

I stood there and waited, five, ten minutes. Nothing came out. I didn't hear anything else. But it was over a half hour before I dared to go back down the trail, and then it was with a fear that made each of my steps an act of will. I couldn't find any sign of it. There was no trace of it except for that single roar. But I had seen the other tracks, and it was a roar that set my hair on end.

I got my pack and started up the trail, trying to understand what had happened. It had caught my scent? I had walked past that bear, below it. I was two hundred yards upwind from it when it roared.

I had sensed anger in the Crows before I went in, an anger in the darkness back among the peaks, an anger surrounded by the seventies, beset by the seventies, the only place left where it could survive. And just now maybe I had heard it.

THAT NIGHT I built a smudge fire and slept under a pine tree down by the creek, making the test. Four times I woke up, and each time I thought to myself: Why would that bear want to eat me tonight? It has no reason to eat me tonight. Mist came up from the creek, and the growing half-moon floated low through the fog, casting a strange yellow light among the trees. I watched for a moving form in the mist, but saw none. I listened through those haunted woods, but all I heard was the sound of the creek, washing forever over the rocks, sound of the stars, trickle of the universe. Ticking through the wilderness night.

When dawn came I was infinitely glad. I had the vague feeling that I had passed something. I packed up and climbed higher, rising out of the timber. At midmorning I hit the end of the drainage, the top, a glittering silvery lake from which arose countless oval boulders, some of them as big as houses, like giant eggs rising up from the lake toward the jagged granite rim above. There was a notch in it to the north that it looked like I could get over, but I didn't know if I would get rimrocked once I got up there. The sun came out from behind a cloud and I sat down in the rocks and warmed my hands.

The lake was dead, no fish. I felt too weak to make the climb out that day. I built a fire and baked bread with the last of the flour, and made a big jerky-and-rice stew, and stretched my things out in the sun to dry. I took off my shirt and let the sun soak into my body. Medicine.

That night I listened while the moon went down, but whatever the bear feeling was, I had left it behind. The next morning I climbed up through the rocks, above still pools, above rock slides and ridges of boulders, and up through a long stretch of dwarf junipers just under the top, those low evergreens that dig their roots down through the rocks and into the earth, and dig their fingers into it and grab ahold, and that maniac wind comes along at eighty miles an hour and tries to tear them out of the ground, and they just stay low and keep their roots in the earth, and the wind can't tear them loose. Dwarf jupiters, I call them. I climbed up through them dwarf jupiters growing out of the rocks, till I hit the stones just under the rim, and walked out onto the edge.

I clumb off my charger and took a look. She was peaks, peaks ever'whar, an' it seemed like I war at the top o' creation. The wind come up over from afar and hit through my buckskins, and the sound of it carried a loneliness like I never knowed, a far loneliness like I'd come up into another world, a world I never seed the like of, nor felt, afore. Some of the peaks was shinin' in the sun; others of 'em was layin' in the shadow of clouds. White misty clouds was hangin' off some of 'em away off in the distance. They was spirit mountains all right, sure enough they was spirit mountains.

I seed a long dark ridge on the right side. It looked to me like I could see smoke comin' off'n that ridge way on down, but it war so far I couldn't make out if it was smoke or mist. The whole lay of it give an eerie feelin', but it war the only way south. Reckoned I'd head for that smoke and see if old Gabe got turned into mist.

I made a big fire behind some rocks down out of the wind, roasted some more deer meat and et my fill. Warn't for that deer an' I'd be powerful hungry about now. Reckoned I'd stay up here high tonight an' make medicine. I set down cross-legged by the fire, an' I brung out my bones and feathers.

Peaks was turnin' dark and silvery all as far as I could see, an' I set thar lookin' at 'em. The wind come up over the rocks with a hiss, it come from far away and it war an autumn wind, turnin' cold. I put my hands up in it so's I could feel it on my fingers, I closed my fists on it, an' I asked it for its power. I asked it inside me and I asked it aloud with my voice, and I felt it in my arms and in my spirit. Give me your power that blows from afar, that don't know no bounds, that runs free from peak to peak and don't never end. Blow inside me and give me your strength to keep me goin', for I need some new medicine. I felt it far away comin' from them dark and silvery peaks, and I felt the power of it blowin' inside me. And it war comin' good medicine, I could feel it. Gabe war always a friend of the wind, and now that wind war givin' him its medicine. I shet my eyes an' felt it blowin' over me, and I listened to it, and I let it more inside me, and it war a good, far feelin'. An' afore long, away off somewhars, I begun to hear a sound under that wind. I didn't know whar it was comin' from nor what was makin' it, but I heared it, and it war soothin' an' good. It was a song of things I knowed, forests and rivers and sun and plains, ranges up and down the Shinin' Mountains,

*all the country I'd ridden and the wild animals that had the run
of it, that kept me alive, it war all in that faraway song that
come in under the wind. It war good medicine all right, even if I
couldn't find no reason in it, no explanation for it. Reckoned it
war a song o' life.*

NOT FAR across the haze rose a series of shark-toothed peaks,
rimmed together, like a strange outgrowth in the divide. To the
west were peaks, gray and misty, everywhere. Beyond to the
north lay a high and barren plateau country, a mixture of
thudded peaks, massive windswept ridges. Straight north after
the head of the valley I saw a long hulk of a ridge with a dark
streak in it, running north, and when I saw it I felt the old
tingling of the Crow Mountains, their dark spirit. That was the
only way north. The way I would go.

This was it, the rugged interior of the range. *Up and down the
mountains through the seventies;* all those miles and the years of
searching, the spiritual poverty and anxiety of the decade—it all
led to these windswept mountains standing in front of me, the
mortal number of footsteps that led through them to the north.
And looking out over it and trying to sense what it was, all I
could feel was a vast sense of emptiness, and over it the play of
the wind.

I started down a steep snowfield with a fresh layer of powder
on it, down over a slide and into the high head of the valley.
Right at the bottom it was grassy, but it soon broke into hills of
rock, little timber-fringed ridges, rising and falling with subalpine ruggedness. I jumped a grouse and it burst away without
the chance for a shot; I jumped two more and the same thing
happened. They flew away from me as if they had seen a ghost.
It was as if, even though I was hungry, something had turned,
some medicine had put them out of my reach. I felt in a deep
way that I wasn't going to get one. No fresh food.

I explored for two or three hours and found no human signs,
no horse sign. A little bit of deer sign, no fresh elk. There was
hardly any big game up here at all, so little that I could hardly
count on it if I got stuck in the big snow.

I was sitting on a rock when a black shadow passed overhead,
and I looked up and saw a lone golden eagle winging toward

one of the shark-toothed peaks: five or six wingbeats and then a glide, five or six wingbeats and then a glide, over and over, till it was gone in a gap between the peaks. And I thought: *Maybe the wind.*

I ate a bunch of jerky and started to climb, toward where it had gone. I was climbing up steep channels in the rock that trickled springwater; if it snowed I would be stuck up there until it melted. The sky was scattered with huge cloud fragments that were floating in from the southwest, so that the sun shone weakly now and then. I climbed steadily for a long time, and by the time I came to the top it was evening and my shirt was soaked with sweat. A steady cold wind came over the top, chilling me so I shivered, and I got out my wool shirt and windbreaker and put them on. It was coming from far to the west, and it hit the two peaks rising up on either side of me and poured through the wide gap that I was standing in. 'Lo, wind. Are you my friend?

There was cover from the west, a line of boulders with a mat of dwarf jupiters growing in front of them. I cleared the bigger stones out and made a bed in among the jupiters, a hard bed, but one where I couldn't be blown away. I was up above 11,000 feet; the wind left trailways through the granite chips, and during a bad storm it picked them up and hurled them through the air like little bits of metal. I ate some more jerky, then tied my pack into the jupiters and snapped my poncho closed around my sleeping bag. When I had it set the way I wanted it I crawled in and settled back to wait.

The darkness came slowly. It settled into the shadows among the peaks, deepened among them, turned them silvery and awesome into the distance. It rose up above them and spread through the sky. The wind came out of it, and it made a high, infinite hissing sound off the peaks above me. I lay there and listened to it as it came and went in the darkness. In it was all the power and emptiness of the heights, the huge sweep of it, the earthly silence in between gusts. A few windblown stars shone through the clouds. I kept waiting for it to begin to rise, to begin to stream through the gap, but long into the night there was only that great hissing sound that came sometimes high off the peaks, and the stars, windblown stars. All I could sense was its great, empty power. The tissues of my body seemed paltry against it. A region of emptiness; few deer, few elk, peaks rising into more peaks, the windswept loneliness of space. I woke to it through the night, but the wind didn't rise.

A streak of red in the east; another dawn, and I felt that I had passed. I stood up and dressed in the wind that was still hissing, the cold autumn wind that I could still feel on my skin. *You are my friend,* I thought, *and I am yours.*

I went down the other side, a two-hour descent. The ridge with the dark streak in it lay to the northeast, and I climbed toward it, down a steep jumble of rock hills, under a big dry waterfall, up through long scattered rocks and timber, steeper and higher. Another grouse burst away without the slightest chance for a shot; hunger medicine. I felt close to exhaustion.

When at last I came over the top of the back ridge I was looking down into a strange lonely-looking valley that ran north for three or four miles, then ended against the folds of timbered mountainsides in lower country. There was something about it that struck me immediately; an extreme feeling of isolation. It looked as if hardly anyone ever went down into it. It looked lost, like a forgotten valley.

Below me spread a long expanse of boulder fields and slides. Up the hill it broke into cliffs; there was no other way except to angle down over the slides to the right. It was a long way down, and looking at it I felt it aching through my back and shoulders, my knees. I knew it would be hard, and exacting. I rested for a while, drinking some water, and then started down.

A half hour later I was sweating heavily and I felt light-headed. I kept thinking it was going to end but it didn't, and the piles of rocks and boulders that sloped far and wide seemed to be swimming before my eyes. The peaks around me seemed to be floating with a maddening air of loneliness, emptiness. My laboring body was all that was real, and it was starting not to seem real to me. My muscles felt as if they were losing their core of strength, and I was getting careless, starting to lose my grip on myself without even realizing it. And then a voice inside me said, *Maybe the rocks.*

I stopped. I was breathing heavily, sweat dripping off my head, and I stood there looking around, regaining my conscious-

ness again. The voice had come from deep in my subconscious. I
stopped and rested, splashed some water in my face, cleared my
head. I was starting to get mountain sickness; when the loneliness and the wind and the vast stretches of rocky nothingness
start to drive a person ringy. That was what was happening.

With an act of will I brought my concentration and instinct
back up to the surface, and I started down again. I concentrated on every step I made, and I used my instincts to sense
which rock might turn under my foot, or which big rock might
not be lying solidly. I kept going like that for another half hour,
concentrating on everything I did until I started to get a head-
ache, but working consciously over the piles of boulders, holding
on to that spark of determination in me that said I was going to
make it. Holding on to my consciousness. And somewhere
toward the bottom I paused to rest, leaning on a long boulder
that must have weighed eight hundred pounds, and as soon as I
put my hand on it, it started to go. It slid downward with
grating noises that sent out spurts of granite dust, falling off the
boulder it had been resting on and crashing into the rocks below.
When it hit it sent other rocks clattering down the slide, and the
echos rolled off the mountains, off their empty heights, and on
down that strange lost valley. It would have cut me in half.

I sat down and looked at the sky. I looked all around at the
mountains, and I shook my head. I tried to go back and retrace
my footsteps and see what made me pass above that boulder,
instead of below it. There was no answer in it; it was all gravity
and chaos, a chaos of boulders falling off the top of the mountain for a long, long time. The fate of the Crow Mountains. I
thought for a long time, and all I could think was that you could
will confidence into being. That if you weren't foolish about it,
even if it seemed gone, you could will confidence and passage
back into being.

*Rode down that valley for three days, days o' dark skies, many a
time thinkin' I oughter turn back. I was gittin' deep into the
spirit of them mountains, and eerie they was, my backside tinglin', wonderin' all the time what that smoke was up ahead. It
war a mighty strange country all right, the timber war deep,
warn't a sign of Injun nor white man. I'm wonderin' if'n I'm
gonna see them waters o' spring agin.*

*Afore long I begun to see that smoke up thar in the distance
through the timber. It war comin' off that long dark-streaked
ridge, about a third o' the way up, whar the ridge come down to
a gap. It was comin' right out'n the beginnin' of that gap. It
warn't no Injun smoke, I knowed that. It was smokin' day and
night, I seed it goin' in the moonlight, an' thar was a feelin' of
somethin' awful an' powerful in it. I clumb off my charger and
stood thar a-lookin' up at it. Storm clouds was comin' in so's the
sky was turnin' low and dark; that smoke come swirlin' through
them trees up above, some of it white and some of it yellerish,
like a warnin' that a body hadn't oughter go up thar. Like there
was somethin' big and dark that lived up thar on the other side
of that smoke, an' it war best to pass by it an' count your bless-
in's as you went.*

*Reckoned I'd find out what it was. I unpacked the mule an'
pulled the saddle off'n my charger, and tied 'em both off good
so's they could git at some grass. I et some deer. Then I set off a-
climbin' up through them trees, carryin' my Hawken ready in
both hands. Bullthrower was my Hawken's name, and I cocked
it, an' I patted it on the stock for all the fixes it seed me through.
Figgered if thar war an evil spirit up thar, an' the son of a bitch
was gonna git me, it'd catch a ball afore I went down.*

I WALKED among the last of the rocks scattered through the
grass, to the beginning of the pines, and looked down into the
valley. I didn't want to go down into it. There was something
about it that I didn't like, a feeling that it was lost from time, that
no one ever went into it. I was exhausted, and I didn't want to go
through with it.

I got out the maps and tried to figure out where it went to
down at the end. I couldn't make the country I could see down
there correspond to what the map showed. I tried for an hour,
turning the map this way and that, using the compass, but I
couldn't make it fit, or get its relation to the Boulder watershed.
I knew that if I couldn't find it, all I had to do was climb east
and I would eventually come out on the Boulder River. But I
knew too that if a big snow came it would make steep climbing
impossible. I would be stuck down there till it melted.

I looked at the sky. Off to the southwest a high gray mass of
cloud was moving up the sky. I couldn't tell if it was a storm

mass or not. It was up very high, moving slowly and imperceptibly, and it had already covered a third of the sky. Big lonely gusts of wind came over the high jags of the divide and poured through the trees, raining needles and sticks, and then died away. Was it the forerunner of a big storm? I couldn't tell. It was a misty white around its edge, dark near the middle. It gave me a strange feeling. Why had it come now, just when I got to this valley? It seemed like too much of a coincidence.

I began to feel more afraid. The map showed that there was a trail running through this valley; I left my pack and walked up toward the upper corner to find it. After looking quite a while I saw three or four switchbacking cuts in the grass near the top, but I couldn't find it down below where I was. Finally I climbed up to it and started following it. There wasn't any horse sign, no tracks at all. After it left the steepness the trail disappeared without a trace.

Maybe your own footsteps.

No one used this valley. No one had been down through it in years.

The sun was setting, gone behind that high cloud mass. I walked back down to my pack and sat looking down into the valley. It would be the valley a grizzly sought out, one where people didn't go. I was sure there was a grizzly there. It would be the valley I had been looking for ever since I came out west —one that was wild, one where there were no people. That only struck me as ironic now, for I was deeply afraid of it.

The valley I had been looking for.

Darkness was coming down. I made a bed inside the trees and lay there with the hard lonely wind blowing, feeling stranger than I could ever remember feeling. I didn't know if I had the courage to go down into the valley. That trail was there above me, and everything in me was longing to go up it and out that way and save myself. I was bone-weary, run down to empty, and I didn't think I had enough jerky left to wait out a big snow. With snow would come tracks, but there were hardly any deer in this country. I might not be able to find one before my muscles gave out. I could wait a long time by a fire if I kept my head but sooner or later I would have to find the strength to make my way out.

All those thoughts were running through my head, but beyond them all was the spirit of the Crow Mountains, riding over my subconscious like that dark and silvery cloud mass high in the stratosphere. It seemed to be hanging there, waiting on my decision. The image of the trail disappearing in the grass kept coming to mind, and I felt hollow inside, as if there were nothing left of me, as if the wind and peaks had triumphed over my spirit. All night I wrestled with it, dozing, waking up, turning over, waking again and lying there looking at the high cloud mass. Wondering if I would go down through that valley.

Come up through the trees an' I begun to hear a bubblin' sound. Smoke was comin' through the trees thicker, an' it smelled bad. Trees all around was dead, ghostly-like in that smoke, an' the ground was ash an' white powder, crusty. Come up to the smoke an' I seed a big pool o' bilin' mud, yeller mud! Hair rose on my neck. Thar was other pools about, an' steam comin' out'n a cone in the rock. I crep' around with Hawken ready to fire, but I didn't see nothin'. It war the ha'ntin'est place I ever seed, made me so's I was walkin' on coals and turnin' around ever' other step. I figgered if'n them Injuns was right, this was whar the big evil son of a bitch would be livin' all right.

Well, I didn't find no tracks, and thar warn't no sign of him anywhar that I could see, so I turned around to head down. An' that damn voice in me switched around, an' it says to me: "Now, Gabe, you don't know for sure that thar ain't an evil spirit up here, and you ain't gonna make your medicine till you find out. Spirits don't normally come out during the day—they come out at night. You can't say there ain't no evil spirit in these hyar spiritful mountains less'n you spend the whole damn night up here."

Son of a bitch. I knowed it war right. I went back down to the animals, packed 'em and brung 'em up the hill, an' tied 'em thrice around to some live trees out at the edge. Sun war settin' behind some storm clouds that was comin' up from the so'west. Got me my robe and sat down in the ash agin a dead tree, not fur from that bilin' mud pot, an' waited while the darkness come on. Last o' the twilight I seed a handful of crows circlin' off a mountain across the valley, raisin' a ruckus. Then darkness come down, an' I war alone with that infernal bilin' in the earth.

Mist begun to rise. Them storm clouds was slowly comin' in closer, thunder rumblin' off in the distance, far-off flickers o' lightnin'. My hair begun to creep 'cross my scalp. I jest set thar tight, a-lookin' around, hands on my Hawken, hatchet on my right an' pistol on my left. Low yeller moonlight war comin' in through them dead trees. I jest set thar waitin', longer into the night till I lost track o' time, the thunder movin' closer. Thought I seed somethin' move once but I reckoned it war my imagirnation. Told myself thar warn't no sech thing as a evil spirit, them Injuns was superstitious as children an' they didn't know no better. Told myself I war a mountain man, and I warn't scairt o' no evil spirit. Told myself that more 'n once, by thunder.

Truth was, I war wrestlin' with the urge to hightail it on outta thar.

A HAND tapped me on the shoulder, and a voice said gently in my ear, "The wind is blowing, and there's enough light to see." I sprang awake, twisting around to see who it was, but there was no one there. All the loneliness of the surrounding peaks, the aloneness of my predicament, swept over me for a moment, then passed into the morning light. The hand and the voice had been real enough to shock me, to make me think that there was someone really there. Yet it had been my subconscious. My subconscious had tapped me on the shoulder and spoken into my ear.

I got up. There was gray light all through the trees, steel-gray light off the peaks. I looked all around and didn't see anything moving, or hear anything. I walked out into the open and stood there thinking, looking at that high, dark cloud. It had scarcely moved, but seemed to be hanging there. I decided I'd go down into that valley.

Two grouse burst away at my approach. As soon as I got into the trees I felt something lightening in me, rising into my body and my perceptions. My head cleared, a new tone came into my muscles, and my hands felt quick and sure. I worked down the old blazes in the trees, sensing and watching, and the further down I went, the lighter and more certain I began to feel. My pistol was loose in my holster. When I got down to the bottom I saw an old pole off through the trees, and I moved toward it.

I walked out into a clearing and saw an old, deserted hunting camp. No one had used it for years and years; the forties, the fifties, the sixties had rained down upon it. The trees had grown around the corral poles; the weather had split the stumps they used for stools. Grass was growing up where the fire had been and there was part of a strange old syrup bottle half buried in the ground. The whole camp was overgrown, sinking into the earth. For a moment I felt as if I had entered a twilight zone, a deserted realm of history. I remembered the emptiness of the high peaks over the last several days, the far-reaching emptiness of the wind, and I thought back to that night in the Swans, up on the ridge after I had seen the goats, when the Milky Way was like a cloud of mist and the stars seemed to be pulsing with life, with mystery, filling me with the longing to know what was up there. I walked among the overgrown corral poles and tried to picture the scenes, the sounds of elk fighting under the first evening stars, and men running after them with guns, oblivious to those stars. Always the same stars, from Taos to Wind River, up to the Crow Mountains. In the valley of fate there was a hunting camp that had been deserted for thirty years.

It was as if after the first half of the range, the mildness and beauty and feelings of creation, the second half had been like a journey into the future, past Bullwinkle and the glints of the seventies, through the eighties, hinting at emptiness, toward the year 2000. Something had been drawing me in these mountains, pulling at me like a magnet, calling me until I got to this valley. Whatever it was, I knew this was it. The calling had ended at a deserted hunting camp. It stood like a warning, rising beyond all I had experienced. While I followed an old dream. All the pain and disappointment in the search through the decade, trying to be a mountain man in spirit: as the American system dug into the Shining Mountains in the seventies, it was reaching a point in history where it was beginning to eat its own soul, bury its own dreams. Dreams of mountain men, dreams of pioneers. Dreams of the wild. When the land was stripped those dreams would be gone; in a certain amount of time it would be too far gone to resurrect. People who loved the land had to stop them, before it got too late.

The seventies were just beginning to pour into the Crow

Mountains, and the eighties would hit them harder. I had dreamed of a range where I could travel wild with a pack and a gun, like a mountain man, where it would feel wild and remote enough to take a deer when I got hungry. I was too late. There was no range like that left in the lower forty-eight. The population now was too large to do it, and big game was going downhill. It was true of the Crow Mountains as well, the wildest range left.

And I realized then that was why I had Gabe traveling south in this range while I was traveling north. We were going in opposite directions. He was riding back into history, toward a dream I had when I first came to the Rockies. And no matter how much I longed for it, I couldn't ride backward in history. I had to ride ahead, toward the future.

I stood up, looking around at the overgrown stumps, the weather-cracked poles. That was the spirit I found in the Crow Mountains. The spirit of the future: the sunrise, the singing in the fog, the hawks in the wind, the black shiny moose at dawn near the hunting camp. The mild spirit of creation hidden in the mountains, a spirit of grass, blue skies, morning breezes, and the wandering life of a bear. A spirit that called to me from the future, a spirit that was still there.

But I knew now that it had no power, no dark anger. The eighties, the nineties, and the rich developers would do to it whatever people let them do. It was helpless to protect itself. Only people who loved it could protect it. It was a spirit that found its highest expression in people, its mirror in people. It didn't exist separately from the land. It could be ruined, and it could be lost. It is a spirit that can't save itself. Only humans could destroy it, and only humans could save it.

I STARTED on again, and the further down the valley I went, the more a feeling of completion rose up into my being. It was the end of the search. For the first time I felt like I was going to make it through the Crow Mountains, through the seventies. I had the feeling that I had passed the test, that a dark veil of superstition that had been haunting me all through the seventies had lifted. It was bad all right, but not so bad I couldn't sit down and pick my way through it. I had to find my way through it, and hold on to my spirit. And stars of the sky or stars of Fort

Hollywood, I knew which way I wanted to go. For it was glamour and status that were destroying the spirit of the land.

I came down to a clearing where the creek wound through the grass, a mild-looking clearing with sharp square chunks of shale falling down into it on the close side. As I came up to it, it began to glow with bright sunlight, while all the timber and rocks around it remained dark in cloud shadow. It glowed like that for ten seconds, then went out. I was at the end of the valley. I stood there remembering the sunrise, the singing, the spiritual feeling of the spring. There was something about the way those things happened that I couldn't explain.

Below the clearing the valley spilled into deep timber. I lost the faint trail several times in tangled log piles, but stayed on the blazes. After a long time I dropped down into a timbered flat, and there I found fresh horse tracks on another trail. I followed them across the creek to the east, then hit a side trail which left off from them and began climbing the ridge due east. I figured it must be the one that led over toward the Boulder drainage. This was where I had been afraid I would get hit by a snowstorm, the trail I wouldn't be able to find, the trail leading out of the valley of fate. I started up it and had not gone more than four hundred yards when I looked up and saw a big lone deer coming down the trail toward me. It was a doe. I froze. All through the whole trip I had wondered in the back of my mind if I would get to a place that felt wild enough to justify taking a deer. I had wondered that before all of the trips, wondered if that experience would be a part of the book. I had seen deer on the first day in the Crow Mountains, and I hadn't seen any since. The country I had just come through seemed empty and windswept, void of life. Now, on the last day, after the last test, a deer was walking toward me close enough to shoot with the pistol. It was as if that spirit that had run through all the ranges, that I had trailed through all the seasons, now finally raised its head in the Crow Mountains and spoke to me. *Don't take one unless you need the meat. If you would have gotten into trouble down in that valley, if a snow would have come, you would have had this deer that is walking toward you. It would have meant life to you. As long as you don't need it, let it live. There might come a time when you'll be glad it's there.*

Medicine of the Shining Mountains.

It stood forty feet away, daylight gleaming in its black eyes, raising and lowering its head again and again, first low to the ground and then high, trying to get wind of me. Trying to figure out what I was. Finally I waved it on up the mountain.

And then, climbing higher, I remembered Gabe. In a flash I realized I had just passed him by. Without even thinking about it I had pulled ahead of him. I left him in the night, back at the head of the valley that lay behind me; back in those swirling mists of North American history. Back down the elk trails of time, toward the earth's oldest superstition.

'Bout time, by thunder. I set thar with my finger on the set trigger, lookin' side to side with wide eyes, tryin' to see through that ghostly yeller mist. That storm kept edgin' closer, an it warn't like no storm I ever seed. Seemed like a big snake was sneakin' up on me in the dark, through them rumblin' clouds. I set thar a-shakin', tryin' to tell myself thar wasn't no evil spirits, tryin' to tell myself them Injuns was jest superstitious, and I knowed better. And right when I war a-tellin' all that to myself thar come a crack o' lightnin' that lifted me off'n my seat, boom o' thunder and the ground begun to rumble, I heared a whinnyin' laugh somewhars, and of a sudden the earth exploded with water and mist flyin' ever'whar, and right through that mist I seed the tail end of a red cape slip behind a tree.

Lord bejesus, it was the devil. Oh m' God. The hair stood up on my neck and my gut shriv'led up like an old man's fist, and I set thar shakin' all through my body like a pizened dog. I war paralyzed with a fear like I never knowed. I'd forgot all about the evil son of a bitch and now he war comin' to git me. He'd heard me 'n' Fitz plottin' to bust outta hell and now I warn't even gonna git to see the gangplank o' heaven, nor feel St. Peter's holified boot. That devil war gonna drag me right down to the coal pits straightaway.

I seed two sparks move through the dead trees an' a little cry o' fear come out'n my throat like a mouse before a hawk hits. I had that Hawken in my hands so's my knuckles was white, but I couldn't move it. I jest set thar shakin' like a leaf, countin' my last moments on earth.

I got to my feet, and I stood thar still a-shakin', but pointin' that Hawken an' tryin' to spot whar he was. Didn't see him nowhere. Wind come up and swirled the mist, thunder boomed in the sky. Then another big flash come and I seed red off to the right. Raised up and fired. The smoke no sooner cleared into the mist when I heard that whinnyin' laugh off to the left. The son of a bitch was ever'whar at once!

Reached down slow-like, fingers tremblin', an' picked up my hatchet and my pistol. I begun callin' on my medicine. 'Lo, sun, 'lo, rivers, the Evil One's after old Gabe. Whar are ye, son, whar's your spirit? 'Lo, sun. Come back, boy. You ain't goin' down without a fight, are ye? You ain't gonna set thar like a whipped dog while that spark-eyed cacklin' son of a bitch lays his hot hands on your neck, are ye? No, sir. You ain't goin' down without a fight.

I begun to git mad. I could feel anger comin' into my arms, and into my teeth.

"Come on, you pitchforked son of a bitch," I says. "Come on out here whar I can git my hands on you."

I circled slow through the mist, hatchet in my right hand, pistol cocked in my left, teeth gritted with my medicine. I seed a flash o' red, but I held my fire, waitin' for a good shot. Then I seed them two beady sparks right in front o' me through the mist.

"Take this, you fire-breathin' devil!" I yells, and I let go with a pistol shot straight into his gut. Echo was no sooner lost in the thunder than I felt a hot smokin' finger tap me on the shoulder.

I dropped the pistol and come around with that hatchet hard enough to lop the head off'n a bull ox, but thar warn't nothin' thar but thin air, he'd already vanished. Hatchet flew way the hell 'n' gone through the trees. I heard that whinny o' laughter through the swirlin' mist.

I scooped up some o' that hot water in my hat and begun stalkin' him. "Come out in the open, you bat-eared son of a bitch!" I says. "Come on out of that smoke and I'll give ye a taste o' water. You ain't gonna drag this poor child down to hell without knowin' you done some draggin'!"

A puff o' fiery breath hit me in the back o' the neck. I spun around and throwed, but the son of a bitch was gone again, cacklin' over in the mist by that mud pot.

I throwed the hat down. All I had left was my two fists. I looked into the deepest part o' that mist, and I seed them two sparks, jest standin' thar, lookin' at me. I raised both my fists. I seed his arms folded in his cape as I walked closer, his bat ears through the mist, pointed tail twistin' behind him, little goatee beard, them sparky eyes and the smile o' evil acrost his face, jest a-standin' thar lookin' me on, as if to say, Now's the time, Gabe. Now you're goin' down. I raised my right fist an' when I got close enough I let that son of a bitch go with everything I had in me, right fer his smilin' teeth. It was the last thing I remember. I seed the Milky Way flash through my head, like one big throbbin' heartbeat full o' stars. Then ever'thing went to darkness.

Well, when I woke up my head was achin'. I didn't open my eyes; I jest layed thar an' lissened for the moanin' an' gnashin' o' teeth, an' all them ouches echoin' through the mountains o' hell. All I heard was birds. Didn't never think thar was birds in hell. Opened my eyes an' instead o' coal smoke I seed blue sky, a big open blue sky all the way across above the trees. I sat up, rubbin' my head. I was sittin' in front of a dead tree. Thar was the mud pot, bilin' away. Thar was my animals. By thunder, I was still on this old earth.

Got up and looked around for his tracks, but he didn't leave a one. Thar warn't a sign of him. I must've knocked the son of a bitch clean out!

Well, I'll be goddamned. I looked at my right fist. Blood on it, an' sore. Reckoned I hit him a lick all right. Reckoned I knocked that cacklin' son of a bitch clear back down into hell!

Well, I was feelin' pretty good. Picked up my hat, brushed the ashes off, hunted up my pistol, and begun packin'. Looked around, but I never did find that hatchet. Mebbe he grabbed it and took it with him on the way down.

Wait till I tell the boys, I'm thinkin' as I packed. Wait till I tell 'em the story of the putrified forest, an' the story of the night old Gabe fought the devil! One hell of a fight it was, boys!

Well, I rode on down that little river, an' end of the day it opened up into a valley that struck me to my bones, wild an' mild an' purty it war, plenty o' grass for the animals. It war like I'd come home.

I camped at the head of it that night, took me a splashin' in a little hot pool I found thar, and let the animals eat their fill, then dawn come an' I started on down. Frost was meltin', sparklin' red an' blue as I come through, an' thar was a big bull moose out in the willers; elk a-fightin' an' clackin' their horns up on the mountainside, an' deer runnin' ever' which way, black bears rootin' around whar the creeks come down—more wild critters than I ever seed in one place afore. It war like old Gabe had come out'n the place o' twilight an' back to life in the Shinin' Mountains. Rode on to whar the valley spilled down through the timber, an' come onto rollin' open hills, sage, an' buffler. An it war lookin' famil'ar to me. I rode out for a day, looked around, and then I knowed whar I war. This was the very country whar White Grass hunted buffler in the fall, an he warn't come through yet. West o' here would be the trail to the Three Tits an' Pierre's Hole.

An' sittin' thar back in country I knowed, thinkin' o' all I'd come through, thinkin' o' my knees an' the winter comin' on, thinkin' o' the look on White Grass's face when he come up an' thinkin' o' Mountain Lion, thinkin' o' my medicine, I got me an idee, I got me an idee. My name warn't Runs Like Wind no more. No, sir. My name warn't Runs Like Wind no more. It was White Wolf.

I rode back up into that valley clippin' along, my mind a-workin' on it, layin' it out. Right whar that hot spring war I'd build me a little cabin, start layin' in logs right today. When she got colder I'd hang me up a deer an' an elk, an' I'd haul in some buffler from the hill country. Kill off a griz or two so's they wouldn't run me out, and then I'd have me lamp and saddle grease. Smoke some fish if'n I had time, an' git in a pile a moss afore it froze in. Meantime git my medicine suit ready. Couldn't wait to see the look on White Grass's face. Reckoned he'd like to faint dead away.

Old Gabe warn't done roamin' yet, by thunder. Even if'n he couldn't trap no more, nor run like the wind. He warn't done roamin' yet.

I STARTED up a huge wash and found the trail again, climbing back and forth up steep switchbacks. The Boulder River should be twelve miles down the other side of this ridge; it was the last ridge I had to climb. As I labored under the pack I thought of my medicine and Gabe's medicine, the ride into the past and the ride into the future. We had both fought with superstition, and we had both won. But he still believed in it; I didn't.

There wasn't any dark and angry spirit in the Crow Mountains. It was in the times I was living through. Superstition was a form of oppression, whether psychic or political; all through history superstition has led people to make fools of themselves. So now in the back of my subconscious Gabe is thinking that if his plan works out he will have quite a power over White Grass and his bunch; he will be able to get whatever he needs from them. He knows there is no power on earth like the idea of a spirit, and now he is thinking that a steamboat full of whiskey and trading goods couldn't lure White Grass away if he thinks Gabe's medicine is stronger than the Evil Spirit.

When I finally walked over the crest I saw the Boulder River valley far down the drainage that lay below me. I turned around and looked back across the wilderness of peaks that lay to the horizon, thinking of the journey I had just come through, the mental and emotional territory I had covered. All I could feel was that it was a deep and extraordinary range.

And I thought to myself: Maybe there are currents in the earth which are only explainable in terms of spirit. Maybe there are certain psychic connections between humans and the earth which can only be explained in terms of spirit. Currents as indefinable as the threads that weave their way into love. It struck me that that was what I had felt that morning the ridge had turned ultraviolet and the gold sun had risen off the mountains. I had felt without even realizing it that I loved it, that it was more beautiful than anything I could ever do or make, that it moved me to the heights of my being. And I felt that burning anger at the lies they were telling about energy in the seventies, about how they were doing everything they could and it had to go to coal and strip-mining before it could go to solar and wind. That was the biggest lie in the seventies. I had thought there was some anger in the Crow Mountains at what was happening to the land in this decade, but it had been my anger, subconsciously projected into the range. The only true anger I found was in the heart of the grizzly. A roar like the spirit of the range. I would keep that anger in my soul.

When I got to the bottom of the ridge I found a motorcycle track, about a week old, coming up the trail. It had roared all the way up that long wild drainage. I looked back around at the ridgetop, the weather closing in; maybe that dark cloud taking over the range behind me was the eighties, coming on, and I had better dig in and get ready for it. Maybe the eighties were going to be harder on the mountains than the seventies were.

A vision of my mule floated into my head. Something about it was dawning on me, the way I had held on to it through the years. I had to take a look at that poor old thing when I got back to Fort Hollywood.

I started down the trail, and it seemed like hours of one foot-step after another, thousands of footsteps. Pains shot through the cords in my neck, my back ached, my ankles and knees felt like there were thistles in them. At last I came out on a tremendous mountainside overlooking the Boulder River, but it was another long and aching stretch of time before I wound my way down to the bottom.

When I finally stepped out onto the dirt road it was twilight, and there were summer cabins scattered around. No one home. I couldn't have walked much further. With a sweet sense of the end of the journey I let my pack fall to the ground, and slowly I lay down in the weeds by the side of the road. Spring, summer, and fall, in and out of the seventies. Selway, there is only one Selway in the West, a jewel. Swans, moon mountains, wild, no wildlife; a little silver griz eating through a hundred and fifty years of history. Gabe. Spirit of the passing seasons, spirit of the earth. Write like him. Crow Mountains, mountains of the spirit, future of the Rockies. Fort Hollywood. Seventies, eighties, black skies. Stars at night. Belief in history, belief in the future, seeds of the future. The spirit of the land. Muscles aching, aching and sinking, tired, sweet exhaustion, sinking, sinking into the ground.

Something made me raise my head. Something that I didn't hear or see. Out in the meadow by the road two young deer came skipping out into the twilight, hurrying, looking around for danger as they went. But playful together, going lightly through the twilight, like a glimpse of the future. Life for the mountain men, and now food for thought, my truest link with them. They had come out in the evening to eat a little bit of the earth.

It was one last touch of the spirit.

GOODBYE, FORT HOLLYWOOD

AND A long, long way it is from that wild spirit to the streets of Fort Hollywood. Down from the last big range left in the Rockies, trailing an ageless dream of the mountain men, the modern fear and wonder up there and the wrenching of my spirit, the final breakthrough at last—all that suddenly switched on the moment to the sights and sounds of those streets again. Bright colors, noise, honks, hurried footsteps, the subconscious profit fever streaking everywhere in the streets. It surprised me; I walked around and took it in, a return to modern existence. It was unexpectedly uplifting.

For about a day and a half. I soon noticed that Fort Hollywood was starting to spin like a top gone berserk. Lunch hour on Main Street looked like "The Gong Show"; more and more new people hurrying to buy richer clothes, shinier gadgets, trying whole hog to catch up with the stars. More and more noses traveling around up in the air. If dirty looks could fracture picture windows, well, it was getting to be a very breezy town.

I got in old Sixties and took a ride down that frenetic high-class street. Before long those new people were laughing and pointing, guffawing at how beat-up and out of style that mule was, nothing at all like the class those stars had. And it was limping all right, coughing and stalling at the stop signs, its eyes cracked and dazed, ribs ganted in, having a hard time getting going again. I held on to my pride, patted it on the dash and whispered encouraging words in its ear. I noticed that the latest thing in the store windows was an automated stainless-steel nose picker, going for only $19.95. Selling like hotcakes too.

"*You're not the one who is wrong,*" I whispered. "*They are.*"

I rode that mule back to my lodge and tethered it out by the shed. I put the blanket back over its tired shoulders, and I put some clean oil in it. By God, that mule would ride again, I said to the sparrows.

But there was something deeper in me whispering, something from the spirit of the Crow Mountains. *You can't ride an old mule into the future of America. You have to ride with the times. Even if you don't like 'em.*

I didn't like that voice. How could I ride a different mule? After all the miles we'd been through, all the times we'd seen? I didn't see how I could let go of it. That mule, like the wild mountains I had seen in it, was a feeling in my heart. I saw the connections, and I feared if I let go of old Sixties I would be letting go of my hope for the Rockies. I searched my memory, back through the places I had been, the wild rivers like veins in the flow of my memory, trying to call up something essential, something that would crystallize out of the experience. But it was too soon, it wasn't coming. I couldn't see the direction yet.

THE TAIL END OF
A MONTANA RENDEZVOUS

SATURDAY NIGHT came along and I figured I'd drink on it. I walked on into the fort with a neon haze starting to fill the sky, heading for the Waste o' Time bar. The best foot-stomping band in the valley was billed in and it figured to be quite a night. The Waste o' Time bar was also known as the Strangler, and when that band came in there on Saturday night something usually flew before the night was over.

It was already crowded when I got there. I gave four bits to the Buddha by the door and went on back to a table with some people I knew, smoke rising, the band stringing and tuning, warming up. The crowd was excited, restless, getting that alcohol flowing into its veins. The band kicked into a couple numbers, exploring, feeling the crowd out, looking for direction.

People were waiting in an unconscious way, talking up a storm, checking outfits to see who looked the most like a star. The band kept toying with it, poking around for the right place to dive in. And just when it looked like they were ready to take the jump, a strange supernatural glitter flashed through the room.

Lord bejesus, it was the stars. In they came single file, all dressed up as country folks, suspenders, overalls with patches, they even had some fresh cow shit on their boots, skipping out onto the dance floor to kick up their heels. Whispers ran through the crowd like wildfire, people elbowing each other and pointing low-like so no one would notice. The band sort of froze for a minute, and in the meantime the stars moved out onto the dance floor, spread their elbows a little, and took it over. Finally the band swallowed, one of them came up to the mike and said, "And now we're gonna play some *shit*-kickin' music!" And they got on it like a music box full of black dex.

Well, it was something to see. They were mostly millionaires, or hundred-thousandaires, one or two fifty-thousandaires, and you could tell they knew it. Some of the women had white satin peasant blouses, which was what gave the room that supernatural glitter. At first glance you couldn't have told them from any other country folks, but you got to looking closer and you noticed that the patches on their overalls were cut out of hundred-dollar bills, and that shit on their boots was imported from France. One or two of the women had little stars pasted on their cheeks; they could've passed for country perfume ads. They wanted to be country folks all right, but they also wanted you to know that they were quite a bit better than country folks too. They wanted you to know that they were the stars.

THE MYSTERY GUEST

I SAT THERE for a while and watched, danced a little, couldn't really get it going, too distracting. Before long in comes a man dressed in a fine sweater and moneyed slacks, wearing a cowboy hat. He looked like an advertising executive trying to convey the idea he was a cowpoke. Sweating a little, seeming as if he were in pretty shallow water. He put his hat down on a chair close by, smiled, went out and started dancing with the stars. Pretty soon a rumor ran through the crowd like prairie fire, from one person to the next: *It's the Governor!*

Son of a bitch, it *did* look like him. I went up to the bartender and said, "Is that the Governor?"

He nodded, wiping the bar. "It's him all right. Came up and introduced himself."

"Well, what do you know about that."

The bartender shrugged. "I don't give a shit if it's the King of Africa, as long as he pays for his drinks."

I was about to tell him that Africa had more than one ruler these days, but I thought better of it. Went back and sat down. I realized that I had arrived at the tail end of a Montana rendezvous, circa 1977; and the real end of my long search up and down the Rockies, a search that led me to the tops of the wildest peaks left. And as I watched them dance, spinning around with an air of how contemporary they thought they were, a vision of the Selway River floated into my mind. It was the first time I saw it, ebbing the banks at high water, bucking and plunging, twenty-foot rooster tails lofting into the sunlight, its thunder pounding into my heart. I remembered its pure feeling, and it struck me watching the dance floor that this tryst in front of me, the glamour and the politicians who courted it, was the vital element in the degradation of the Rockies through the seventies. They acted as a smoke-screen, turning people's eyes toward glitter and glamour, away from the way the land was being ruined. Their glamour served as a diversion for the rich industrialists and developers, who ultimately, one way or another, signed their checks.

And then it started to come home to me, something about egotism I had learned on the trips, the gleam of a crystal from the wild, some direction at last. It was starting to coalesce in me. But the action in front of my eyes was fast and furious; it wasn't a place or a time for contemplation. I took a deep breath and shook my head, climbing back down to reality.

Boys, the Strangler bar hadn't seen such excitement since the night old Casey Dangerfield puked up a steak dinner on the pool table right during a tournament. People were buzzing and pointing, snickering; no one could believe it, but there he was. The Governor of Montana.

I sat there thinking that I didn't care for Fort Hollywood any more. I had seen its essence. I didn't want to be like the stars, and I didn't want to rub elbows with the Governor. *I wanted to be my own self.*

A LOCAL MOUNTAIN MAN!

BUT IT WASN'T over yet. Speak of the devil, in walks old Casey Dangerfield. People's eyes turned. Casey was in his twenties, a big hell-raiser with a devilish set to his jaw, thick beard, shoulders like a wagon yoke. He was a native Montanan, dressed in a beat-up jeans jacket and black cotton logger's pants stitched with patches—*real* patches—and the rivers and mountains of Montana flowed in his veins. It was generally recognized that Casey had thrown up more times in the Strangler on Saturday night than anyone else on record, and for that and other mountain man feats he carried a certain mystique. Nothing was sacred when Casey was around.

Somebody poked him and pointed out the Governor. "It's really him—there's his hat!"

Casey's eyes went from the man dancing with one of the women stars to the hat resting on a chair. For a few seconds a devilish glint shone in his eyes, then it went away. He sidled up to the chair, yawning, and sat down squarely on the hat.

People almost choked. Casey just sat there sipping his beer, looking tired, stretching now and then. Pretty soon the dance ended and they began to fan back toward their tables. The Governor walked up and began hunting empty chairs. Casey yawned. The Governor got close to Casey and it clicked in his brain that Casey was sitting on the chair where he had left his hat.

"Have you seen a Stetson?" he asked, with the smile of a politician.

The people around Casey were frozen, looking away. He patted the last of a yawn, sat up sleepily, and looked around on the floor. When he didn't see it there he raised up a little and felt underneath with his hand. He paused for a moment; slowly he pulled out the flattened hat.

"*Damn.* Sorry, bud. Didn't even see it sitting there."

The Governor turned it over once, tip to tip, and gave a diplomatic little laugh. "That's all right. It'll pop right back out."

But he looked grave as he walked away.

People around the table buried their faces. You had to hand it to old Casey all right. He knew which way the cart was rolling.

A MOUNTAIN MAN'S STATUS

CASEY GOT UP and hitched up his pants. "Let's get to dancing!" He jumped out onto the floor and began moving as if he were trying to stomp out a forest fire, throwing his elbows, spinning around from one place to another like a human tornado. The stars had to sort of move out of the way; that glitter didn't get in Casey's eyes. Pretty soon more and more people were jamming onto the dance floor, sweating, bumping, pressing toward the magic hour, the hour of eruption. Casey was in the middle of it, and the stars were getting bumped just like everyone else. People were getting that frenzied look in their eyes, like they were seeing stars up toward the ceiling. The energy just kept building higher, more frenzied, ticking toward the breaking point.

All of a sudden Casey Dangerfield yelled out in a gurgling voice: "*Look out!*"

People moved away like a flock of chickens. He spread his arms, pushing someone aside, and his shoulders heaved. A warm splash hit the dance floor, followed by a retching sound and another big splash. With one voice the crowd gave a sickening groan. The energy that had been rising was defused like a camp-fire in a thunder shower.

But then something else began growing in the crowd, a cheer which rose from person to person until everybody was whistling and waving their hats. Casey stood there swaying, smiling, wiping his mouth. I didn't know what was going on till I asked somebody.

Casey had broken one hundred! He had thrown up 101 times in the Strangler on a Saturday night. Lord knows what his record was if you counted the other nights of the week.

He stood there weaving dizzily, tears running down his cheeks, his big fist raised in the air. In a brawling voice he yelled out, "I can outpuke any son of a bitch in this whole bar!"

Cheers and whistles followed. It was a claim to status which the stars apparently found distasteful. They left, followed by the Governor. The last I saw of him he was reaching down to brush off the cuff of his slacks as he walked out the door. Well, it was good to see him get down amongst the people for a night, anyway.

That night didn't turn out so bad after all. You never knew what was going to happen in the Strangler on a Saturday night.

THE COTTONWOODS all up and down the Yellowstone River turned yellow, and the first snows came to the high country of the Crow Mountains. At about the same time, Steve McQueen came to Fort Hollywood to work on a new script with one of the screen-writers. Word had it that he was toying around with the idea of buying a thousand acres for a million dollars. I was looking for some time to draw out that crystal of my experience in the wild, but the pace in Fort Hollywood seemed to be ever accelerating as the seventies drew to a close, with rampant distractions. News of McQueen's presence spread through town like wildfire, and before long the real estate agents could be seen skipping down Main Steeet in an ecstatic frenzy, throwing carefully measured handfuls of pennies to passing children. Six more fashion shops opened up in less than an hour. The bankers closed themselves inside their private offices and began doing handsprings around their desks, shooting jellybeans at each other with rubber-band slingshots. The price of a fancy new four-wheel-drive pickup went from $10,000 to $11,000. The new-car dealers grinned from ear to ear. What was good for business was good for America, they were heard to say. Richard Brautigan, who lived near Fort Hollywood, started to work on a new novel. Irony had never had it so good.

Out in a valley that was as beautiful as any paradise, where Steve McQueen wanted a thousand acres, a few of the ranchers stopped to lean against their fences, pondering the peaks of the Crow Mountains. The price of fertilizer was killing them. Taxes were killing them. The price of everything was killing them. How could they go on? Of course, a guy could always sell out to someone like McQueen and ride the rest of the way in on Easy Street, but that didn't sit right with all of them. They were ranchers down to their bones, down to their children's bones, and they wanted to stay ranchers. But what could they do? Hollywood was moving in, and the bankers and the stars had all the money.

And I thought: Five years from now, ten years from now, how far back in would you have to go to find a place that was truly wild, a place where you could feel that wild spirit? What would the top of the Swans be like in ten years, and the Selway? Where was this rampage of development leading to? Stardom, and oblivion? That crystal of the wild involved my ego, leveling my ego, putting myself on the level of wild rivers and wild animals, feeling under the influence of the wild that I was an ordinary human among millions of humans. A sort of wild specific gravity, places where I could feel the earth's spirit and feel myself in communion with it in a positive way without feeling egotistical. A place where I could knock down false ego buildups, and still repair the weird lacerations of the American social scene. I was beginning to see the wild mountains as a place where I could humble myself, and at the same time feel good and positive. That was what I felt over and over back in those mountains, a leveling of myself. A status of the wild.

ANOTHER DISTINGUISHED GUEST

BUT BEFORE I could get a further grip on that concept Farrah Fawcett-Majors breezed into town. Things were happening fast in Livingston, Montana. She ate at one of the local restaurants, and word had it that she got miffed when one of the waitresses didn't offer the proper respect before she served the food. She left town; all the faucets leaked for days after she departed. The fact that she didn't settle there meant that maybe one certain rancher could hold on for another two years.

And I thought: It was all over in Fort Hollywood. When you see that a tide is going a certain way, and is bound to go that way by forces already gaining massive momentum, there's no sense in going down with the ship.

And pondering those same dark blue peaks that the rancher was pondering, peaks that humbled me, I thought to myself: *You can't ride a mule that was past into the future of America.* You had to ride with the times, no matter how bad they tasted.

And I knew then what I had to do.

IT WASN'T EASY. All the way back to my lodge I was thinking about the mighty chain of mountains I covered with that mule, the cabin we searched for, dreams of mountain men, of wild mountains—a myth that I rode all through the hard times of the seventies. As I climbed the stairs to get the pistol it all came back, wave after wave. Times when oil was getting scarce, ideals were going down the drain, and you had to make do with what you could, scrounging greasewood and cottonwood bark, and stealing gas out of Cadillacs in the night. Holding to your beliefs. That mule was a feeling in my heart.

Old Sixties stood there in the last sunlight of the day, half asleep, flicking its exhaust pipe at a blowfly now and then, lost in some dream of far green prairies in America that were free as the wind. I untied it and climbed in, the pistol wrapped up in a blanket and hidden in my rucksack, resting next to me on the seat. I patted it gently on the dash.

"We ain't got far to go now," I said in a soft voice, "and it won't be a hard ride. Giddyup, now."

THE LAST RIDE OF OLD SIXTIES

W E RODE on out of the fort, limping along, and I let it go at its own pace, enjoying the ride and the countryside. And ganted up as it was, it was still ready to go on riding, just thumping along with its aerials perked up listening for enemy phone trucks, thinking that maybe we were finally heading out of Fort Hollywood for good, heading for greener hills and new country to the west. When it came right down to it, that mule always did have guts; it was ready to try the eighties. But I knew better. The eighties would break its spirit plumb in half.

We rode out toward the junkyard west of town on a country road, a flock of blackbirds gathering along the phone wires, the evening wind rattling through dry autumn leaves along the roadside. There was a big pile of dark clouds building up back to the west. I passed a gravel pit and some storage tanks, the sun hanging red on the horizon crowded by those clouds, the sky in the east beginning to settle into a steel-gray twilight. I looked at the Crow Mountains in the distance and thought of the trips I had made, and I felt numbness and sadness for the wild places I had seen. What scars would the eighties leave in those places? I tried to hold on to that crystal I had seen, that I had brought back; I tried to hold to it beyond what I had to do now.

Way up ahead I saw the entrance to the junkyard, and something inside me turned around. "No, I won't give it up!" a voice in me cried, and I held on to the wheel with my spirit. But something stronger in me kept on driving steady, toward that weedy turnoff to the junkyard. Something from the Crow Mountains. Maybe it was the singing that came in with the fog, or the bear in the morning, or the spirit of that moose. Maybe it was something in all those things, the spirit of life that lived in those mountains, that turned my eyes toward the future. Whatever it was, it gave me strength.

But that mule had a hold on my heart. When I turned past the mailbox and weeds and started in toward the end, a flood of memories came in on me. Times and feelings, things that we rode through that you knew were true even if the newspapers were saying they weren't. An angry reaction in that mule that was beautiful, a rearing up of the human spirit, before the system caught the reins and began to sell the revolt in news magazines and boutiques. All those times that you knew in your heart, and all the millions of people who did what they did because of something in their hearts, and not because they wanted to get into the limelight. They were your soul, old mule, and you spread across the land.

And then came the seventies and you rode on through the seventies, and even though you took a beating, and your spirit got lonely in these times, you still kept on riding with it up high, the same millions of people, still trying to ride toward what you felt in your heart. You had guts and vision, and you knew the truth of things that other people didn't want to see.

THE LOAD ON ITS TIRED BACK

I QUIETED THE TREMORS in my stomach and drove slowly on in toward the piles of wrecked cars, past a little shack with a light on, a man sitting inside engrossed in a copy of *Penthouse*. A part of the load. Greasy car parts jammed the shelves around him, timing chains and flywheel gears hanging from wires, nude women on the walls with greasy thumbprints on their thighs, a desk cluttered with papers and used radios. The man scarcely noticed me as I rode past; he had put aside his copy of *Playboy* and turned to *Penthouse* because it showed direct shots into the human vagina, rather than just hints, and that was something new to him. He was staring at one of those shots now as if he were gazing into a crystal ball. Actually in conformation the vagina in the picture was not much different than his wife's vagina, but its full-color portrayal in a national magazine allowed him to fantasize in a way that was completely disconnected from reality. The fact that he was so engrossed in it gave me some leeway, made it easier to do what I had to do.

I rode down between the rows of wrecked cars, over grease-packed dirt and shards of broken safety glass, searching for the right place. Here was a forlorn radiator leaning against an old bumper; there was a stack of worn-out tires, etched with bald spots. I passed broken windshields, cars with the wheels gone, sinking amid rivers of rust into the earth. The image of the deserted hunting camp came to mind for a moment. I kept going, and finally I found a place next to an old, strong-looking panel truck, out of the wind. Slowly I backed it in. When it was settled good I patted it on the steering neck, got my rucksack and blanket and pistol, and pulled the ten-year load from its tired back. As soon as I shut it off it shook for a while, then rolled in the dirt tracks some. Finally it just stood there gurgling its oil. It was happy. I got everything together and stepped out into the open air.

The sun was low down on the horizon, shooting red beams through the big dark clouds. The light on in the shack was growing more prominent, and the man was still engrossed in his copy of *Penthouse*. From far across the northern plains a lonely wind had escaped the sinking sun, and now it whistled through the abandoned metal parts with a sound that made me pull my capote up tighter around my neck. A few tumbleweeds came rolling through among the rows of wrecked cars, their rusting roofs catching a few of the sun's last glints. Up in the sky a golden eagle was flying to the west.

I hunkered down in that cold October wind and made a last, lonely camp. I burned a little sage. I roasted a sausage, and I heated some water for coffee. It was just like any camp we made down through the years of the seventies anywhere in the Shining Mountains. Like that camp in the high mountains above Leadville when the snow came through the trees thick as feathers; like the camp on that strange old river down in the Taos country when the spirits threw a pan over the edge of the canyon and scared us clean out of there. And hightailing it out of the Vail country before money and fancy people ate us alive. All the time looking for some mountains that were still wild enough to take a deer, to live wild. With the seventies that was gone now, and the eighties were on the way.

THE HEART OF A DECADE PAST

I PICKED UP the blanket roll and stepped back a few paces. I felt its heaviness, and my hand was trembling. A lonely wind devil swirled through the silent rows of wrecked cars. Slowly I slipped the pistol free of the blanket, and with one click I turned the cylinder onto a live round. My face turned pale, and I began to speak in a voice that caught in my throat.

"You were a good mule, Sixties, strong and true to your blood. You did some riding all right, and you saw some historic times. You rode hard all through the seventies, and the further you rode, the harder it got for you. But you just kept your head up high and your heart up strong, even though the times were rising up against you, and your rings were getting worn and your valves were getting burned out. You were still trying, in whatever your everyday life was, to live those things that you felt, even though they were going out of fashion. You kept on trying, and you kept on going with your spirit.

"And now people are laughing at you and saying that you're all done in, that you didn't really mean anything, that you were just a mistake in history that they could erase and make fun of and tell the way they wanted to. That wasn't the truth of it, Sixties. You were a magnificent mule! You had guts and a soul that felt other people's pain; you saw the size of the injustice, and you got out in the streets and fought it with everything you had. There was a war that was a pack of lies, and as soon as you saw what lies they were telling, your eyes turned red and your heart began to burn, and you got out there and fought them beyond thoughts of your own safety, losing your job, getting your head split open, going to jail, and the more they tried to push you down, the mightier you kicked back, and in the end you beat them. You made them end that war. On your back, Sixties, the American people took on the government and the corporations with nothing but their bare hands, and they won. *You mustn't forget that.*"

My knuckles had grown tense around the pistol. I looked in through the cracked windshield to the torn spots in its seat. A tear of old forgotten rage ran down my cheek, and I wiped it away.

I went on in a softer voice. "And now, Sixties, they're trying to say you were nothing, and a whole new generation is coming up that never heard of you. They're trying to put the blame for that whole thing on someone else's doorstep. But you knew in your heart where it belonged. It wasn't the American people who wanted that war. It was the government and the corporations who wanted it, and they lied to get the country into it. You saw that, and you stayed true to your feelings in what you did."

I stared at the rusty grill, the moths and bugs stuck to the radiations in its chest. I felt an ache start to rise in me.

"Don't you listen to them now, the way they're going. You did your time, Sixties, and you were a good and beautiful mule! You weren't perfect, but then what was? Maybe you made a jackass out of yourself in front of the television cameras sometimes, and maybe you brayed into the microphone once or twice just to hear the sound of your own voice on the news. But don't let that hurt your spirit now. Maybe those were things you had to learn about yourself, a part of your growing up, coming of age in the seventies. At least you had the courage to get out there and put yourself on the line for what you believed, and for that you can look back and feel good about yourself. Feel inside that you were right after all, and you did good."

I looked with fondness at its battered finish, the pheasant feathers I had woven into the visor. The last of the sun's red rim clung to the horizon, as if waiting to see what would happen. A strange glowing haze began to show to the east. Up above me a sparrow did a sudden loop-the-loop and began flying in the opposite direction. Slowly the trembling pistol came up to a level. A muscle in my forearm began palpitating.

My voice came out in a whisper. "The times are rising up against you, and they're going to bury you for a time and the truth that you knew and lived with your heart. It seems like you were a peak, a peak shining both dark and silver like all the peaks I saw, and now the times are sliding downhill away from you through the seventies, past even the wild mountains that I searched for your spirit in, and they're going to slide even lower down in the eighties. It's time to let go of you now. But I'll remember your lesson, old mule, and I'll hold on to it through the times that are coming. I'll remember that what I feel in my heart is always deeper than the fashion of the times."

Both hands were on the pistol now, and my knuckles were white.

"I have to let go; I have to find you in the future now. But I'll put it down for you. You were brave and good, you had a magnificent heart, a human heart, and you fought a good fight. A fight you won. There wasn't anything wrong with you, Sixties, not in the long run. You were a truly historic mule."

And so saying, I cocked that big .357 and fired it square between the headlights. There was a numbing explosion in my hands and a flash of flame; Sixties gave a metallic screech and rocked back on its haunches, then rolled to a standstill. A dripping sound began, and its lifeblood drained out into the dust.

A wind devil swirled past. The sun dropped behind the horizon. A distant clap of thunder sounded in the dark mass of clouds. A cricket jumped into an exhaust pipe. Somewhere in the night America screeched around the corner to the right. A bull moose fell to its side in an empty meadow. An Indian retreated to the high mountains after losing a battle. Two mountain men parted company for the winter at the big bend in the Yellowstone. The Governor did the twist. Gabe left in the spring for the Nez Percé country. A division of troops steamed off toward the Spanish-American War. A working ranch became a California amusement park. A river ran dry. A shiny new corporation sprang up on the horizon. A new subdivision sent out full-color brochures. An elk starved to death. Deep in the Crow Mountains one of the last-remaining grizzlies roared in anger.

And the man in the shack threw down his *Penthouse* and came running out into the twilight. "What in hell do you think you're doing?!!"

It took me fifteen minutes of fervent explanation to keep him from going back in and calling a padded wagon. I told him straight out that I came out west to be a mountain man in the early seventies, and explained that the old station wagon with the dripping radiator was the Spirit of the Sixties and I was full of it. I told him I thought the country would change after that decade, turn a different direction, and so I kept riding that mule. But it didn't. It went back to the same thing it was before the sixties; it was as if American history were going backward after that experience, back into the fifties. And so I had to lay old Sixties to rest in my heart, and look to the future. Look beyond the dark clouds building up on the horizon.

There was still somewhat of an indignant glitter in his eye as he listened, but at least he didn't seem as if he were going to call the police. The fifties, the sixties, the seventies, they were all the same to this man—the struggle to earn a living. He grumbled something, glancing at the license plates, and with a final warning about shooting that pistol around his junkyard he walked back toward the shack.

"*The starter and generator are still good in that mule!*" I called after him.

I was alone. I wrapped up the pistol and shoved my coffeepot and blanket into the rucksack. For a while I sat there looking at old Sixties, lifeless now, its headlights glazing over, beginning to drain its spirit into the lonely emptiness of the junkyard. The sun had gone down, and a twilight wind came in from across the Montana prairie, blowing over those distant coal-fired generating plants on the northern plains. I had done what I had to do. It was finished now.

I had thought I would feel remorse, but instead I felt a slowly awakening sense of liberation. A cycle had dawned on me in the Crow Mountains, and now at this spiritual parting with old Sixties it was gaining clarity. American history travels in thirty- to forty-year cycles, I thought, staring at the now vacant headlights. Twenties, fifties, eighties; the way it was shaping up the eighties would be something like the fifties. Then it went to ferment: thirties, sixties, *nineties*. The nineties would be a key decade. The two-thousand-year cycle of Christianity was nearing an end, women were rising, and the Chinese were speaking of war with Russia. Everything in the world was building toward the period around the year 2000. A human evolutionary climax. Something big was brewing, and it was only twenty or thirty years away. Because I had been looking backward at Sixties, holding to it, I hadn't been able to see it fully, the way it was building beyond the darkness of the eighties.

I turned my gaze to the pheasant feathers in the visor. I would let them go free, into a space that was past. *"I rode you three or four years longer than I should have,"* I murmured. *"Maybe I did. But I learned your lesson the hard way, the lesson of staying true to my heart, and that was a good lesson. At your best you were always free in spirit, and you're free now. The same way history is free. And in my heart you feel good now, and you will always."*

I stood up with that rising sense of liberation, hoisting my rucksack up on my back. I took a last look, sensing all the grandeur of the Rocky Mountains in that mule, and then I walked away, toward that strange new glow to the east. The man was back in the shack just before closing time, hunched over his copy of *Penthouse.* On an impulse I cupped my hands and called out through the gathering dusk, from everything I had learned:

"You can't separate those old back-to-the-land myths from the times you're living through! If you do, there won't be anything left."

That was the truth of the seventies all right. I turned and started walking on in toward Fort Hollywood, toward that strange glow. Walking with the pack brought back fresh images of the trips, feelings from those wild mountains, and for the first time I could look back on them without feeling that sadness. I remembered the intense, exhilarating aloneness as I climbed along the top of the Swans in the sunlight, the feelings that welled up in me as I caught sight of the next basin, the lonely beauty of it, wild, unscarred, untrampled. I recalled the Selway River pounding through my spirit those first few days, the wonder of it, and I felt again the great pouring of spring as the waters came down off the top of the Bitterroots, so awesome, so much more moving than anything people could build in this century or the next. Those places, those feelings began to solidify in me now, to take their place in my memory as something precious in my life. Something beyond the damage that would be done in the eighties, the trampling, the tossing away of plastic wrappers, the lack of awareness, the clear-cuts. I held to those feelings as I walked on in the growing dusk, beneath the silent phone wires, along a country road that was fast changing into a suburban road, and I believed in the power they gave my spirit. I remembered that somehow the tremendous depth and power in the Crow Mountains had finally made me let go of old Sixties and look to the future, and I realized that there was power for the human spirit in the earth, that there was still something there that I could believe in and unite with. The trips began to come home to me in a way that I could feel good about, wild places that I could remember and draw hope from, wild feelings that I could call back into my life. That crystal from the wild was at last gaining its true brilliance: the wild mountains that were left were a place for me to merge my spirit with that of the earth, to let go of my ego and feel the simple but profound flow of existence, outside the social lacerations of everyday life; feel the life force, and my connection to the earth and its history. What it meant to be a human, and where it was going. That was what was coming to me along that road back toward Fort Hollywood, after parting with my long-time mule. They were places away from the struggle where I could find my spirit again.

BUT THERE WAS one other matter concerning the parting that I hadn't yet resolved. I had to pick out a new mule.

TWENTIETH-CENTURY FUN, INC.

THAT STRANGE GLOW to the east that I thought might have been some supernatural aura surrounding the death of old Sixties turned out to be a neon haze emanating from the new and gaudy signs they were starting to hoist up around the fort. It was beginning to look like Fort Capitalism, where I had started out in the Rockies seven years before, riding on Sixties. And indeed, it seemed to be fast going beyond that stage, toward the bizarre. It was back to reality for a would-be mountain man.

By the time I hit Main Street full darkness had settled and I noticed that the real estate agents had big bonfires crackling away on the roofs of the banks, and they were having marshmallow roasts up there with gold-plated willow sticks, burning up old homestead deeds. The bankers were pacing around with them, smiling and tossing down free all-day suckers to the passers-by on the streets. A carnival had come to town, and people were wandering around with cotton candy and caramel apples. I was thinking about that new mule as I watched the scenes, trying to decide what qualities I wanted it to have, and I began drifting through the crowds toward the area of the car lots. I thought I might pick out a sleeper, and get a good deal on it.

Turned out there weren't many good cheap cars left. The dealers were parading around some brand-new models that they'd just had airlifted in that night, that cost $12,995 Detroit. Now, $12,995 was a lot of money to pay for a new pickup, a salesman admitted to me, but at least it wasn't $13,000, and these new trucks were absolutely guaranteed to make your neighbor faint with shame when you drove them up the drive way. He said they even had a special low-interest finance deal rigged up so your kids could take over the payments when you passed away. All in all it sounded like a good deal, but I passed on it. Later on someone saw one of the stars pull into the Safeway in one of them—paid cash for the damn thing, they said. People stared with dreamy eyes as the beautiful vehicles passed by on the streets, steered by remote-control computers so you thought there was something supernatural about them. It looked like a hell of a deal, if only you could get financing on one of them.

I wandered on through the streets. The phone company had sent out emergency overnight crews, and they were whipping up a special telegraph line all the way from Madison Avenue to Fort Hollywood. Soon it was clacking away with all kinds of good news. An Indian got thrown out of a bar onto his face. A railroad executive drove a golden spike into the heart of the

West. Somebody plowed their car into the statue of a famous city patriarch. A woman screamed with delight. Down in the bowels of the courthouse UPI reported a secret meeting between the Forest Service, some rich people, and the Hollywood stars; they were trying to work out a law which would make it illegal to set foot in the mountains unless you made $95,000 a year or better. Outside people were whooping and hollering, shooting off fireworks. Casey Dangerfield had climbed up to the top of the flagpole on the courthouse, and he looked a little pale. There was a carnival air all over the fort, and all those old homestead deeds were just about burned up. The real estate agents were ringing the church bells and throwing down free biographies of themselves. Out on one of the private roads beyond the fort some of the stars were having a race in the moonlight toward the Crow Mountains, boys against girls, pushing authentic old $500 musket balls along with their tongues.

It seemed sort of decadent after a while.

OLD EIGHTIES

I WENT on out to a low-down used-car lot on the outskirts of town while the celebrations were still going on, and began looking for a new mule. I wanted it to be more compact than Sixties, run quieter and burn less energy. Sixties was sort of a grandstand mule in its way, rolling down the highway showing off, steaming and braying out its indignation for all to hear sometimes, letting everybody know how funky and rugged a mule it was. A lot of Sixties energy went into its external self, how it thought it looked when it rode down the highway, and I realized that it was doing just what those people in the Cadillacs were doing. So I wanted this new mule to have a completely *internal*-combustion identity; to have its identity secure within itself, so it felt good about itself and didn't feel any need to show off. A mule whose life force worked from within, instead of being wasted on outside looks.

I poked around here and there and finally found a tight little blue mule, a compact wagon with a rebuilt engine. Didn't look funky at all—just another mule, four-door, six-hoofer, eighteen peaks to the bucketful. I gave four hundred plews for it and rode it back up to my lodge, tethering it out by the shed. Looked it over for a while, listening to its rockers and lifters, and gave it a can of STP to make friends with it. To look at it you wouldn't have thought it was anything special, but this time I knew I had a mule of the future, and it would carry me through. I named it Eighties, and I left it there to regurgitate that STP. As I walked away I felt that twinge of sadness, that there was a new mule where Sixties once stood. I didn't think that was still in me.

I could still hear the fireworks exploding in the distance as I climbed the stairs to my lodge, the real estate agents and bankers ringing the church bells. I thought to myself: How much longer? Twenty years? Thirty years? But my spirit was moving ahead of it, and I no longer felt its despair. I had the right material in that mule to get me through it.

The place I was looking for in the mountains, the feeling of wildness that I sought after on the trips, turned out to be a place of the spirit. Public land, national forests: the wildest peaks left in America. On paper they were owned equally by all Americans, and could be used equally by all Americans. For the rest of the dream, the cabin in the wild, the rich and the movie stars would own all the private land around the Crow Mountains by the time the eighties were through. You would have to be a movie star or a politician to be able to afford any of it. That was the way it was going everywhere in the Rockies. A new class of landowners, almost feudal in nature, was forming in the seventies. I had to have the wind and the sun in my spirit. But that national land feeling wasn't a place I owned. I didn't have the exclusive rights to it. It was a place of the spirit I had found on the trips, and it belonged to the future of America. I had to find out how my spirit fit into that, riding old Eighties.

I listened to the whoops, the squealing tires, the explosions in the distance. It wasn't here. You could tell which way the cart was rolling here. And at last I felt that my mountain man spirit was ready to take flight. It was the resolution to what had seemed an endless search. You couldn't escape Fort Hollywood geographically, because it was spreading everywhere. You had to leave it in spirit.

I started packing up my outfit, and I did some housecleaning while I was at it. I carried that old TV down into the moonlight and got a sledgehammer from the shed. For a minute I stood there looking at it, thinking of all the broken souls it stood for, all the ads for motorized vehicles tearing up the mountain slopes I had seen in the Swan Mountains, the Bitterroot Mountains, the throwaway cans, the throwaway consciousness. Finally I raised up with that sledge and came down with everything I had. Plastic exploded into splinters, glass and broken tubes went flying. I hit it again and again, until there wasn't anything left but tangles of wires, broken plastic, splintered wood. I shoveled it all into the wheelbarrow and dumped it in the garbage can. It was out of my life for good now.

I went back upstairs and threw out all the dirty looks in Fort Hollywood that led people to struggle to get a bigger piece of the mountains. I threw out all the Hollywood magazines with pictures of the stars, one for every clear wild stream that I waded across in the Selway. I crumpled up all the dreams of status and money that were floating around Fort Hollywood, and I burned them all up in the stove, for the Yellowstone River, that it would remain clear and wild, always flowing into the future of Montana. I swept up all the dust that came with fancy new $12,000 vehicles and unlimited monthly payments, and I threw it out the window onto the night breeze, for all the wild animals I had seen on the trips, for the silvery young grizzly and the wild haunting basin with the waterfall where it lived and fed. Because the forces behind all those things were the very forces that were eating away the wild mountains. The times might be going toward Fort Hollywood, but my spirit wasn't.

I got my outfit all trimmed down to just what I would need to get by, and I got it all loaded into Eighties. The rear end was sunk just a little, but it looked like it would ride all right. I wondered how it would handle, and how I would feel riding it after being with Sixties for so long. Well, I would soon find out, for the time was at hand. It was goodbye to Fort Hollywood.

The streetlights were burning late, one or two house cats

prowling around the garbage cans. I rode on in toward Main Street, figuring to catch the last of the celebrations.

But it was all over. A sad scene prevailed in the predawn darkness. The streets were empty and littered with plastic wrappers and junk. A shiny new pickup was wrapped around a telephone pole, the radiator dripping the last of its fluid into the gutter. A lone workingman came staggering up under a streetlight, holding on to his guts. Hungry dogs roamed the streets, sniffing at the fresh vomit outside the bars, and a discarded newspaper came rolling along and stuck to a fence, with a headline about China and Russia. Here was a lost wallet with the money and credit cards gone. There were the tumbling ashes of an old homestead deed. An Indian lay unconscious in an alley. A train whistle sounded in the distance. Special Boy Scout crews hired by the bankers were just starting to scrub the scorch marks off the tops of the banks. A rooster crowed three times. A convict fell out of his bunk in his sleep. An ex-President took off for California. And the truth of an entire decade was stricken from the public record.

But I rode through those times, they couldn't erase them from my feelings. Out of the sixties and through the seventies, into the eighties: America was back on the track again, the track where profit ruled over public consciousness. Steaming toward the year 2000. And it was getting real hard to make it any more. I would ride with it on old Eighties all right, but not with my soul. My soul was standing with those wild peaks. And that separation, I realized, was the real lesson of the seventies. You had to find a mule that would keep your fighting spirit strong. Or gradually, over the years, it would break you.

THE THREAD OF THE DECADES

I RODE on out of the fort, out into the darkness of the plains. I was heading for the Nez Percé country, the place where big rivers joined. Shadowed forms of dreaming mountains rose up to

the south, an occasional barn light winking in the hills. I swung
the wheel back and forth; Eighties cut good sharp curves, and it
seemed a well-balanced mule, turning quickly on short notice. It
ran quiet and smooth, without the belching and farting that
Sixties sometimes indulged in to get attention when we passed
Holiday Inns. Eighties just purred simply down the highway,
seeming as if it were at peace with itself, as if it knew itself in a
way that old Sixties didn't see. But I wondered: Was it the rebel
Sixties was, did it have that fierce and beautiful streak of anger
running in the rivers of its soul? By God, it did. I crowded it
into a drift on a wide curve, pressuring the tires until they
squealed with the tremendous excess weight, then cut it back
sharp. It bounced left and right, straining against the shocks,
then settled back down to the highway again, running true and
straight. It had it.

And then, miles later, like the pink streaks that were beginning to show in the east, it began to dawn on me about the
decades I had come through. *They weren't separate.* There was
some of old Sixties in Eighties. That loud and courageous, that
self-confused mule was one twentieth of America's history, and it
wasn't sitting finished back in that junkyard in Fort Hollywood.
It was in the bloodstream of history, a part of history, and it was
flowing forward, invisibly, toward the future. It had reached up
to Eighties and touched it, and now Eighties was on the road,
riding on where Sixties had left off. When I saw that and felt it I
experienced a wave of happiness, and at last the negative emotional hold that Sixties had on my heart was gone to freedom.
There was some of old Sixties in Eighties all right, and it was
riding free with its spirit reborn, a quicker and smarter mule.

I rode on, relieved, tired from the packing and the emotional
release, but wanting to keep going through the sunrise, the rising
of the red atom off the last big wild range, the one that turned
my soul. The image of the tumbling newspaper came to mind
again: China and Russia were becoming increasingly bitter
enemies. I wondered as the miles slipped past if history would
make it past the confrontation that was brewing between those
two giants toward the end of the century. America, even Wall
Street America, was probably the only country that could stop
them from going to war, a war which in the emotional bitterness

of their national feelings might break into a nuclear free-for-all. But only if America wasn't bankrupt by then.

Weariness, sweet oblivion, kept toying with my vision. Still I steered old Eighties straight down the highway, trying different tricks to stay conscious. I shook my head sharply from side to side; I counted telephone poles out loud until the sound of my voice became boring. When I started to doze off again I slapped myself in the face. I kept waiting, and waiting for it.

And at last it came. A great red sun rose off that big range back to the east. *Faith in the earth.* Long live those wild mountains, sanctuary of the last of America's spirit. I rolled the window down, glancing at that sun in the rearview mirror, feeling the wash of cold air, and I kept on going.

A NOTE ABOUT THE AUTHOR

David Thomson has worked as a reporter for the Newark *Evening News* and was a free-lance correspondent in Vietnam. He is currently employed as a guide for the Thunder Mountain Wilderness Service in Livingston, Montana. *In the Shining Mountains* is his first book.

A NOTE ON THE TYPE

The text of this book was set on the Linotype in a new face called Primer, designed by Rudolph Ruzicka, who was earlier responsible for the design of Fairfield and Fairfield Medium, Linotype faces whose virtues have for some time been accorded wide recognition.

The complete range of sizes of Primer was first made available in 1954, although the pilot size of 12-point was ready as early as 1951. The design of the face makes general reference to Linotype Century—long a serviceable type, totally lacking in manner or frills of any kind—but brilliantly corrects its characterless quality.

Composed by Maryland Linotype Composition
Company, Inc., Baltimore, Maryland
Printed and bound by The Book Press,
Brattleboro, Vermont

Designed by Camilla Filancia
Map by Mark Livingston